GIN
Glorious
GIN

How Mother's Ruin Became The Spirit Of London

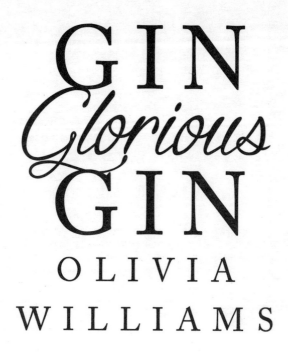

GIN
Glorious
GIN

OLIVIA
WILLIAMS

How Mother's Ruin Became The Spirit Of London

headline

First published in 2014
by HEADLINE PUBLISHING GROUP

1

Cataloguing in Publication Data is available from the British Library

Hardback ISBN 978 1 4722 1533 8

Typeset in Adobe Garamond by Palimpsest Book Production Ltd,
Falkirk, Stirlingshire

Printed and bound in UK by Clays Ltd, St Ives plc

Headline's policy is to use papers that are natural, renewable and recyclable
products and made from wood grown in sustainable forests. The logging
and manufacturing processes are expected to conform to the environmental
regulations of the country of origin.

HEADLINE PUBLISHING GROUP
An Hachette UK Company
338 Euston Road
London NW1 3BH

www.headline.co.uk
www.hachette.co.uk

For Mam and Dad.

Acknowledgements

WITHOUT THE BACKING of my publishers this book would not exist so I am eternally grateful to Sarah and Georgina at Headline, for their great ideas and encouragement, as well as my ever-enthusiastic agent, Claudia. I would also like to thank the various gin experts and archivists who answered endless questions, especially:

Joanne McKerchar and Alia Campbell at Diageo
Ian Hart and Hilary Whitney at Sacred
Tim Stones and Desmond Payne at Pernod Ricard
Susan Scott at the Savoy
Dr Andrea Tanner at Fortnum & Mason
David Connell of The Distillers Company

My family, friends and colleagues have been supremely understanding while I have buried myself away in my work, and I am very lucky to have them. In particular, my boyfriend has put up with all the long hours on nights and weekends when I have been working in silence – thank you, Luke.

Looking further back I owe so much to my teachers, and a few really stand out. My primary school English teacher Mr Ralls, whose flair and humour deserved a far wider audience than his class of 11-year-olds, was remarkable. He told my parents that he wanted the royalties from my first book and, if you are reading this Mr Ralls, then do get in touch about that cheque. I also had the wittiest, most diligent history teacher who you could ever wish for, Mr Hobbs. I found history lessons both a pleasure and an inspiration. By the time I had finished four years at Oxford I was more in love with history than ever, and for that I must thank Dr Davidson, Dr Davis, Dr Gauci and Dr Holmes. I hope this book is, in some infinitesimal way, worthy of how impressive you all are.

Where it all began: The slums of St. Giles, in the heart of London, was the eighteenth century home of gin making

'Gin! Gin! a Drop of Gin!
The dram of Satan! the liquor of Sin!'

THOMAS HOOD, 1799–1845

Contents

1: The Ginnaissance

A MODERN G&T
*Fill a balloon glass with a generous double shot of gin and chunky
ice cubes, then choose a garnish that picks up the main flavour of
the gin and run it around the rim of the glass before stirring it in*

To BE A gin-drinker in this day and age is to be born at
exactly the right time. For the past 300 years the British have
been making and drinking gins of varying quantities and
qualities, but they have never been so deliciously diverse as
they are today. Every month a new, beautifully packaged gin
arrives on the scene, vying to earn its place at the bar. Of the
200 commercially available in Britain, many have only existed
for a matter of years. In a short time we have come a long
way from the classic trinity of Gordon's, Bombay Sapphire
and Beefeater.

Since its lowly birth in London's Georgian backstreets, gin
has clawed its way up to respectability through gin palaces,
gentlemen's clubs and the cocktail parties of the Bright Young
Things to become the most subtle spirit at the modern bar.
The story of gin is a rise from grime to grandeur, from
notoriety to acclaim, from recourse for the desperate to

accessory for the fashionable – it has quite literally been a journey from the slums to the Savoy.

What makes gin such a useful prism through which to view London's history is the range of scenarios in which Londoners, of all walks of life, have turned to it. Say 'gin' to one person and it will evoke the wretches of William Hogarth's *Gin Lane,* say it to another and they will picture flapper girls sipping Martinis, or the Queen Mother clutching a G&T on a day at the races. Despite the glamour that gin acquired during the twentieth century, it retains an intriguing aura of melancholia and seediness, left over from its earliest incarnation as 'mother's ruin'. It has taken on layers of cultural significance so that its current image of sophistication co-exists with historic connotations of drunkenness and despair.

By the time that gin was first mentioned in the *Oxford English Dictionary* in 1714, it was already defined as 'an infamous liquor'. It would eventually overcome this gin craze stigma, but it was such a traumatic, vivid event in London history that its memory has not quite been forgotten. Many modern drinkers, for example, still insist that gin has the power to make them more maudlin than any other alcohol. Given that there is no scientific explanation for that idea, it is simply gin's dark history that makes people believe in that effect.

As with so many things that we hold as quintessentially British, gin in fact had its origins abroad. When the malty Dutch import genever was crudely imitated in the tenements of Georgian London under its new guise of 'gin', few contemporaries would ever have believed that what they were making would become the symbol of British refinement around the world that it is now. Although recently barns, garages and garden sheds the length of the country have been transformed into micro-distilleries, historically gin has been considered an English, more than a British, drink. Back in 1834 the *Spectator* noted the difference between the Celtic fringes and their whisky, and the particular Englishness of gin, which 'is so much more congenial to the palate of John Bull'. Gin's history is strongly one of Englishness and more precisely of London as the hub of both gin-making and gin-drinking. Even now almost twice as many people drink it in the south east as in any other part of the country.

Not so long ago, however, it seemed that gin's ties with the city of its birth may be severed altogether. After the Second World War, when sales went into steep decline, it became difficult to find a London Dry gin that was actually made in London. One by one the distilleries closed down or moved away as they were priced out of town. All but gin's most dedicated older fans had moved on, and what makes this current boom, which shows no sign of relenting, so remarkable is that gin was totally neglected throughout the 1980s and 1990s. Vodka was the order of the day, although it has little of gin's charm. Gin is very much a drinker's drink – complex not only in cultural associations but in its flavours. Unlike vodka, it does not lend itself to being a wallflower in a sickly cocktail or playing second fiddle to a soft drink; it has its own distinct taste to be relished. Vodka is in fact very close to being neutral grain spirit, which is just the base for many gins. So where vodka stops, gin starts – with the addition of all the botanicals that give gin its breadth of possible flavours, its subtlety and its character.

Until its twenty-first century renaissance gin was a sad, unloved spirit, and with its popularity in long-term decline it would have been a sorry end for a spirit with such a rich 300-year history. However, gin has weathered many a storm in its long life and fortunately the vodka boom of the 1960s has not proved the one to finish it off. Thanks to enterprising distillers, adventurous bartenders, and enthusiastic drinkers, gin has dusted itself off for a comeback and now production across the country has risen a quarter in the past decade.

In London there are currently six important gin distilleries, with Beefeater as the grand dame. Of all the great Victorian gin-makers, Beefeater has been the only one to hang on in the city since it was founded in 1863. All of the 2.6 million cases of gin that it sells around the world every year are made at its imposing distillery in the shadow of The Oval cricket ground. A gin that is steeped in history, there are reminders of its earliest days everywhere in the building to this day. A diminutive still that belonged to Beefeater's founder James Burrough is in use even now; his recipe cards and notebooks covered in carefully written instructions are kept out for inspiration in the office; and the staff still share their Christmas lunches with the thirty-seven Beefeaters, also known as yeoman warders, who work at the Tower of London. With such rich heritage, no wonder the current master distiller Desmond Payne says that he can always feel Burrough 'watching over him' – in a comforting way, he quickly adds.

The current flurry of gin-drinking has been fuelled by a blossoming scene of independent distillers, including Dodd's Gin, Sacred, the City of London Distillery and Sipsmith, which all make their own brands. Of these, Sipsmith is the eldest, at only five years old. The new distilleries themselves are as individual as the gins that they produce – from Sipsmith's copper pot distillery, which started off life in a garage on a street in Shepherd's Bush, to Sacred which is made using laboratory equipment in a living room in Highgate. Down the road from Beefeater, the Thames Distillery in Clapham does not make its own brand, but produces forty different gins in small batches. It works for big players including Fortnum & Mason and Marks & Spencer, alongside newcomers such as Portobello Road, the world's first organic gin Juniper Green, Little Bird and Oxley.

The flavour, of course, is vital to a gin's success but so too these days is the story of how it came to be made, and the thought and ambition behind it. In the same way that people have become very curious about the provenance of their food, the same is now true of their drink, which makes these carefully crafted gins all the more appealing. In a time when we know very little about so much of what we consume, it is perhaps comforting to know that there is a human, hand-made element to a drink like gin.

There are so many innovative brands emerging in London, but the inspiration for it coming back into fashion this time around came from some unexpected corners of the country. The first two British boutique brands to test the water were Hendrick's, up in the wilds of Ayrshire, and Martin Miller's in the Midlands. The stunning success of Hendrick's in 1999 gave other distillers the courage to experiment with high-quality, unusual new gins. Its evocative apothecary-style dark bottle and offbeat ingredients set the bar thereafter for all those entrepreneurs with a dream of making gin. Miller described launching his eponymous brand, when Hendrick's was the only other artisanal gin out there, as the result of 'love, obsession and some degree of madness'. A man of diverse talents, his other ventures included owning hotels and writing books such as *Success with the Fairer Sex*, and *Miller's Antique Price Guides*.

Perturbed by the irony that only Beefeater made its own London Dry gin in London anymore, the founders of Sipsmith were the first of the new-wave distillers to set up shop in the city in 2009. Unlike Hendrick's however, they wanted to revive a more traditional flavour. Brimming with enthusiasm the three Sipsmith founders, Sam Galsworthy, Fairfax Hall and master distiller Jared Brown, applied to Customs and Excise for permission to get going, but heard nothing for six months. Eventually explaining the hold-up, Customs told them that no one had applied for a gin distilling licence of that kind since 1823. They added that the quantity that Sipsmith wanted to make was so small that it was, legally speaking, moonshine.

The restrictions that Sipsmith were up against had been set in place when strict regulation was needed to prevent Londoners using illicit little stills to avoid paying duty. The Sipsmith founders were finally ready to make gin when they secured a change in the law after another two years of negotiating. Aiming for the top, Sipsmith headed to the Dorchester to pitch their newly minted gin, and to their amazement its venerable bartender, Giuliano Morandin, gave them a chance. With the Dorchester as their first client, many others soon followed, and Morandin is very proud to have championed them.

So many newcomers have started up since 2009 that Sipsmith

already seems like a veteran of the scene. Just after its fifth birthday, it had outgrown its Shepherd's Bush garage and moved its copper pot stills, Prudence and Patience, to an old brewery in Chiswick. Prudence and Patience can produce 300 bottles a day each, so Sipsmith can now get up to 900 a day with the help of a third, new still, Constance. Sipsmith has also branched out to make sloe gin and the wonderful Summer Cup, which is like a less sickly version of Pimm's. Even now, however, it still only makes in a year what Beefeater can produce in a morning.

One unusually uplifting upshot of the recession was that it gave us all another exceptional new London gin. When work began to dry up for City headhunter Ian Hart whose main client, Lehman Brothers, collapsed in spectacular fashion in 2008, he turned his hand to an activity about which he had always been curious. Hart's father used to distil and had left his 1940s textbooks to him, so Hart dug them out and constructed his own six-foot still at his house in Highgate with equipment from a laboratory supply specialist.

The resulting gin, Sacred, is very eighteenth century, as it is made 'at home' rather than in a dedicated distillery and is unique for that reason. It took Hart twenty-three attempts to perfect his recipe – with a little help from his natural sciences degree from Cambridge and enthusiastic guinea pigs at the local pub, the Wrestlers. He started by delivering bottles around north London on his bicycle and then by bus around the rest of London with his partner Hilary, which they continued to do until recently. An inspiration to independent gin-makers the world over, Hart won a double gold medal in 2013 at the Oscars of alcohol – the World Spirits Competition in San Francisco. Despite great international acclaim Hart still makes his gin by himself in the sitting room and keeps his ingredients in the garden shed and his children's old Wendy house.

Hart's formula of twelve botanicals is so fresh and intriguing that it has become a bartenders' favourite for Martinis, particularly with Alessandro Palazzi at the Dukes Hotel in St James's. Hart has since developed a Sacred Spiced English Vermouth, Rosehip Cup, Cardamom Gin and Christmas Pudding Gin, among other Willy Wonka-esque innovations. He says that he can produce about 300 bottles per day, meaning that Sacred has the potential to produce 100,000 per year. At the moment, with help from Hilary, he manages to make about 25,000 bottles.

Across the river in Battersea, Dodd's Gin is made in the equally genteel surroundings of a Victorian dairy, using a copper still called Christina. The brainchild of distiller Darren Rook, Dodd's is named after Ralph Dodd, a serial entrepreneur who tried to start his own Battersea distillery in 1807. Dodd founded his Intended London Distillery Company to 'manufacture Genuine British Spirits and Compounds' but to contemporaries he was best known for his failed attempt to build a tunnel under the Thames between 1799 and 1802. Poor old Dodd was a laughing stock and sadly his distilling company was no more of a success. Following a complaint by a distillery in Essex, a case was brought against him under the 1720 Bubble Act because he was offering transferable shares. He was very unlucky to be taken to court over it, as the law had not been used for eighty-seven years at the time. After raising all the necessary funds, mustering the staff and buying the Old Water Mill at Nine Elms, no distillation was allowed to take place after all.

By 1812 his company was disbanded and his dream of making gin was over. Now, at last, we can raise a glass to Dodd's efforts with a gin that bears his name.

Of the newcomers the most centrally located is the City of London Distillery on Bride Lane, which is tucked away behind Fleet Street – an area that used to be famous for its gin-makers, thronging gin shops and ostentatious gin palaces. From the C.O.L.D. bar, which offers a dazzling stock of gin, you can see the two highly polished copper stills that have been producing their gin and vodka since 2012. It was the first working distillery to open in the City itself for over 200 years. Their stills can make about 200 bottles per distillation, so they are at the very smallest end of commercial distilling. By contrast, a big player like Bombay Sapphire can make 2,000 litres each run.

For all the new gins that are launching every month, there seems to be unlimited space on the shelves for more. There will come a time when this growth becomes unsustainable and some will inevitably become a mere footnote in gin's long and chequered history. For now though, the prospect of setting up a new gin is still very attractive. It is relatively cheap to start making, will not go off if it does not sell immediately, and what makes it particularly appealing is that entrepreneurs can commission a batch to be made at another distillery before establishing their own. Many gins that have 'Distilled in London' on the label are in fact made in the same place, by Thames Distillers in Clapham. It has proved a valuable start-up for fledgling distillers who want to see how popular their recipe is before they take the plunge and invest in their own.

Charles Maxwell, the master distiller who oversees all the brands made there, says that he is now approached on a weekly basis with pitches. Although he does not share a surname with any of today's famous brands, his family started distilling 300 years ago when they founded Finsbury London Dry Gin and Stone's Ginger Wine. Aspiring gin-makers have all sorts of flavour ideas – one even asked him if they could distil cocaine. Although he tries to accommodate most botanical requests, Maxwell has drawn the line at class-A drugs. The main criticism of having several gins made in one distillery is that they can taste similar because most of them will be made in the same still at the same temperature. By contrast, distillers who make their own have the flexibility to tweak the recipe and experiment on a daily basis.

For all the rocky patches that British gin has weathered over the past fifty years, Britain has held its position as the largest gin exporter in the world, dispatching 373 million pounds' worth to 180 countries every year. Gordon's has proved particularly robust as it remains Britain's bestseller, shifting one million nine-litre cases a year on home turf alone. Despite all the newer brands snapping at its heels, it accounts for nearly half of all the gin that British people drink. Its closest competitor in Britain is Beefeater, followed by Greenall's Original London Dry Gin from Cheshire.

Rather than cutting out the luxury of drinking during the past recession, people have found more solace than ever in the gin bottle – and not just any old bottle. Even when disposable incomes dropped, drinkers proved unwilling to compromise. Rather than switching to cheaper brands, they started consuming less but better. Analysts coined the term 'weekend millionaires' to describe this kind of shopper –

people who prefer to trade down on everyday items, and use the saving to buy high-end products. So rather than spend money drinking a lot at the pub, 'weekend millionaires' would rather buy a bottle of premium gin to enjoy at home, or just one or two expensive cocktails when out socialising. Spain, Europe's other major gin-drinking nation, saw the same phenomenon. Despite record unemployment and profound economic strife, its gin market managed to grow 20 per cent in 2012. It is this desire to maintain little luxuries through times of hardship that has kept the premium gins climbing the fastest of all in Britain, and indeed globally, with sales soaring in the emerging markets of China, India and Russia.

THE MASTER DISTILLER

Whether a big beast like Gordon's or an artisan operation like Sacred, the lynchpin of any distillery is the master distiller. He monitors the taste of the gin, works on creating new flavours, collaborates with bartenders to develop cocktails and, of course, keeps the secret of the recipe. While the gin is being made, even in the large distilleries, the master distiller and his assistants will personally check the quality of each run by sampling a small amount that comes into a glass box called the spirit safe. From there, they can smell, taste and look closely at the spirit, while a computer will check that its alcohol levels are correct. Historically only the master distiller and the tax man would have held keys for the safe, as this was where the amount of duty to be paid on the gin was agreed.

Virtually all master distillers these days are men, as they always have been, but there are a handful of women in the role working outside London. Lesley Gracie created Hendrick's,

Laura Davies of the Penderyn distillery oversees Brecon Gin, Brecon Botanicals Gin and Brecon Special Reserve, while Joanne Moore works at G&J Greenall, where she makes Greenall's Original London Dry Gin, Berkeley Square, and the floral Bloom Gin. When master distillers secure that coveted top job, they tend to hang on in there for a very long time. Moore is only the seventh master distiller at Greenall's, even though the company was established over 250 years ago.

In the past, master distillers would also have gone travelling to find natural flavourings for their gin, known as botanicals, as part of their work. Most large companies now commission a team of buyers to go shopping around the world on their behalf, although Bombay Sapphire has a master herbalist who is solely responsible for buying all their ingredients. One very traditional master distiller who does still nose through the juniper and coriander himself, however, is Desmond Payne of Beefeater, with a team of four or five to help him.

Now in the industry for over forty-five years, Payne is Britain's most experienced distiller. He came over from Ireland in the 1960s, where he took his first job at the wine cellar of Harrods. From there, he found his true calling in gin at the now-closed Seager Distillery in Deptford, south London. A job offer from Plymouth Gin managed to coax him out of his beloved flat in Chelsea and out to Devon. He stayed there until 1994 when he returned to take up one of the industry's most-coveted jobs, master distiller of Beefeater – a post that he has held ever since. As well as his usual duties, Payne has overseen Beefeater opening its doors to the public for the first time in 2014. For gin enthusiasts visiting London, the distillery tours are a great chance to watch the process, ask questions and, of course, sample the fruits of his labour.

HOW GIN IS SERVED NOW

A vital component in gin's resurgence is the accoutrements with which it is served. Until a few years ago, outside the very best bars it was difficult to get a good cocktail or even a decent gin and tonic. A single shot of lukewarm Gordon's with Schweppes, a bit of waxy lemon and a few lumps of rapidly dissolving ice was standard fare. Much has changed however. Now all aspects of the once-humble G&T are up for debate – from the type of glass, to the garnish, even to how the ice is made.

For tonic, Schweppes is still the market leader, as it has been for decades. Although, because Schweppes has subcontracted its production around the world, it has created variation in the taste – in many cases not for the better. The American version is particularly sickly as it is sweetened with corn syrup, while in Britain sugar and saccharine is used. Artificial sweeteners like saccharine can leave an unpleasant aftertaste, particularly when coupled with artificial quinine, which most big brands use.

Although all of today's tonic water contains a medically insignificant amount of quinine, it still affects the flavour. In Japan they do not use quinine in their tonic at all, which makes it unpleasantly sweet for Western palettes. The Japanese market was, in fact, the inspiration for Sipsmith's high juniper, high alcohol Very Junipery Over Proof gin because they needed the extra kick of 57% ABV, or alcohol by volume, to cut through that Japanese tonic.

Packaging is the other major drawback for many tonics because the plastic bottles mean that they lose their fizz disappointingly quickly. Between the sweetness and the flatness, many distillers feel that the big brands can blanket the subtleties of their recipes. One such frustrated man was Charles Rolls, the ambitious former managing director of Plymouth Gin.

Rolls and his business partner, Tim Warrillow, set about filling the gap in the mixer market with Fever Tree, the now-ubiquitous alternative to Schweppes in upmarket restaurants and bars. With their flat tonic bugbear in mind, they were determined to make their own brimming with bubbles – so many, in fact, that in the test run the caps would not stay on and kept flying off the bottles. For the tonic itself, they took inspiration from scouring historic recipes in the British Library. Their research convinced them that they needed to track down a specific type of real quinine, which they found in a plantation run by German settlers in the Congo. Like the gin distillers, Warillow and Rolls keep the exact botanicals in their tonic to themselves. They use marigold oil, bitter orange oil from Tanzania, cane sugar, and water from the Buxton hills, but the other ingredients are closely guarded. After a year of tasting and experimenting, and with £100,000 of Rolls's own money, they launched in 2005. Carting the bottles around to bars and shops from their base in Chelsea on Rolls's motorbike rapidly paid off, as early adopters included the Ritz, Claridge's and Waitrose.

A sign that they were truly on to a winner came from the ultimate flattery of being served at elBulli, the finest restaurant in the world at the time, in the form of a granita – *sopa de Fever-Tree tonica*. By chance Richard Hamilton, the father of British pop art, was a Fever Tree fan and had taken a bottle with him to Spain to show to his friend Ferran Adrià, elBulli's chef. Fever Tree then went on to collaborate with Adrià on their Mediterranean Tonic, made with rosemary and thyme.

After Fever Tree came a wave of other premium tonics. Peter Spanton launched his eponymous mixers in 2010 after running cult 1980s restaurant Vic Naylor's in Clerkenwell. Entertaining regulars such as Tracey Emin, Sam Taylor-Wood, Jay Jopling and Stella McCartney at the bar had taken its toll on Spanton and he ended up checking himself into the Priory with alcohol addiction in 1999. When he was out socialising again afterwards, he realised as a non-drinker how few mixers there were, and became bored of endless elderflower spritzers. He has now developed several tonics, such as his Cardamom Tonic, Lemongrass Tonic and Mint & Bitters Tonic.

There are plenty of intriguing brands on the market now, which go to all sorts of lengths to become the connoisseurs' new favourite. Spanish 1724 tonic does not just use real quinine, but quinine found at 1724 metres above sea level on the Inca Trail. You would need a pretty well-attuned palette to discern such subtleties, but perhaps it does make a difference.

Hailing from Thornbury in Gloucestershire, 6 O'Clock Indian Tonic Water is unique in having its own brand of accompanying gin. Both the gin and tonic are made by Michael Kain, director of Bramley and Gage, which he runs with his wife and children. Kain, who started his business making fruity liqueurs, was inspired by his great-grandfather, the Victorian engineer Edward Kain, to make gin. After retiring from the Merchant Navy, Edward would take to his armchair at six o'clock every day with a G&T to ponder his possible designs, hence the name. Like many of these entrepreneurs, the Kains developed their drink in a makeshift manner, perfecting their recipe using a SodaStream at home to carbonate the proto-types. Kain's plan for success was not to stray too far from drinkers' preconceptions of how tonic should taste. In the same way that however innovative a gin may be, it still needs to please gin fans, Kain found a similar balancing act for making tonic: 'Too esoteric and we faced disaster, too bland and we faced being a facsimile of what was currently available.'

The alternative to all of the fussing with tonic is to go for the really traditional approach of drinking gin with water. This came heartily recommended by bon viveur and author Kingsley Amis in his 1983 ode to alcohol *Everyday Drinking* as 'an all-round improvement on gin and tonic: cheaper, less-fattening and less filling'. He railed against the fashion for any kind of tonic: 'To pour sweetened fizz like tonic water into such a masterpiece of the distiller's art makes about as much sense as putting tomato ketchup on caviar.' He used to have his gin with a dash of Malvern water and no ice. This is certainly an acquired taste. However, it is one perhaps worth acquiring if you want to be scientific about finding your favourite brand. Many distillers will try a new gin in this way, to make sure they pick up all the subtleties behind the tonic.

In terms of glasses, some London bars have ditched the traditional highball, following the lead of the Spanish. Together Britain and Spain account for over half of all the gin sales in Europe and both take their gin preparation very seriously. In the bars of Barcelona, you will find gin served with fresh garnishes, lots of ice and only a little tonic in big, open balloon glasses. Happily, this is catching on in London too. The wide glass, along with the garnish, is believed to deliver more aroma to your nose and the ice will not melt so quickly as in a highball if held by the stem. However, there is no need to throw the trusty old highball away just yet – the jury is still out. After all, the tonic loses its fizz faster in a wider glass and many London bars are reluctant to adopt the fashion for that reason.

Even more dramatically improved than the humble G&T is the gin cocktail. Its revival has been so popular that it has helped gin sales at pubs, bars and restaurants to spike up 12 per cent in a year, with the keenest guzzlers in London, unsurprisingly. Shaking things up on the cocktail scene are experimental proprietors such as Tony Conigliaro of 69 Colebrooke Row and the Zetter Townhouse who pioneers new flavours at the Drink Factory, his laboratory in Pink Floyd's former studio in Islington. As well as macerating and infusing cocktail ingredients, Conigliaro dabbles in molecular mixology, which has earned him the plaudit of being 'revolutionary' from the doyen of molecular mixology himself Heston Blumenthal. Conigliaro experiments with deconstructing flavours and remaking them as foams, aromas or reductions to give his cocktails the edge. The results are rarities like his Woodland Martini, in which gin is laced with bitters made from three different types of bark, and the Barbershop Fizz, a cocktail of patchouli-infused mint and Beefeater 24 infused with pine. Such bespoke ingredients are a strong feature of London's new cocktail bars. Tristan Stephenson's Worship Street Whistling Shop in Shoreditch has even created its own cream gin inspired by Victorian gin palaces, where gin was often mixed with cream and sugar and left to infuse in barrels before being served neat.

In the 1990s, cocktails were fashionable if they were casually thrown together, or at least appeared to be, with minimal decoration. Now the spectacle of ordering a mini-masterpiece is no longer dismissed as old-fashioned. One sign that the old rituals are back is the renewed love of cocktail trollies. Once the epitome of starchy formality, now the gleaming trolley and the fussy preparations at the bars of the Ritz, Dukes, Shoreditch House, Quo Vadis, the Connaught, and Bring Your Own Cocktail in Covent Garden are winning a wider, younger audience.

In much the same way that classic gin brands have been spurred on to innovate by the newcomers, classic cocktail bars have been revitalised by the competition. Eighty years after head barman Harry Craddock wrote his seminal *The Savoy Cocktail Book*, the hotel's American Bar is still a beacon of cocktail-making – the present head bartender, Erik Lorincz, is winning world-class accolades and the bar is buzzing. However, the Savoy cannot afford to be complacent; it has a great deal to compete with around London.

Over in Piccadilly the Ritz's Rivoli Bar, an homage to gold leaf and Lalique, underwent a drastic overhaul in 2011 to bring it up to date with all the changes in cocktail-making. A new Portuguese bar manager, Luis Simoes, shook up the menu, taking the plunge of halving the number of cocktails and making sure that the staff perfected a smaller selection instead. Simoes' cocktail cull paid dividends very quickly. Over the next two years, cocktail sales soared from 1,000 a month to up to 6,000. The old list had not changed much in over ten years, but now it is reviewed quarterly. House drinks are sacrosanct however and will be safely on the menu for years to come, such as the Ritz 100, which was invented to celebrate the centenary of the hotel and is made with Champagne, vodka, Grand Marnier and peach liqueur, topped with 24-carat gold leaf.

Like its more casual counterparts, the Ritz is now keeping up with cocktail trends as never before. This involves making many ingredients in-house and seeking out the latest gins, the most popular of which with Ritz drinkers are currently The Botanist from Islay and No. 3 London Dry Gin, made for London wine merchants Berry Bros. & Rudd. The gin list leans so far towards the high-end that there is no Gordon's – or so it appears, until you catch sight of a familiar green bottle on their cocktail trolley. They do have Gordon's, but it is sixty years old. So if you have ever wondered what it was like to drink a Negroni in the 1950s, you can order their £90 version made exclusively with ingredients of the period. Despite the inherent formality of the Rivoli, Simoes manages to coax fashionable drinkers in with creative presentation. When he arrived one of the first things that he did was to investigate what treasures lay in the hotel cellars. Alongside rare spirits for the vintage drinks list, he found the silver room, and the miniature shakers and treasure chests from there are now used to serve the Manhattan cocktails.

Francisco Santos, Simoes' deputy, is thrilled to find that drinkers are far more open to trying new gins now. These days if you order a simple 'gin and tonic' the Ritz waiters immediately suggest four different brands that may be to taste. The new gins are so popular that the bar is introducing a separate menu of their favourite combinations of gin, tonics and garnishes, including a gin-based tribute to Margaret Thatcher, who lived at the Ritz in her final years.

At the Langham, the hotel bar has undergone a similarly comprehensive makeover. Artesian has been transformed from a dowdy polo-themed bar into a low-lit, velvet-lined drinking den with bartenders Alex Kratena and Simone Caporale at the helm. Like the Rivoli, they reduced the old menu to fewer than half of the thirty-five cocktails that it used to offer. Instead of trying to cover all the bases, they focus on presenting their new cocktails as memorably as possible. In fact, they almost certainly serve London's most outlandish concoctions. The Forever Young comes concealed behind a mirror so that leaning in to drink from the straw gives the drinker an up-close view of themselves, and Opium incense sticks are tucked behind the mirror to create a smoky, mystic feel. Artesian's Super Panda cocktail is also a sight to behold. The drink is served in a tumbler sitting on top of a small paper cushion filled with a tangerine aroma. As the tumbler crushes the inflated paper, the aroma is released to accompany the cocktail. Plastic stirrers, glacé cherries and paper doilies clearly do not cut it with today's drinkers.

Thanks to the enthusiasm of bartenders and distillers, London is both the gin and cocktail capital of the world. Artesian has now won the title of best bar in the world for two years running, and London bars make up four of the top ten in *Drinks International*'s all-important rankings. It is no coincidence that London's gin and cocktails have experienced a revival at the same time. As effusive Italian bartender Giuliano Morandin, who has worked at the Dorchester for twenty-eight years, explains, 'There is no real flavour to vodka as such,' but with gin, on the other hand, 'there are so many weird and wonderful things that you can mix with the spirit that makes it so creative to work with.'

As well as exploring conventional cocktail bars, gin lovers are also discovering how gin is made and how they can blend their own at places such as the City of London Distillery, the London Gin Club and the Ginstitute. Weekly master classes and tastings, such as the Juniper Society at the Graphic Bar in Soho, Gin School in Chiswick and the Gin Ramble walking tour are invariably booked up months in advance. At the moment the Guinness World Record for the world's largest commercially available gin collection is held by the Feathers Hotel in Oxfordshire with its 161 bottles. However, the Graphic Bar in Soho is now snapping at its heels with a tally of over 180, hoping to bring the accolade to gin's spiritual home.

So how did Londoners become hooked on the spirit in the first place? Remnants of past gin drinkers and makers are to be found all over the city, it is just a case of knowing where to look . . .

2: The Trouble Begins

GENEVER

*Malty and smooth, Dutch genever would have been served neat,
at room temperature*

WHEN WILLIAM OF Orange arrived on the coast of Devon in 1688 to rule Britain, he heralded a rather inglorious revolution in drinking. Once the new Dutch king had made himself at home at Hampton Court Palace, one of his first major decisions was to liberalise gin distilling. This fateful move in 1690 led directly to Britain's first binge-drinking epidemic – one that would take sixty years to finally wrestle under control.

Thanks to William's new rules, with only ten days' notice and a token fee to Customs, anyone could make spirits out of British grains. This new lax approach had the benefit of rewarding William's landowning supporters because the excess grain, and ones not fit for food, that were grown on their land could now be sold off to make cheap spirits instead. Landowners and farmers thereafter had strong shared interests with the distilling industry, and it became a tricky alliance to defeat. Whenever anti-gin campaigners argued for a clampdown in the decades to come, they would have to make an assurance to the landed gentry that they would not suffer financially. For William, this encouragement of the gin trade was an expedient move. For London, it would prove a disaster.

The idea of drinking a juniper-flavoured spirit recreationally came from William's native Holland, and until he opened the floodgates for the British to make their own, they had to rely on imported genever, also known as Hollands. It was only available on a very small scale, so it was naturally the preserve of upper-class drinkers; the very fact that it was imported gave it a sophisticated aura. An inability to grow grapes in Britain also made wine and grape-based spirits such as brandy and port into elite drinks, leaving a limited selection of alcohol for everyone else. In the nineteenth century the British would manage to create a new product altogether – London Dry – but in the meantime they would make do with a rip-off version of the Dutch original.

Just as no one person can take the credit for inventing vodka or whisky, genever's Dutch roots are similarly murky. It is often attributed to Dr Franciscus Sylvius at the University of Leiden, with the claim that he was the first person to intro-duce juniper berries into alcohol at his laboratory, in the hope of treating kidney and bladder complaints. However, so far no mention of 'genever' has been found in Sylvius's papers from his fourteen-year stint at the university from 1658. In any case the 1650s seem too late a date, because even in Britain there were already similar spirits being made on a small scale for medicinal purposes. Precisely when the British elite found a taste for genever is uncertain, but the phrase 'Dutch courage' is thought to come from the Thirty Years'

War (1618–48), when British soldiers fighting alongside the Dutch adopted their custom of fortifying themselves with a tot of genever.

To this day, Dutch genever and London Dry gin remain very distinct. The Dutch still hold genever dear as a national drink, in the same way that London Dry now symbolises a certain kind of Britishness. When a Dutch delegation brought traditional items to the Lord Mayor of London, Sir Frederick Rowland, in 1950, he was presented with a stone bottle of Dutch gin and a keg of twelve herrings by a girl in national costume. Subtle it was not, but it did make the point that we should not forget gin's Dutch connection. For all the popularity of London Dry, the Dutch are resolutely proud of their own genever and to this day it is still the Netherlands' best selling spirit.

However, not only would the British create their own ways of making gin, they developed their own drinking culture around it. 'Antisocial behaviour' is a modern term, but eighteenth-century Londoners were all too familiar with what they referred to as 'brawling'. The first Licensing Act, passed under Edward VI back in 1552, was triggered by the 'intolerable hurts and troubles' that arose in 'common alehouses', and ever since successive parliaments have struggled to curb Britain's culture of heavy drinking. As recently as 2012, the coalition government published a strategy for implementation in 2015 to grapple with this national problem as British people's bingeing levels remain some of the highest in the world.

However troublesome the alehouses had been, when the gin shops sprang up, they were an entirely new low in badly behaved clientele. Until the gin shops came along, for centuries alehouses had been the most basic drinking holes, with taverns one cut above because they generally sold more expensive food and drink, and sometimes offered accommodation. Inns were at the top of the hierarchy as they were akin to basic hotels. The ale at the 'common alehouses' was cheap and routinely drunk throughout the day from the early morning, but it was fairly weak stuff. If legislators felt that the behaviour from too many ales was 'intolerable', they were in for a very rude awakening.

For gin created a 'new kind of drunkenness', as a fearful Henry Fielding, the author of *Tom Jones* and one of London's most active magistrates, would describe it. It proved all the more frightening for taking hold among Londoners on the perilous fringe of self-sufficiency, at a time when society could offer precious few safety nets. Throughout the gin craze period, the upper classes would continue to get merrily drunk on sherry, brandy and claret without interference as heavy drinking in elite circles never made it on to the political agenda. Gin, however, had different connotations; it became synonymous with the darkest aspects of London – its poverty and desperation.

Not only was gin cheap to make, but it also had little competition, particularly while William was at war with Louis XIV of France. With duties on French wine ratcheted up and brandy banned altogether, gin provided one alcoholic alternative. However, Londoners' early attempts to make it were of such poor quality that anyone who could afford it carried on paying for the Dutch import. British gin would not become popular with the upper classes for another 150 years. To keep them well-oiled while heavy taxes remained on their favourite drinks, the 1703 Treaty of Methuen established favourable duties for Iberian fortified wine, allowing port and sherry to come into their own for the first time.

Until William's free-for-all, only a select group of wealthy Londoners were allowed to distil spirits within twenty-one miles of the city. A Royal Charter granted by Charles I had bestowed the Worshipful Company of Distillers the power to run a monopoly of those making any 'Aqua Vitae, Aqua Composita, and other strong and hot waters'. The distillers' regal connections went further than just its royal charter. Among its illustrious founders were Dr Thomas Cademan, Henrietta Maria's physician, who became the first master of the company, and Sir Theodore Turquet de Mayerne, physician to James I and Charles I. One of de Mayerne's own recipes for a typical aqua vitae, Latin for 'water of life', survives. It must have been a very sweet-smelling, not to mention expensive, concoction given its extensive and exotic ingredients: rue, sage, lavender, marjoram, worm-wood, rosemary, red roses, thistle, pimpernel, valerian, juniper berries, bay berries, angelica, citrus bark, coriander, sandalwood, basil, grain of paradise, pepper, ginger, cinnamon, saffron, mace, nutmeg, cubeb, cardamom, galingale.

Pulling out juniper, cinnamon, cubeb, cardamom, coriander, grains of paradise, citrus bark and angelica from the list would have made an excellent gin – not that de Mayerne would have wanted to create such a thing. Before William's intervention, distilling spirits had been a respectable medical endeavour to create liqueurs and cordials, and was never conducted on a large scale. The company described itself as supplying 'those that be aged and weak in time of sudden qualms and pangs' and the 'King's ships and merchant ships for use shipboard and for the sale to foreign nations.'

The history of home distilling had not been in the least scandalous. It was even an acceptable hobby for ladies of leisure. In courtier and alchemist Sir Hugh Platt's recipe book of 1602, *Delightes for Ladies to Adorne their Persons, Tables, Closets and Distillatories,* he included a recipe that, like de Mayerne's, featured many botanicals that we would recognise in today's gin. For his 'spirits of spices' he instructed: 'Distill with a gentle heat either in a balneo, or ashes, the strong and sweete water wherewith you have drawn oile of cloves, mace, nutmegs, juniper, Rosemarie, &c after it hath stoode one moneth close stops, and so you shall purchase a most delicate Spirite.' Lady Margaret Hoby, whose diary is the earliest known to be written by a British woman, noted between 1599 and 1605 that she often 'went about my stilling'. Her diary does not reveal whether she used any recipe books, although there would have been a few around. One of the most popular soon after was writer and poet Gervase Markham's 1615 guide to household management, *The English Housewife.* It was full of suggestions for aqua vitae that a 'compleate woman' should be able to rustle up at home in case of ailments such as 'wind colic', 'dangerous coughs' or 'any infection at the heart'. Markham singled out juniper as good for restoring sight, when mixed with fennel and gromwell seeds into ale and dropped into the eyes.

Juniper and cures for colic continued to be so closely linked that as late as 1729 a report presented to parliament referred to 'Cholick Water, which in short was Geneva'. It was widely believed to remedy all sorts of digestion problems. In his diary for 10 October 1663, Samuel Pepys recorded in unpleasant detail his attempts 'to make myself break wind and go freely to stool'. He was in such discomfort with his stomach that his friend, Sir William Batten, 'did advise me to take some . . . strong water made of juniper', although Pepys could not immediately tell if it had improved his complaint.

These days we treat botanicals as mere flavourings, but juniper, and other ingredients that make modern gin, had serious medical purposes before the gin craze. London herbalist and physician Nicholas Culpeper took up the mantle of home distilling with evangelical zeal, publishing his books in English rather than Latin to reach the widest number of people possible. He argued in his most popular work, *The English Physitian* in 1652, that anyone could treat themselves with the right herbal remedy. If Culpepper had been in the room with Pepys at the time of his indigestion, he would have advised the same remedy as Batten. He believed that there was 'scarce a better remedy for wind in any part of the body, or the cholic, than the chymical oil drawn from the [juniper] berries'.

Like Markham, Culpeper also recommended juniper for improving sight, and for a whole range of other ailments. To him, the berries were an all-purpose wonder drug. They were 'admirably good for a cough, shortness of breath, and consumption, pains in the belly, ruptures, cramps and convulsions. They give safe and speedy delivery to women with child, they strengthen the brain exceedingly, help the memory, and fortify the sight by strengthening the optic nerves; are excellently good in all sorts of agues; help the gout and sciatica, and strengthen the limbs of the body.' It seemed there was little Culpeper thought juniper could not do.

Culpeper lived and worked on Herbal Hill, a street that still runs off the Clerkenwell Road, and he collected his herbs from nearby Clerkenwell Green. It was this area of London, with its fauna and fresh water springs, that would go on to become the hub of London gin-making, although it was not until William Y-Worth's *Compleat Distiller* in 1705 that the earliest British recipes for gin as a recreational drink were published.

Appropriately, it was also around this time that one of the earliest descriptions of a gin-induced hangover emerged, discouraging people with the threat of a horrendous morning after:

> *His skull, instead of brains, supplied with cinder,*
> *His nose turns all his handkerchiefs to tinder . . .*
> *His stomach don't concoct, but bake his food,*
> *His liver even vitrefies his blood;*
> *His trembling hand scarce heaves his liquor in,*
> *His nerves all crackle under's parchment skin;*
> *His guts from nature's drudgery are freed,*
> *And in his bowels salamanders breed.*

Far from realising the legislative blunder of 1690, parliament had pressed on. The raising of tax on beer in 1694 made it more expensive than spirits for the first time, and a few years later the Worshipful Company of Distillers' remaining regulation of the industry was completely withdrawn. However, buoyant from all their tax breaks, a group of distillers published a pamphlet that deemed the policy a resounding success. They claimed that spirit-making 'hath greatly increased, and been of service to the Publick, in regard to her Majesty's Revenue, and the Landed Interest of

Great Britain'. They were not the only ones in self-congratulatory mode. Parliament was so pleased that it urged more production, reiterating in 1713: 'Any person may distil . . . spirits from British Malt.' To add yet another incentive, the 1720 Mutiny Act excused tradesmen who distilled their own gin from the inconvenience of having soldiers billeted on them.

Binge drinking en masse had never been a phenomenon until the advent of cheap gin, nor indeed of the masses themselves. Parliament's encouragement, low grain prices and the ease of making gin (or something that tasted reasonably like it) came together with the rapid growth of London to create a perfect storm. Once the gin took hold, it would prove extremely difficult to rein back in. While beer and ale could only be purchased in licensed premises, the selling of gin would go unregulated in backstreets for decades. The scene for the gin craze was set.

3: A Slow But Sure Poyson

ROT-GUT GIN

'Oil of vitriol, Oil of almonds, Oil of turpentine, Spirits of wine, Lump sugar, Lime water, Rose water, Alum, Salt of Tartar'

Recipe for Beaufoy, James & Co. gin

STANDING ON THE gallows on a frosty day in February 1728, Joseph Barret looked out on the crowd, seeing London for a final time before the blindfold slid over his eyes. The hangman tightened the noose around his neck, and the horse-drawn cart holding him up pulled away. Barret, a 42-year-old labourer, had been found guilty of killing his son James.

In Barret's last confession, recorded at Newgate prison, he explained that before James's death, he and his wife had been beside themselves as James stayed out 'Night after Night coming Home in the greatest Disorder imaginable', that 'he beg'd Money from People and bought Gin with it, drinking till he appear'd worse than a Beast, quite out of his Senses'. To rescue him from this self-destruction, Barret 'prepar'd a Cat of Nine-Tails for his Chastisement', a skill he had acquired in the navy. He had 'no evil intention . . . only to

reclaim him (if possible) from his wild Courses', but Barret
beat his son so ferociously that he took to his bed and died.
James was only eleven.

In St Giles in the Fields, where the Barret family lived,
James's behaviour was tragically unremarkable. The pastoral-
sounding parish was in fact the most notorious slum in the
country. Barret acknowledged that James's drinking was
'extravagant' for a boy his age, but nothing more. Fittingly,
William Hogarth would choose St Giles as the nightmarish
setting for his iconic etching *Gin Lane* twenty years later.

On the scaffold alongside Barret that day was 22-year-old
George Weedon, who was hanged for burglary. In his last
confession, Weedon insisted that he had never stolen more
than an apple as a boy, and that he had enjoyed a Christian
upbringing and a good education. When asked how he had
then become such a 'vile wretch', he furnished the increasingly familiar explanation – gin. By the time of his last theft
of 'Eight Pewter-dishes, and Twenty Pewter-plates', Weedon
had left his mother's house, abandoned his bookbinding
apprenticeship and moved in with a gang of thieves whom he
had met at a gin shop. Weedon's sorry conclusion was that
gin shops had 'prov'd his Ruin'. It was just the kind of slide
into destitution from which Joseph Barret was hoping to save
his own wayward son.

These 'death row' confessions to the Ordinary of Newgate
prison were published for the public as moral lessons, available to buy as a kind of grisly theatre programme to accompany executions. Weedon's confession of a gin-lubricated slide
into criminality played well into the notoriety building up
around London's newest spirit. Londoners became fearful of

the repeated narrative of serious criminals starting off as petty thieves and ending up perpetrating the most heinous crimes. Gin was portrayed as the ultimate corruptor of the poor, and the gin shop was, accordingly, London's most notorious crucible of criminality. As James Baker, a twenty-year-old hanged for robbery a few years later put it, having 'too much liberty' he was 'one of them who frequented Gin-Shops' where he 'got into the acquaintance of the vilest Company in the World, who for two or three Years past, drove him headlong to destruction and into all kinds of Villanies'.

These confessions confirmed the worst fears of the London grand jury, whose role it was to decide which cases would go to trial at the Old Bailey. The jury noted that 'Most of the Murders and Robberies lately committed have been laid and concentrated at Gin Shops,' and warned that 'fired with these Hot Spirits' criminals were 'prepared to execute the most bold and daring Attempts'. On a more sympathetic note, Henry Fielding, in his capacity as chief magistrate at Bow Street, felt reluctant to sentence these gin-addled unfortunates: 'I have plainly perceived, from the State of the Case, that the Gin alone was the Cause of the Transgression, and have been sometimes sorry that I was obliged to commit them to Prison.'

However, with such a fragile structure in place for keeping law and order, any hint of subversion or violence was deeply feared for the havoc it could quickly cause. The state's growing inability to control gin-drinkers exposed just how vulnerable the city was to disorder. There was no idea of a professional police force for London yet. The streets were patrolled only by nightwatchmen, untrained men who were paid a token amount by the parish, and by Beadles during the day.

The gin itself would have varied greatly from bottle to bottle, batch to batch, and recipe to recipe, because the methods and ingredients were so improvised – but the perception was the same. The very word became sullied with connotations of alcoholic squalor; a shorthand for everything that was wrong with London's urban underclass. Drunkenness from gin was far worse than a silly overindulgence. It was toxic, literally and metaphorically. What had been a rarefied spirit drunk by the elite in the seventeenth century evolved into a recourse for the desperate and disenfranchised in the eighteenth. Henry Fielding, who saw many sad cases, described it as 'The Poisoner of a Fountain, whence a large City was to derive its Waters'. Clergyman Thomas Wilson, who presented an anti-gin pamphlet to parliament, warned that it was an 'infection' that permeated the lives of the working poor. It was a 'slow but sure Poyson' that entered the very marrow of drinkers, destroying their appetite and weakening their nerves. He described it as a drug, 'both in its Nature and in the Manner of its Operations'.

Until now, outside religious circles, drunkenness had been depicted as a fairly benign, even comical state. With gin, it took on a new resonance as nihilistic. Heavy gin-drinking was not celebratory in the way that other drinking was portrayed. On annual holidays, Londoners traditionally drank excessively to relax, but the culture surrounding gin was not about drinking for an organised knees-up, but as a relentless, grim way of life. It was the first time in British history that a spirit had been so cheap and loosely regulated, and the result was a crisis of alcoholism that became entrenched in London's poorest areas.

4: Gin Geography

DOG'S NOSE
1 pint of warm pale ale or porter, a shot of gin,
a sprinkle of nutmeg

BY THE TIME that the gin craze was becoming widespread in the 1720s London was the fourth largest city in the world, home to 10 per cent of the entire British population. Thanks to a deluge from the countryside of budding job-hunters looking for work as apprentices, labourers and servants, its population became young and transient. For these new arrivals, with few friends and little spending money, cheap gin shops were an attractive place to wile away long nights in a strange city.

For centuries, the prevailing wisdom had been to contain the burgeoning city within its Roman walls. It was an area of only around one square mile, so this resulted in warrens of courts and alleyways tucked behind the main streets as Londoners struggled to squash in. It was in these backstreets, crammed with dingy tenements, that the unlicensed gin shops flourished unchecked. As a quick release from the drudgery of everyday life, they proliferated across the slums of the West End, into east London and across the river to the notoriously run-down area of Southwark. London was a city that boasted theatres, pleasure gardens, fairs and elegant shops, but they were never too far away from a gin shop, gambling den or brothel. As west London became more popular with the wealthy, drawing them out to tranquil Kensington and Chelsea, central London became ever more socially mixed. There, affluence and poverty existed side by side, and superiors found the visibility of drunks in public places highly distasteful.

Daniel Defoe, the author of *Robinson Crusoe*, was horrified by 'the abuse of that nauseous liquor among our lower sort' that he observed when he walked through town, thanks to 'the prodigious number of shopkeepers whose business is wholly and solely the selling of spirits'. When London authorities did eventually investigate the scale of the problem with their creaking bureaucracy in 1751, they found 17,000 'private gin shops' in a city of only 600,000 people. The High Constable of Holborn reported 7,066 of them in his patch alone, so roughly one house in every five there was waiting to relieve Londoners of their meagre wages. These figures did not even include all the inns, taverns, alehouses and private homes where gin was available too. The temptation to drink was everywhere. It was little wonder that those who could afford it were moving out to the west London suburbs – the middle of town was bedlam.

There were shockingly few curbs on the gin shops, which were potentially open twenty-four hours a day, seven days a week, until 1839, when the first Sunday Closing laws were enacted. It would also only be in the Victorian era that children were legally protected from alcohol, and even then the laws were not strictly enforced. All this laxity meant that in the 1720s around 2.5 million gallons of gin were produced annually in the capital. As the gin craze gained a frightening momentum the amount that Londoners were drinking per head every year quadrupled between 1720 and 1730, and nearly doubled again in the 1730s.

Drinkers, in fact, did not have to even take the trouble to find a gin shop or public house to get their fix. Many chandlers, who were supposed to stock household items and basic food, sold it too, keen to make a little money on the side, and opportunistic street hawkers were selling it everywhere, turning up wherever there was a crowd with their portable supply. Hot gin and gingerbread became a ubiquitous pairing from these sellers as a winter warmer at fairs and executions, which were then considered family days out.

The gin and gingerbread was a particular highlight of the Frost Fair, which took place until 1841 whenever the Thames froze over enough to support stalls, tents and shoppers. Even when it was not frozen, gin was still available on the Thames. Boatmen sold a cheap, warming drink to sailors on the barges and small rigged boats called the Dog's Nose, a cheap mix of ale and gin, which was heated on the boatmen's stoves before being decanted into pewter pots.

Of all the places where Londoners could seek out a dram, St Giles was undoubtedly the heartland of it all. The whole network of streets north of the Strand was riddled with slums, known at the time as 'rookeries', after the way that crows nest noisily together. The poet George Galloway disdainfully described these places as clusters of 'mean tenements densely populated by people of the lowest class'. It was commonly said at the time that if a criminal reached its labyrinthine, unsigned passages, the Beadles and nightwatchmen would simply turn back rather than venture in. When night fell, it took on an even greater atmosphere of mayhem.

With the unprecedented number of people arriving in London, these grim tenements strained at the seams. Many families lived in single rooms wherever they could find them – in crumbling houses, damp cellars and drafty attics. Although tame in comparison, the nearest modern equivalent would be Notting Hill in the 1950s and 1960s. Before its 1980s gentrification, Notting Hill was also home to a transient population of newly arrived, poor migrants on the hunt for cheap accommodation. In both cases, as the newcomers piled into the area, once-respectable dwellings became sub-let out of all control. The ensuing problem of a community full of sex workers, thieves and addicts who were unable to get regular work was one that was shared by Georgian London centuries earlier.

In both St Giles and Notting Hill, unscrupulous landlords carried on dividing up houses until they became unsanitary, rickety warrens, in urgent need of repair. The main difference was the ethnicity of the migrants. In post-war Notting Hill the main group arriving was from the West Indies. In Georgian London most arrivals were from the English country-side or from Ireland, although there were a few freed slaves too, nicknamed the St Giles blackbirds. The Irish's mini-ghettos within the rookeries earned nicknames such as the Holy Land and Little Dublin.

Slums such as Bedfordbury and nearby Porridge Island, behind the church of St Martin-in-the-Fields on Trafalgar Square, would not be cleared away for another century. Eventually, in 1845, New Oxford Street would be built through the middle of St Giles, to open it up to the rest of the city. Even then, a century after the gin craze, the area was profoundly impover-ished. Some residents grouped together to write to *The Times* in 1849: 'We live in muck and filth. We aint got no priviz, no dust bins, no drains, no water-splies, and no drain or suer in the hole place,' they pleaded. Archeological evidence suggests that their landlords were indeed in the habit of covering over cesspits to avoid the expense of cleaning them out, which must have been revolting for the inhabitants.

It is tricky to establish just how much gin people were also making at home for private consumption. In an area like St Giles where gin was so prevalent, as well as drinking what they could buy ready-made, people used very rudimentary distilling equipment at home – from small copper stills to improvised 'balneos' or hot-water baths. In St Giles High Street, where the multi-coloured Central St Giles development by Renzo Piano now stands, many drinking bottles and jugs of the period have been excavated. One of London's most modern looking buildings, its foundations are sunken into a rich seam of eighteenth century relics that suggest a prolific drinking culture. Most evocative among the recent finds is an earthenware 'fuddling cup'. Found at the former heart of the rookery, the vessel was fashioned of three cups that were intertwined at the bottom. 'Fuddling' meant to confuse or stupefy, so it was clearly hoped that by mixing the contents of the cups, drunkenness would be accelerated. There is little sense that Londoners of this period were drinking to appreciate the flavour of the gin – they were drinking to lose themselves.

5: Into the Georgian Gin Shop

BASIC GIN

'Take of juniper-berries three pounds, proof spirit ten gallons, water four gallons. Draw off by a gentle fire till the feints begin to rise and make up your goods to the strength required with clean water'

Ambrose Cooper, 'The Complete Distiller'

As IT WOULD be another twenty years before many large-scale professional distillers would emerge to make 'proper' gin, most of it was made at this time by opportunistic amateurs. Served with no hint of finesse at gin shops, it was usually drunk neat and at room temperature. It was gulped and re-ordered by the dram, a small draught that roughly equated to a quarter-pint. The upper classes would carry on drinking imported genever throughout the gin craze, while the poor made do with their coarse, improvised version, which had rarely been within a mile of any real juniper. If London's amateur gin-makers had walked out to Finchley and Dulwich, they would have found juniper on the windswept commons, but few seem to have thought it worth the trek.

Gin was not the only product of which shoppers had to be very wary. Food adulteration was a widespread problem, with chalk used to thicken watered-down milk, and alum to colour bread. Even expensive brandy was frequently tainted, or in the worst cases something else entirely. Imitation brandy could be rustled up from stewed oil of Cognac, orris root, black tea, prunes and rose leaves. It was given ironic nicknames such as 'French Cream', or ones that described how nasty the taste was, such as 'Ball o' Fire' or 'Cold Tea'. However, brandy, Holland's and sherry were much harder for bootleggers to imitate than gin simply because they were more complicated to make in the first place.

Making counterfeit gin was relatively straightforward. Without the costly ingredients needed for the real thing, Londoners improvised alternatives that were easy to come by. Turpentine and sulphuric acid were often used to replicate its flavour and warming sensation and although these unappetising ingredients were much maligned, there was good reason for them. Turpentine, for example, was not as peculiar a substitute for juniper as it sounded. It is distilled from pine resin, which means that it shares one of juniper's most prominent components, pinene. The sulphuric acid, or oil of vitriol, is indeed as unpleasant as it sounds, but it does not distil, so it could be used to purify the alcohol without ending up in the actual drink. It can also react with alcohol to produce diethyl ether, which tastes sweet and is not harmful in carefully controlled amounts. Large amounts of diethyl ether would certainly be toxic, but the amount needed to add flavour is unlikely to have poisoned people.

Even if they were not quite as bad as they sound respectable Londoners were horrified by these shortcuts. In *The Complete Distiller* handbook, Ambrose Cooper informed his readers that 'the common sort' of gin was 'not made from juniper berries as it ought to be but from Oil of Turpentine'. He went on to give a description of 'what is sold at the alehouses' and reflected, 'it is surprising that people should accustom themselves to drinking it for pleasure'. He recommended instead a simple recipe with proper juniper: 'Take of juniper-berries three pounds, proof spirit ten gallons, water four gallons. Draw off by a gentle fire till the feints begin to rise and make up your goods to the strength required with clean water.'

Even over a century later William Terrington, in his cocktail book *Cooling Cups and Dainty Drinks*, observed that 'almost every distiller . . . has a mode of his own in making Gin . . . giving it his own characteristic flavour with the aid of oil of turpentine or other aromatics'. As Terrington grouped turpentine with 'other aromatics', he did not seem to have been quite so horrified by it as Cooper, his gin-craze-era predecessor.

Gin shops were set out for customers to drink quickly, standing up, or to fill up casks to take away. The emphasis on hasty drinking reflected the kind of clientele that the gin shops attracted, as a large number of these inner-city Londoners were strangers to each other. The shops were not the welcoming centre of a neighbourhood in the way that well-established taverns and alehouses were. Their quick, cheap service was in keeping with how the urban poor ate their food as well. Unable to pay for upmarket taverns or inns where they could sit in comfort, and without the space to prepare food at home, they often bought ready-made food from 'cook shops'. A typical dinner would have been boiled off-cuts of meat brought home from the cook shop, washed down with gin and water.

For the poor living in the middle of London, the gin shop around the corner was one of the few places that they could afford as a change of scene from home or work. The gin shop itself was often little more than a wooden bar in a spare room so these bustling, ephemeral drinking holes left behind very few physical traces. However, so many crimes took place in them that they left an invaluable paper trail at the Old Bailey, giving a sense of their clientele and atmosphere. One such customer whose case ended up at the Old Bailey was bricklaying labourer Benjamin Gosling.

After a night of carousing, Gosling was weaving back to his rented room in White Horse Alley off Drury Lane. Covent Garden, where he lived, up to Holborn and Charing Cross, had become a thriving entertainment district with a distinctly seedy undertone. Between one and two o'clock in the morning on a bitter January night, Gosling was approached on Drury Lane by Phyllis Noble from St Clement Danes, a slum behind the Strand. 'How d'ye do my Dear – 'tis bloody cold weather – I wish you'd give me a Dram,' she coaxed. The subtext of her street-corner invitation was not lost on Gosling. The two struck a bargain and headed to the nearest warm gin shop.

There, the landlady had a private room alongside the bar for just such a liaison. Although gin shops offered little in the way of comforts, a private room was often available to hire for brief encounters. The total bill came to 8d, although Gosling was not impressed with Noble's services. He ungraciously reflected in court, 'I must needs say, I might as well have gone home to any Wife.' To make an unsatisfying evening worse, Noble had made off with his brass money box and two guineas. Noble, for her part, told the Old Bailey that she was already in the gin shop – to warm up on a cold night, she added defensively – when Gosling, who was 'very drunk . . . fain would have been rude with me'. Noble said that he threatened her with a pistol to have sex with him outside the shop, but the jury did not believe her. Through crimes like these we get a detailed picture of who went to gin shops and what they were hoping for when they did. It gives us a rare insight into the underbelly of Georgian society.

Thomas Tutty had a very similar experience. He was walking in Coleston's Court, also off Drury Lane, in the early hours of the morning in October 1723. There he met Katherine Speed and an unnamed woman from St Giles in the Fields, who stopped to ask him for a dram. After spending half a crown on gin, Tutty ended up in bed, 'betwixt them, in a very loving Posture', in a room above the gin shop. Tutty recounted that Speed then 'thrust her Hand down his Breeches and pull'd out all that he had, which was 18s 6d'.

When Tutty gave chase, he found the pair at another gin shop, buying themselves a congratulatory drink. Low-grade prostitutes like Phillis Noble and Katherine Speed charged only a pint of gin and a few shillings, but clients often found themselves parting with much more. Noble and Speed were the lowest kind of prostitute. Women further up the pecking order worked from their own rooms or bawdy houses, with a few regular clients, rather than soliciting strangers on the street.

The infamous slogan that was said to advertise many gin shops at the time was 'Drunk for a penny, dead drunk for two pence, clean straw for nothing.' It does seem that the clean straw was indeed needed on occasion. It provided a soft corner in which customers could pass out until they were sober enough to walk home, and it was not unusual for customers to sleep there on the floor after a heavy drinking session. An unnamed man accused Elizabeth Strawbridge and Hannah Armstrong of stealing two pounds and fifteen shillings from him in January 1726. He insisted that he was on his way home to his wife at 4 a.m. after a night out when the women took him by each arm and carried him to a gin shop in Crown Court, St Giles. After an hour of drinking, he said that he went to sleep there in the shop, presumably on that inviting straw, and woke up in time to walk home to bed by 6 a.m. His wife, fearing the worst, had searched his pockets to find only a penny left. He must have been far from alone in waking up at the gin shop hungover, full of regret, and not entirely sure what had happened the night before.

6: Madam Geneva's Women

GIN AND PEPPERMINT
To a pint of gin add 2 ounces of mint leaves and steep for a month before decanting.

'One may know by your Kiss, that your Ginn is excellent.'

Peachum to Mrs Trapes in 'The Beggar's Opera'

THE PRESENCE OF women at all at gin shops, let alone the prostitutes, added an extra layer of revulsion for respectable Londoners. As eighteenth-century social commentator Bernard de Mandeville observed, gin charmed 'the inactive, the desperate and crazy of either Sex'. Unlike taverns and inns, rough and ready gin shops did not develop an acceptable code of conduct or discreet, designated areas for women – they were just up at the bar, drinking with the men. Women could buy as much alcohol there as they wanted without gender politics getting in the way.

Gin and female promiscuity became a firmly embedded cultural association during the gin craze. Bishop Thomas Secker complained that as well as the main bar, each gin shop had a back room or cellar, where men and women mingled without inhibition. 'Here they might commit what wickedness they pleased,' Secker stormed in the House of Lords. A royal proclamation that railed against gin shops had similar complaints: 'Women have been seen exposing their sex in such a condition, that 'twas an offence to every modest eye.'

The very fact that a woman was drinking gin was cause enough to suspect her of lasciviousness, never mind the fact that so many women at the gin shops really were prostitutes, out soliciting trade. There were so many prostitutes around Covent Garden that from 1757 to 1795 a directory was printed annually, which unsurprisingly sold rather well. One historian has estimated that *Harris's List of Covent Garden Ladies,* as it was delicately titled, sold at least 250,000 copies altogether. It guided readers through the 120 best-known ladies, describing their skills and appearance.

The whole notion of women going out drinking unaccompanied tapped into a wider fear of freedom from male control. Many female migrants would have arrived in London without their families and therefore without the close moral guidance that Georgian society expected. The compact area of central London and its higher wages meant that women were also much more mobile and independent than in the countryside. For contemporaries, this reinforced the dichotomy of the countryside as an idealised, wholesome place where propriety was maintained, while the city was full of sinful, gin-swilling freewheelers.

As the craze gathered momentum gin acquired a feminine identity, as suggested by its 'Madam Geneva' nickname. This femininisation could have simply arisen from the perception that more women than men drank gin, or perhaps because of that older, biblical notion of women's power to corrupt and seduce – as exemplified by the original temptress Eve in the Garden of Eden. Madam Geneva represented that same ugly, dark side of femininity that had the power to lead men into temptation.

For female drinkers themselves, it gave them the reputation not only of promiscuousness but of bad motherhood. From legal cases, we can see that Madam Geneva's powerful cultural symbolism was a useful way to stain a woman's character. When Matthias Brinsden was charged with murdering his wife Hannah, he alleged that she had a gin addiction in an attempt to garner sympathy from the jury. Accused of stabbing her in the chest at their home in the parish of St Ann Blackfriars, near St Paul's Cathedral, Brinsden said that he reached for the knife because Hannah was 'half Speed', or 'half cut' in modern parlance, and that she wanted 'to go to her Companions at the Gin Shop' so she 'endeavour'd to slip behind him'. When he saw her making for the door, he decided to restrain her from going to the gin shop. He said that he 'turn'd about with the Knife in his Hand, to prevent her, and she in Strugling to get out, thrust her self against it before he was aware'. On this occasion, the ploy did not work. Brinsden was found guilty after witnesses testifying against him said that he had in fact stabbed Hannah after she was heard asking him for meat for supper, which he was not able to provide. It was not an argument over her drinking at all. Character witnesses told the court that he was a 'very ill Husband, often abusing and beating his wife'.

In literature, one of the earliest mentions of gin's appeal to women was in *The Beggar's Opera* by John Gay, set among London's robbers and prostitutes. First performed in 1728, the gin is sloshing liberally throughout the play among the cast of unappealing women. Some maintained a little dignity by claiming they were drinking for medicinal purposes, but others, such as Mrs Diana Trapes, a hag who receives stolen goods, were more brazen. She indulges in flirtatious banter with police informer Peachum:

> Peachum: *Dear Mrs Dye, your servant – One may know by your Kiss, that your Ginn is excellent.*
> Mrs Trapes: *I was always very curious in my Liquors.*
> Peachum: *There is no perfum'd Breath like it – I have been long acquainted with the Flavour of those Lips . . . Han't I Mrs Dye?*
> Mrs Trapes (holding out cup): *Fill it up – I take as large Draughts of Liquor, as I did of Love. – I hate a Flincher in either.*

In keeping with the depiction of gin as a female drink, this even extended to children. In drawings such as Hogarth's *Gin Lane*, behind the central figure of the drunken mother with her baby falling out of her arms, the impish orphan girls are depicted already out drinking in the street; and in the mawkish drawing *Children & Gin* by an anonymous artist, it is a little girl who is shown swigging out of a stone jug outside the gin shop. A younger boy with his toy hoop is at her side ready to emulate her and take a swig himself. In his study *London Labour and the London Poor*, co-founder of the satirical magazine *Punch* and impassioned social researcher Henry Mayhew reported that although all the 'street children' drank a penny's worth to 'keep the cold out', it was again apparently the girls who were 'generally fonder of gin than the boys'.

This particular anxiety over women drinking gin would

continue through to the twentieth century. A government
document from the First World War showed that officers in
London were sent out specifically to make a report of
'drinking conditions among women and girls'. Women
around Woolwich in south London were secretly observed
from 4 April to 1 May 1918. Officers were alarmed by the
queues of women in the streets waiting 'for bottles of spirits
on Fridays and Mondays'. They noted disapprovingly, 'on
these days we have seen such scrambles for the limited
supply of bottles, that until the women tore off the wrappers
from the bottles, they did not know whether they had 10/6
for gin, whiskey, or rum'. Even as late at the 1990s, the sight
of women drinking was still thought of as more distasteful
than that of men, with revulsion over so-called 'ladettes'.

In the eighteenth century, the scientific orthodoxy of the day
was still humorism, an explanation of the human body that
had its origins in Ancient Greece. The theory explained that
women suffered from imbalanced 'humours', which were the
four elements believed to control the body and brain. This
imbalance made them moody, capricious and weak-willed. For
a sex already thought to have a limited ability to reason and to
reject sin, gin-drinking was an especially dangerous premise.

Gin was seen to render men and women useless to society as
productive workers, but for women it had the added concern
of making them useless as mothers too. The press took up the
story, and grim tales of gin-fuelled maternal neglect became
classic fodder. One particularly distressing case in 1734 was
that of thirty-year-old Judith Dufour, a silk weaver from
Shoreditch. As a hard-working but poor French Huguenot
immigrant she was an archetypal Shoreditch resident of the
time. Like many night-workers of the period, she was partial to

a few drams of gin as she worked, to keep warm and pass the time. To raise funds for her increasingly unmanageable gin habit, Dufour hatched a plan with a friend, referred to only as Sukey in court proceedings.

Dufour decided to pay her illegitimate two-year-old daughter Mary a visit at the Bethnal Green workhouse. The wardens were suspicious of Dufour's sudden interest in her daughter. There was a thriving trade for second-hand, often stolen, clothes at the time and Mary had just received a set of new clothes courtesy of the parish. The workhouse wardens waited for the churchwardens to send them a note authorising Mary's release into Dufour's care for the day – on the condition that Mary was brought back before nightfall.

Sukey and Dufour went out drinking, with Mary in tow, after they collected her from the workhouse that Sunday. When they ran out of money at around 6 p.m., they walked Mary out to the fields of Bethnal Green, where they stripped her of her new coat, petticoat and stockings. To stifle Mary's cries, they tied a handkerchief around her neck, and hit her over the head. Pushing the body into a ditch, where Mary was later found dead, they then walked back into town. Seemingly lacking any remorse, they sold her outfit for 1s 4d and spent the proceeds on two quarterns of gin. Grim news stories like this, told in melodramatic fashion in the contemporary press, served only to entrench gin's deteriorating image. The story was recounted in one of the most popular anti-gin pamphlets of the time, and in Thomas Wilson's widely read *Distilled Spirituous Liquers, the bane of the Nation*, which ran to two editions.

Two years later the tale of Mary Estwick caused another public outrage, with her horrifying neglect of a child in her care. Again, her behaviour was put down to her gin addiction. Estwick, an elderly childminder, came home at two in the afternoon 'quite intoxicated with Gin, sate down before the fire, and it is supposed, had the child in her lap, which fell out of it on the hearth, and the fire catched hold of the child's clothes and burnt it to death'. Estwick apparently slept on in a stupor. Neighbours said that when they arrived to try to rescue the baby, Estwick was 'so intoxicated, she knew nothing of what had been done'.

7: *Clamping Down on the Poisoners-General*

GIN FLIP

*3 ounces lump sugar; grated nutmeg; grated ginger; 1 pint strong
ale; 2 wineglasses gin – heated with a hot poker*

IN ALL ITS horror, the gin craze changed the way that the
British perceived drunkenness. Alcohol had long been a
preoccupation for religious writers on moral grounds, but gin
earned itself a much broader coalition of critics. It came
under attack on multiple fronts – as a health hazard, a drain
on the economy, a catalyst for crime, a facilitator of sexual
immorality and a destabiliser of public order. Anti-gin
campaigners became convinced that eradicating it was the key
to solving all sorts of undesirable behaviour among the poor.

Physicians began publishing treatises and pamphlets calling
for everything from prohibition to an early form of aversion
therapy. Later, social commentators, satirists, lawyers and
politicians would join the fray with their suggestions. One of
the first people to ever investigate the physical damage that
gin was capable of inflicting was the corpulent Scottish
physician George Cheyne. He had suffered from health
problems himself as a young man when he fell in with 'bottle

companions' as he called them. His early experimentation with alcohol led him to study its habit-forming properties. After his *Essay on Gout* in 1720, the work that really made his name was *An Essay on Health and Long Life* in 1724. In it, he warned that 'running into Drams' was so destructive that 'neither Laudanum nor Arsenick will kill more certainly'. He exhorted the public to drink in moderation, for the sake of their bodies as well as their souls.

As health fears grew, the following year the Royal College of Physicians presented a petition to the House of Commons, warning of the 'fatal effects of the frequent use of several sorts of distilled Spirituous Liquors'. It was the first time the organisation had been spurred into influencing government policy. Other medical experts soon joined the chorus of disapproval. Distressed by what he saw around him, the natural philosopher, botanist and clergyman Stephen Hales, a teetotaler himself, began a lifelong crusade against the evils of gin-drinking. A very eminent scientist of his day, he would be granted the honour of burial in Westminster Abbey. Like Cheyne, he was insistent that people should stop drinking for both their spiritual and physical wellbeing. In his 1734 pamphlet *A Friendly admonition to the Drinkers of Brandy, and other distilled spirituous Liquors*, written for the Society for Promoting Christian Knowledge, Hales warned readers that spirits cause 'Obstructions and stoppages in the Liver; whence the Jaundice, Dropsy, and many other fatal Diseases' and that they were so addictive that 'when men had got a habit of it, they would go on, though they saw Hell-fire burning before them'. He even had the pamphlet sent out to North America, in the hope of spreading the word as far as he could. Hales would prove instrumental in organising crusading parliamentarians who, like him, belonged to the Society for Promoting

Christian Knowledge. They would come together in 1736 to push through the disastrous Gin Act of that year, which was the closest Britain ever came to prohibition.

Alongside the SPCK, the other early pressure group was the brewers, for the less lofty reason that they were losing business. In 1726 they had started by sponsoring satirical pamphlet *The Tavern Scuffle*. In the *Scuffle*, the gin distiller was depicted as a character called Scorch-Gut, crudely described as 'Scorch Gut by nature; for that his damn'd devil's piss burnt out the entrails of three-forth's of the King's subjects'. The brewers' other tactic was to undermine the economic benefits that the distillers claimed to bring. In 1729 the Company of Distillers fought back by presenting *A brief case of the distillers* to parliament. They openly appealed to their old friendly alliance of landowners and farmers, arguing that 'the Landed Gentleman must be sensible the distillers work for him, since the distilling trade in and about London only, consumes about 200,000 quarters of corn, and that corn necessarily employs 100,000 acres of land'. The distillers had the bravado to argue that it also benefitted the poor by giving them employment, but even they had to concede that there was 'no Apology to be made for Vice, no extenuating of Crimes, no Harangues for Drunkenness'.

Whatever the debates and hand-wringing taking place in parliament, it proved fiendishly difficult to actually initiate any policies to curb Londoners' excesses. From 1690 until the first Gin Act in 1729, parliament had actively encouraged the sale of gin as a rich source of tax revenue. Then between 1729 and 1751, eight acts were passed attempting to undo all of this damage. At their best, the acts were ineffectual; at worst, they made the situation even worse.

The first act, in 1729, raised taxes on spirits to 5s a gallon and restricted gin sales to premises which had to take out a hefty £20-a-year licence. This was intended to drive out the backstreet gin shops, but the toothless new rules went largely ignored. Only a trickle of prosecutions followed and consumption went spiraling up regardless. Because the law specified compounded spirits, distillers avoided the higher tax rate by simply not compounding (adding flavour to the gin after distillation) and by giving it the tongue-in-cheek name 'parliamentary brandy'. London had roughly 1,500 recorded distillers, of whom only a hundred were large enough to have equipment worth £1,000 or more. The vast majority had stills worth less than £100, producing low-quality gin for a rapidly growing audience. Parliament desperately needed to tip the balance away from these cheap, small-time distillers.

Even with the tax increase, it was still cheaper to order a pint of gin than a pint of beer. Some factories even paid their workers part of their wages in gin to cut costs, leaving those of precarious means temporarily sated but with little to take home from the working week. As late as 1831, the practice of paying wages partly in gin carried on in London's poorest areas. Coal-whippers, the men employed to haul coal off ships, caused a riot in Wapping to protest a considerable proportion of their wages being paid in gin and beer.

The failure of the first act was acknowledged when parliament revisited the problem in 1733 and it had no more success the second time around. The years 1733 to 1736 saw a big spike in spirit consumption across the board, from 4.8 million gallons to over 6 million per annum. There was a grain surplus once again, which meant that more cheap gin was available than ever before.

Admitting defeat, parliament put the tax on gin back down and, having failed to close down the gin shops, focused its efforts on street sellers instead. Informers who shopped them to the authorities would now pocket £5 for every successful conviction, half of the £10 fine that offenders had to pay. Over the next two years, some 4,000 claims were made for the reward.

However, many of the street sellers could not actually afford such a steep fine and opted to be put in the workhouse instead of paying up, leaving the informers without their reward and often facing a great deal of anger as they were reviled for telling on their neighbours. Many were pelted with stones and dirt in the street or, if the mob became particularly aggressive, even on occasion ducked into the Thames. A few suffered 'skimmington rides', a ritual humiliation more commonly used to mock cuckolded husbands. It involved a public procession in which the informer was taunted while being marched or carried through the community. One suspected informer was 'set upon an ass . . . while others beat and pelted him, leading him up and down Bond Street'. In August 1734 another was 'horse-ponded', which involved being thrown into a pond that was used to water horses, in Moor's Yard next to St-Martin-in-the-Fields. Between being hounded and abused in their communities and often not getting their money in any case, the network of informers broke down.

As heavy-drinking women were giving birth to sickly children, this aspect of alcohol abuse became the issue of the day. The Royal College of Physicians' petition had warned that gin-drinking was 'too often the cause of weak, feeble, and distemper'd children', in what we now call foetal alcohol syndrome. In 1735 a commission of Middlesex justices took up the cause and reported that drinking during pregnancy meant that babies were now being born 'shrivel'd and old as though they had numbered many years'.

A year later, clergyman Thomas Wilson presented his research, *Distilled Spirituous Liqours, the bane of the Nation*, to the House of Commons. He echoed the Middlesex justices and the Royal College of Physicians, writing that drinkers gave birth to children 'half burnt up and shrivelled' and that the 'fruit of the womb' was too frequently 'blasted before it has seen the light'. Given what we know now about drinking while pregnant, these observations sound plausible, although there would have been other complications at that time, such as malnutrition and poor medical practices, to contend with as well. Wilson countered the supposed economic benefits by arguing that gin-drinkers were bad consumers, who did indeed spend a lot of their earnings, but on gin and little else.

A pamphlet presented to Master of the Rolls Sir Joseph Jekyll in the same year, *The Trial of the Spirits: Or Some Considerations Upon the Pernicious Consequences of the Gin-Trade to Great Britain*, picked up Wilson's theme that gin was causing poor families to waste all their money: 'Why, the miserable creatures, in such a situation, rather than purchase the coarser Joynts of Meat, which the Butchers used to sell at a very easy rate . . . repair to the Gin-Shops, upon whose destructive commodities they will freely lay out all they can rap or rend, till the Parish Work-Houses are filled with their poor, starv'd families.'

In the face of another miserable legislative failure, in 1736 parliament took action to hurry through a draconian act. Gin was to be taxed at the much higher rate of 20 shillings a gallon this time, and the smallest amount that retailers could sell was two gallons in an attempt to close down small producers and sellers. Exorbitant annual licence fees of £50 were brought in for all gin sellers. It was so expensive that only two bought it. Again, the authorities would have to rely on informers to find the street vendors. To improve their chances of getting their rewards this time, the informers were allowed to denounce retailers to the Excise Office, where money would be found to pay them.

For Dr Hales and his group of like-minded SPCK campaigners, this was the landmark victory for which they had been lobbying for years. The most influential member of this faction in parliament was the judge Sir John Gonson, who was immortalised in William Hogarth's *A Harlot's Progress*. Gonson's first crusade had been against gambling houses in 1723. After his success on that front, he spent the years thereafter campaigning against gin with vigour. The SPCK group believed that, with the harsh new measures, finally gin would be stamped out. On the night the act was passed, Hales reportedly 'had tears in his eyes for joy'.

The wording of the act itself explained why parliament was compelled into such a robust response: 'Whereas the drinking of spirituous liquor or strong waters has become very common, especially among the people of lower and inferior rank, the constant and excessive use whereof tends greatly to the destruction of their health, rendering them unfit for useful labour and business, debauching their morals, and inciting them to perpetrate all manner of vices; and the ill consequence of the excessive use of such liquors are not confined to the present generation, but extend to future ages, and tend to the devastation and ruin of this kingdom.' It was alarming stuff although parliament had been extremely slow to react to the scourge of gin in London, it was now seen as a crisis of national importance.

Of course, not everyone was as misty-eyed as Dr Hales at the prospect of a life without gin. The night before the 1736 act came into effect, retailers sold off their last stock in a hedonistic gin orgy. In London, Bath, Bristol and Norwich gin sellers staged mock funerals, lamenting the death of 'Madam Geneva', and a group of drunkards in Newgate Street in London were reportedly arrested for their subversive chanting of 'No Gin, No King.' The following day, greater numbers of people than usual lay about in the streets, apparently too hungover to move.

Britain's first prime minister, Sir Robert Walpole, who personally had misgivings about the act, had feared rioting over the harsh measures. He was so anxious that he doubled the number of guards on duty at St James's, Kensington and Whitehall. The disorder, in the end, did not amount to much, but it showed the aura of anarchy that gin had acquired. Later that year, it inspired the play *The Deposing and Death of Queen Gin with the ruin of the Duke of Rum, Marquis of Nantz and the Lord Sugarcane* in September at the New Theatre on Haymarket, in which the mob bayed for 'liberty, property and Gin forever'.

Many street sellers risked ignoring the act and thrived, while larger distillers and drinking establishments were stuck trying to play by the unworkable constraints on their businesses. The big distillers regularly complained to parliament that the hawkers were no less prevalent. One such wheeler-dealer was Captain Dudley Bradstreet. Bradstreet was an Irish soldier, sometime spy for the English against Bonnie Prince Charlie and an all-round chancer. He went through several careers in his erratic life – from playwright to brewer. He tells us in his autobiography, *The Life and Uncommon Adventures of Captain Dudley Bradstreet*, that he turned up in London in 1736, down on his luck and at a loose end. With all these new restrictions on selling gin, he gleefully saw his chance to cash in: 'The mob being very clamorous for want of their beloved liquor, which few . . . dared sell, it soon occurred to me to venture upon the trade.'

The trick, of course, was to avoid detection. Bradstreet persuaded an acquaintance to take a house in Blue Anchor Alley, from where to sell his gin. Then he had a cunning plan to maintain his anonymity. Buying a wooden sign of a cat, he fitted under its paw a small leaden pipe. Through the little pipe, he could funnel gin from inside the house when the paw was lifted by an eager recipient. Bradstreet spent his last £13 on gin from Langdale's distillery in Holborn, put the word about, and waited behind the cat.

Furtively, the customers came, putting coins in the cat's mouth and waiting for their fix. In a low voice, they whis-pered, 'Puss' and got a 'Mew' in return. It was then safe to ask Puss for 'twopennyworth of gin'. It would seem that Bradstreet was never arrested, even if he did have a few close calls. His cat was so popular that it became a symbol for gin, as featured on Burrough's Black Cat Gin and Boord's, which featured a black cat perched on a gin barrel, and these days it appears on Hayman's Old Tom.

So despite the high hopes, the 1736 Gin Act proved as useless as the others and it was eventually repealed in 1743.

In the seven years that it was in action it had been the worst
of both worlds – professional sellers had been driven out of
business, while bootleggers like Bradstreet thrived. An additional act in 1737 had hoped to rectify this by strengthening
penalties for unlicensed traders. They could now be 'whipped
until bloody' as well as sent to the workhouse, but still they
were not discouraged. Informers were attacked so regularly
that the punishment for assaulting them had to be stepped
up the following year as well. Now attackers could be
subjected to transportation, a relatively new punishment,
which in this period meant being permanently banished to
America.

This move came after a particularly frightening breach of the
peace earlier in 1738, when a mob descended on the house of
magistrate Sir Thomas de Veil at Frith Street, known at the
time as Thrift Street, in Soho. Despite the January chill, the
crowd kept growing around de Veil's house. According to
some accounts, they numbered nearly 1,000. Eventually, de
Veil, who had been attempting to enforce the loathed 1736
Gin Act, was forced to call troops from St James's to disperse
the crowd, who were threatening to hunt down his informers.

The gin craze continued to gather momentum in the face of
these laws, and frustrated Londoners continued to vilify it for
ruining their city. By 1740, production had risen again by a
third in four years. The despairing vice-chamberlain, Lord
Hervey, remarked that the 'Drunkenness of the common
people was universal, the whole town of London swarmed
with drunken people from morning till night.' There had, of
course, been drunk people in London since time immemorial,
but the gin-drinker was more feared than any other. Despite
general talk of the evils of alcohol in parliament, gin was the

only drink that was politicised and specifically legislated against.

A truly alarming sign of how much Londoners were drinking was the ultimate barometer of health – the mortality rate. Despite the droves of people moving in, London's population was declining because so few people were surviving into old age, even by the low standards of the time. The blame fell on gin, not only for these adult deaths but for the decrease in the birth rate and the increase in infant mortality, which was already historically higher than in the countryside. The Bills of Mortality showed a rising number of christenings up until 1728, but then a decline until 1750, which coincided with the years that the gin craze was at its peak. The weekly bills were not perfectly representative, as they only recorded Anglican baptisms and burials, and missed out parts of London, such as the parishes of Paddington, Kensington and Tottenham. However, from the numbers that they did register, they showed that there were roughly three burials for every two baptisms. Crusaders against gin seized on this as yet more evidence of the harm that it was inflicting. It was popular to use the bills to suggest that gin was directly responsible for killing people, as Thomas Wilson did when he singled it out as the reason for London's death rate being so much higher than that of any other European city.

By 1743, gin consumption was at an all-time high of 8.2 million gallons, while prosecutions for illicit selling had dropped to a trickle. With a sense of hopelessness in the air, parliament went back to the drawing board. This time they aimed to curb demand without taxes being high enough to encourage more black-market activity, as had been the mistake last time. The duties per gallon were to be lowered from twenty shillings to a few pence. The traditional drinking places could afford the new licences, which were slashed from £50 a year to £1. In only a year, 1,000 were taken out in the city. To limit the numbers, only public houses and traders who had previously been granted a licence could buy the new ones. This approach led to more respectable firms embarking on the business of distilling and retailing, which was a vital step in giving gin a leg up out of the gutter.

However, this new act only passed through parliament after a long, impassioned debate in the House of Lords. Anti-gin campaigners were predictably outraged by the new soft approach. They perceived it to be essentially giving in to popular demand in favour of deriving as much tax as possible, which they found morally reprehensible. Bishop Secker was incensed by 'the most unchristian bill that was ever brought in by any government', and took it upon himself, 'as a Christian bishop', to give battle against it 'in the most open and express manner' that he could. Bishop Sherlock lamented that parliament had 'defeated any endeavours for the suppression of wickedness'. The Bishop of Oxford railed that 'the liberty of selling liquors, which are allowed to be equally injurious to health and virtue, will by this law become general and boundless'.

Like many who joined the debate, Lord Lonsdale painted a hellish picture of London under the influence of gin as he voiced his disgust: 'Whoever shall pass among the Streets, will find Wretches stretched upon the Pavement, insensible and motionless . . . [or] others who think themselves in the Elevation of Drunkenness intitled to treat all those with Contempt whom their Dress distinguishes from them, and to resent every Injury which in the Heat of their Imagination they suppose themselves to suffer, with the utmost Rage of Resentment, Violence of Rudeness, and Scurrility of Tongue.'

He also pointed out that the discriminatory nature of legislation made people 'more fond of dram drinking than ever; because they then began to look upon it as an insult upon the rich'. This comment again suggested that the ruling classes feared gin as a drink that emboldened the poor against them, that it was in some way the spirit of anarchy. Warming to his theme, Lord Lonsdale continued that to look upon gin-drinkers is 'to see men enfeebled and consumed, or rioting in the most horrid sorts of wickedness: to see women naked and prostituted: to see children emaciated, starved or choaked'. He warned that gin shops were little more than 'traps' set up 'for drawing the unthinking vulgar into the excessive use of this liquor'.

Even if parliament stood to gain from more tax revenue, Lord Hervey pointed out the immorality of such an advantage: 'We are to establish the worst sort of drunkenness by a law . . . It is an experiment to discover how far the vices of the population may be made useful to the government.' He used the popular image of gin as toxic as he wondered 'what taxes may be raised upon a poison, and how much the court may be enriched by the destruction of its subjects'. He appealed to the pragmatic problem of not clamping down harder because, after all, gin prevailed 'most among our most necessary and useful sort of people'. Hervey was tapping into the self-interest of the politicians listening by reminding them that gin undermined the poor's utility to the rest of society.

Those in favour of the new act, such as Privy Councillor Lord Bathurst, argued that as people drank whether they were allowed to or not, it would be more civilised if they were at least permitted to do so in licensed places. He suggested that gin-drinkers would be better off at 'Houses visited by publick Officers, observed by the neighbouring Inhabitants, and frequented by Persons of Morals and Civility, who will always endeavour to restrain all enormous Excesses'. Bathurst's reasoning was that pushing gin-drinking 'underground' had made it all the more desperate and seedy.

With characteristic zeal, John Wesley, founder of the Methodist movement, singled out this act for one of his earliest sermons, *The Use of Money*. Unsurprisingly, he did not take the point that moderate policies were the way forward: 'We may not sell any thing which tends to impair health. Such is eminently all that liquid fire, commonly called drams, or spirituous liquors. It is true these may have a place in medicine . . .Therefore such as prepare and sell them only for this end, may keep their conscience clear . . . but all who sell them in the common way, to any that will buy, are poisoners-general. They murder His Majesty's subjects by wholesale, neither does their eye pity or spare. They drive them to hell like sheep.'

For all the emotive arguments in parliament and John Wesley's stirring sermon, the compromise actually worked rather well. Although it did not get back down to 1720s levels, legal gin consumption did start to ease off. It was harder to work out what was going on clandestinely, particularly as the justices of the peace had certainly lost their enthusiasm for pursuing the hawkers. Between 1745 and 1750 in Middlesex, which was then part of the London legal circuit, only two people were prosecuted for selling spirits without a licence. Other evidence suggests that infinitely more than two people were guilty of it, so it seems that the justices had simply given up.

The decline of legal gin sales rattled those with vested interests, most obviously, of course, the distillers themselves, and they orchestrated a campaign to pressure parliament into undoing its own good work. In 1747 parliament gave in and the process of weaning the public off gin was set back once more. Parliament amended the 1743 law to allow gin to be sold at shops again rather than just drinking establishments. This tweak proved disastrous, and sent consumption spiking back up again.

By 1750, Londoners were consuming over eleven million gallons of gin a year, and the city was in turmoil. As emotions ran high, in a sermon delivered to the London Common Council on Easter Monday, the Bishop of Worchester, Isaac Maddox, warned that all this gin-drinking was to blame for the crime wave gripping the city. Echoing Lord Lonsdale's fears for public order in the 1743 debates, Maddox argued that gin inflamed the populace 'against the present Distribution of property' – indeed by 'outrageous Overt Acts, the strongest *Inclination* to bring it nearer to an Equality'. In other words, it was even thought to be giving the poor dangerous ideas of rebelling against the whole current social order. Maddox's sermon and subsequent pamphlet reached a wide audience who feared these unruly paupers, and ran into three editions in six months.

However, not all thinkers of the day were quite so alarmist. In a book of recollections compiled by his confidante Hester Thrale, Dr Johnson gave a trenchant libertarian-style answer when someone asked him, 'What signifies giving halfpence to beggars? They only lay it out for gin and tobacco.'

Johnson replied: 'Why should they be denied such sweeteners of their existence? It is surely very savage to refuse them every possible avenue to pleasure reckoned too coarse for our own acceptance. Life is a pill which none of us can bear to swallow without gilding; yet for the poor we delight in stripping it still barer.'

8: Drunk for a Penny, Dead Drunk for Two Pence

RUMFUSTIAN

1 tablespoon sugar; grated nutmeg; cinnamon, 1/2 pint of old ale; 1 wineglass of sherry; 1 wineglass of gin; grated peel of 1 lemon – heated with a hot poker

❧

AGAINST THE BACKDROP of this legislative wrangling came William Hogarth's extraordinarily vivid engraving *Gin Lane*, which revealed the depths of London's degradation. It was an instant success in 1751 and its horror has been etched in the annals of the city's history ever since. Surprisingly Hogarth himself was by no means puritanical about alcohol. A sociable man about town, he thoroughly enjoyed drinking and dining. However, having experienced life at the debtor's lodgings in Fleet Prison when his father's Latin-speaking coffee house ended in bankruptcy, he felt a solemn duty to report the plight of London's poorest.

There have been accusations that Hogarth was in the pay of brewers to create anti-gin propaganda, including his masterpiece *Gin Lane*. However, with the lack of concrete evidence for this and with Hogarth's energetic campaigning with friend Henry Fielding, it seems unlikely. From his autobiographical notes, Hogarth was clearly impassioned about the subject and heartfelt about his work: 'In gin lane every circumstance of its horrid effects were brought into view, in terorem nothing but Poverty misery and ruin are to be seen, Distress even to madnes and death, and not a house tolerable condition but Pawnbrokers and the Gin shop.'

Hogarth had brought together, in one horrible vision, everything for which gin had been blamed over the past few decades: violence, poverty, crime, disease, debauchery, moral decay, and, ultimately, death. This tragic scene of paupers eking out their lives among dilapidated buildings was naturally set in St Giles. From the landmarks of the scene, it seems that Hogarth had the area behind where Centre Point now stands on Oxford Street in mind. In the foreground the poor are shown carrying their paltry furniture and tools to the pawnbroker, while men brawl in the street in front of the undertaker. Bizarrely a chimney sweep, presumably rendered mad by gin, is brandishing a baby on a stick. Gin did indeed have a reputation for creating wilder reactions in drinkers than other alcohol. Even much later, in 1839, Scottish historian and essayist Thomas Carlyle would still describe gin as 'madness sold at tenpence the quartem'.

In the foreground of *Gin Lane*, above the gin shop door, reads the slogan 'Drunk for a Penny / Dead Drunk for two pence / Clean Straw for Nothing'. Although there is little hard evidence that the advert was widely used, Hogarth was apparently inspired by a gin shop in Southwark, where he saw it written on his travels exploring the city.

The most memorable character in the scene is the central figure of gin as 'mother's ruin' represented by a drunken mother, her legs covered in syphilitic sores, who lets her baby fall as she takes a pinch of snuff. She is the undoubted focal point of the action. As featured in the work of John Gay and satirist Jonathan Swift, gin was already strongly associated with hags in popular culture. As Swift wrote in *The Journal of a Modern Lady*, describing 'fishwives' chattering 'o'er a cup of gin.'

Slumped below the embodiment of mother's ruin on the steps is an ever sicker wretch, a skeletal soldier holding a cask with a ballad called 'The Downfall of Madam Gins' falling out of his basket. Behind him two young orphan girls, who are in the care of the parish, wearing 'SG' (for 'St Giles') badges, are drinking out in the street. Hogarth included these addicted children not only for the emotive quality that it lent the scene, but because it was a genuine problem left unchecked for decades. Rescuing impoverished children was a mission to which Hogarth had a lifelong dedication. His perseverance had already resulted in one of the great philanthropic successes of the age, the Foundling Hospital, for the 'education and maintenance of exposed and deserted young children' in 1739.

Hogarth completed his hellish image with a reminder of governmental impotence in all this. The elegant statue of George I in his Roman dress in the background, looking down at the chaos from the steeple of St George's Bloomsbury, stood as an indictment of Britain's aloof political class. Underneath the image, the original caption for *Gin Lane* warned:

> *Gin, cursed Fiend, with Fury fraught,*
> *Makes human Race a Prey.*
> *It enters by a deadly Draught*
> *And steals our Life away.*

Virtue and Truth, driv'n to Despair
Its Rage compells to fly,
But cherishes with hellish Care
Theft, Murder, Perjury.

Damned Cup! that on the Vitals preys
That liquid Fire contains,
Which Madness to the heart conveys,
And rolls it thro' the Veins.

Gin Lane is so powerful that it is still used today as a trope for many cartoons. Martin Rowson from the *Guardian*, for example, reworked it into *Priority Lane* when the coalition government announced that it was going to 'crack down on "binge drinking" culture' in 2012. *Priority Lane* featured Prime Minister David Cameron as the central mother's ruin figure, with a bank as the pawnbroker, profiting from the poor. Rowson said that he chose to rework the *Gin Lane* setting because it remains such a 'recognised and highly evocative icon of substance-induced societal breakdown'.

The lesser-known drawing of the pair is *Beer Street*, the counterpoint to *Gin Lane*. By juxtaposing *Beer Street* and *Gin Lane,* Hogarth illustrated the growing dichotomy of gin as a drink for criminals and prostitutes, while beer ostensibly remained the wholesome drink of the working man. Alcohol is everywhere in *Beer Street*, but beer had the connotation of being a reward earned through honest labour, which made it socially acceptable. In *Beer Street* food is plentiful, and the poor are healthy, jolly and taking pride in their surroundings. As Hogarth himself explained, *Beer Street* was given 'as a contrast; where that invigorating liquor is recommended, in order to drive the other out of vogue. Here, all is joyous and thriveing. Industry and jollity go hand in hand.' Drinking British beer in large quantities was not only acceptable but was even actively encouraged. It was perceived as a bulwark against the wrong kind of drinking, and politicians would use it to try to wean people off gin in the nineteenth century. The only failing business here is the pawnbroker, suggesting the wider economic benefit of clamping down on gin. The flag seen in the background was the one flown by the church of St-Martin-in-the-Fields every year on George II's birthday, 30th October, lending a sense of celebration and joy to the scene.

BEER STREET.

Underneath *Beer Street*, the poem read:

> *Beer, happy Produce of our Isle*
> *Can sinewy Strength impart,*
> *And wearied with Fatigue and Toil*
> *Can chear each manly Heart.*

Matters would come to a head in the year of *Gin Lane* and *Beer Street*. A petition to the City of London in 1751 claimed that gin had 'obstructed the reproduction of a most useful Class', destroying 'the Health, Strength, and Industry of the Poor of both Sexes and of all Ages'. Henry Fielding melodramatically took it one step further and claimed that there would soon be 'few of the common people left to drink it' if the situation continued. He warned the ruling classes why they must take radical action in his *Inquiry into the Causes of the Late Increase in Robbers*: 'What must become of the Infant who is conceived in Gin? What could an Edward or a Henry, a Marlborough or a Cumberland, effect with an Army of such wretches? Doth not this polluted Source, instead of producing Servants for the Husbandman or Artificer; instead of providing Recruits for the sea or the Field, promise only to fill Alms-houses and Hospitals and to infect the Streets with Stench and Disease?'

Appealing to how it would directly affect the ruling classes was an effective way of encouraging them to act. If the poor continued to be this intoxicated and enfeebled by ill health, what use were they? The great enemy at the time was France and it was feared that the war effort would be undermined by Britain's gin-addled stock of sailors and soldiers. As many other commentators did, Fielding also made a direct link between soaring crime rates and gin-drinking.

The uselessness of the drunken poor was a recurring theme in pressing for action. Philanthropist Jonas Hanway used the same argument to claim that tea-drinking, which was believed to stimulate the brain, risked ruining the nation because of its prevalence among the lower classes. Even something as innocuous as tea was feared in their hands, in case it made them disobedient and harder to govern. Much of Hanway's *An Essay on Tea* was based on the notion that the poor's destructive tendencies must be reigned in, not necessarily for their own sake, but because it would make them more useful to everyone else. The accusations that he made about tea could easily have been mistaken for those about gin when he argued that it was 'pernicious to health, obstructing industry, and impoverishing the nation'.

The final, successful clampdown came later in the year. Based on moderation rather than another attempt at prohibition, many of the regulations proved very worthwhile. Distillers were once more barred from selling gin at shops, it was banned from workhouses and prisons, duty was pushed up and, vitally, spirits could no longer be bought on credit. Licence fees were doubled and only issued to public houses that paid rates of at least £10 per annum to exclude low-rent establishments. In order to further push small-time retailers out, the act specified that debts of less than £1 were no longer recoverable by law, which made them unappealing for distillers to deal with. For all these nuanced good ideas, there was also stringency to back it up. Punishment for hawkers was severe. For second offences, violators were imprisoned and whipped, and for third offences they were transported.

These new laws had immediate results. In 1751 approxi-mately seven million gallons of gin were taxed; the following year, it was less than 4.5 million. By the end of the 1760s, it would be fewer than two million gallons. Finally, five decades of mayhem were coming to an end. Rather than drinkers simply switching to the black market, as they had before, this fall proved a genuine one.

To mark the end of the craze, an anonymous satirical print, *The Funeral Procession of Madam Geneva*, depicted Madam Geneva's coffin moving through her heartland of St Giles because of this 'late Severe Act'. Her funeral cortège included mourning publicans, who walked past brawling women and drunk children. It was actually a tweaked reprint of a cartoon from 1736, when the 'funeral' had been premature, but this time it would have real resonance. As well as the well-considered new laws, what eventually ended the gin craze was a series of poor harvests. This sent grain prices up, which helped to make gin scarce and expensive at the same time as real wages were falling. Beer, particularly porter, and rum, as the second cheapest spirit, were fast becoming more attractive drinking options.

For all the pain and destruction of the gin craze, there were positive developments in the mid-eighteenth century in re-thinking how those on the fringes of society were treated. As contemporary thinkers and commentators had struggled to comprehend what was happening in London's inner city, it changed their attitudes towards the poor. Taboo illnesses and social problems began to be addressed more openly and with greater compassion. The opening of the Foundling Hospital in 1739, in which Hogarth had played such an instrumental part, heralded a reappraisal of how best to deal with illegiti-mate children, for example. Six years later, the London Lock Hospital, for women with sexually transmitted diseases, was

founded, and the Magdalen Hospital for penitent prostitutes
at Whitechapel was opened in 1758. These institutions were
signs of a city that was gradually facing up to its most
difficult social problems.

In the same way, discourse about alcoholism would become
less hysterical and more secular as it moved from being a
matter of sin to a medical condition – although there was not
quite the sense yet that addiction was an uncontrollable
disease, as many believe now. In Dr Johnson's *A Dictionary of
the English Language,* the verb 'to addict' was not passive. We
now refer to 'being addicted', whereas Dr Johnson and his
contemporaries defined it as 'commonly taken in a bad sense;
as, he addicted himself to vice'. The agency of the individual
was still clear then: the individual played a part in 'addicting
himself' and by extension was still culpable.

Like many physicians of the time, Erasmus Darwin, whose
fame would later be eclipsed by that of his grandson
Charles, became an advocate of temperance based on his
work and his life experience. Darwin's first wife, Mary,
Charles's grandmother, was addicted to wine and gin and
died, possibly from cirrhosis of the liver, at the age of
thirty-one. Darwin argued that all liver cancer arose from
alcohol abuse, a subject about which, unsurprisingly, he felt
very strongly. Darwin agreed with the orthodoxy of the time
that alcoholism and gout were hereditary, but he also
insisted that individuals could overcome this through will
power. In his *Zoonomia: or, The Laws of Organic Life,* from
1794, he explained the physical effects on drinkers,
including an all too vivid description of a horrendous
hangover. He likened the experience to seasickness: 'the
inebriate, as soon as he begins to be vertiginous, makes pale

urine in great quantities and very frequently, and at length becomes sick, vomits repeatedly, or purges, or has profuse sweats, and a temporary fever ensues with a quick strong pulse. This in some hours is succeeded by sleep; but the unfortunate bacchanalian does not perfectly recover himself till about the same time of the succeeding day, when his course of inebriation began.'

Even if alcohol has become more sophisticated, it seems that the details of a hangover have changed little: 'The common smells of the surrounding air sometimes excite the attention of these patients, and bad smells are complained of, which to other people are imperceptible.' To encourage others towards abstinence, he told readers of a friend who had freed himself not only from gout but from piles and 'the gravel' (stones passed in urine) by giving up for sixteen years.

Scottish naval physician Thomas Trotter produced a much lengthier study of alcohol abuse in 1804. In *An Essay, Medical, Philosophical, and Chemical, on Drunkenness, and Its effects on the Human Body*, he explained that 'the habit of drunkenness is a disease of the mind'. Trotter was the first physician to go beyond thinking of alcoholism as a physical problem, to identify it as an emotional one. For Trotter, it was brought on not by sinfulness, nor by simple exposure to alcoholic drinks, but by an intense emotional malaise. He thought of it as 'a disease of the mind' whose roots could lie in problems such as loss of self-esteem, or anxiety. Trotter's proposed treatment, then, was not just piety, nor the prohibition of alcohol. It was a kind of counselling, to treat the motivation to drink itself. Trotter stressed also, like the anti-gin campaigners, the harm it inflicted on drunkards' children, both mentally and physically. To overcome the

compulsion to drink, he recommended the rousing of 'particular passions, such as the parent's love for their children,
desire of fame, the pride of reputation, family pride etc.', and
that the addict were deprived 'at once' of all alcohol.

9: A Pint of Purl and a Kick in the Guts

PURL

Two shots of gin topped up with warm beer,
poured into warmed mugs

IN MOST HISTORIES of gin the urban poor drink up and put their glasses down after the gin craze and disappear from the scene. However, there was much more continuity than that. Although increasing numbers of distillers pitched themselves at respectable customers, it did not mean that their old ones vanished. Francis Grose's *Dictionary of the Vulgar Tongue*, from 1811, showed that gin was still ingrained in the inner city when he created an invaluable insight into London street speech. Grose and his assistant, Tom Cocking, were boulevardiers, and they noted down slang words from the darkest corners of the city that they could stomach. Gin prompted a plethora of nicknames with unpleasant connotations:

Blue ruin
Blue ribband
Blue tape
Bowsing ken – gin shop or alehouse
Crank – gin and water
*Diddle Drain (so called from the diuretic qualities imputed
    to gin)*
Frog's wine
*Go shop – where gin and water was sold in three-halfpenny
    bowls called goes Heart's ease*
Jackey
A kick in the guts – a dram of gin
Lady Dacre's wine
A flash of lightning – a glass of gin
*Rag water – gin or any other common dram, these liquors
    seldom failing to reduce those that drank them to rags*
Sky blue
Strip me naked

The nicknames that included references to blueness pointed to
alcohol poisoning, which made drunkards' faces a 'ghostly,
ghastly corpse-like kind of blue', according to nineteenth-
century historian and keen observer of London's poor Walter
Besant. He investigated social evils in the East End, supporting
the work of the Salvation Army, the Ragged Schools Union
and public libraries. In his 1888 publication *Fifty Years Ago*,
Besant offered his own explanation for the reputed blueness.
Although it may sound exaggerated, it showed how dangerous
gin still was in the popular imagination:

> *Among the lower classes gin was the favourite – the
> drink of the women as much as of the men. Do you
> know why they call it 'blue ruin'? Some time ago I*

saw, going into a public-house, somewhere near the West India Docks, a tall lean man, apparently five-and-forty or thereabouts. He was in rags; his knees bent as he walked, his hands trembled, his eyes were eager. And, wonderful to relate, the face was perfectly blue – not indigo blue, or azure blue, but of a ghostly, ghastly, corpse-like kind of blue, which made one shudder. Said my companion to me, 'That is gin.' We opened the door of the public house and looked in. He stood at the bar with a full glass in his hand. Then his eyes brightened, he gasped, straightened himself, and tossed it down his throat. Then he came out, and he sighed as one who has just had a glimpse of paradise. Then he walked away with swift and resolute step, as if purposed to achieve something mighty. Only a few yards further along the road, but across the way, there stood another public house. The man walked straight to the door, entered, and took another glass, again with the quick gasp of anticipation, and again with that sigh, as of a hurried peep through the gates barred with the sword of fire. This man was a curious object of study. He went into twelve more public houses, each time with greater determination on his lips and greater eagerness in his eyes. The last glass, I suppose, opened these gates for him and suffered him to enter, for his lips suddenly lost their resolution, his eyes lost their lustre, he became limp, his arms fell heavily – he was drunk, and his face was bluer than ever.

This blueness that was such a feature of gin's nicknames may have resulted from fermenting old potatoes, instead of grain, to make the spirit base. The bacteria on potato skins could create a dangerous level of methanol. When people die these days from drinking counterfeit alcohol, it is usually because of dangerous levels of methanol. It is a poisonous type of alcohol which is found in anti-freeze, varnish and wiper fluid. It has no taste or smell, so drinkers could easily have unwittingly ingested it. As well as blindness and death, methanol poisoning often leads to blue-tinged lips and fingers. Extreme poisoning from any alcohol can also give the appearance of blue-tinged or very pale skin, caused by a falling body temperature and lack of oxygen getting to the skin. The alternative explanation for the 'blue' nicknames is that the gin itself was that colour, which may have been the case on occasion. If the raw spirit that amateur distillers were using was too acidic, it could have contaminated the gin with copper salts from the still, turning it blue.

From Old Bailey records and newspaper stories it was clear that, much to the authorities' frustration, gin was still quenching the thirst of many a lowlife in the nineteenth century. Long after their peak during the gin craze, remaining gin shops were still feared. As the *Spectator* warned its readers: 'We cannot shut our eyes to the vast increase of crime, which has been solely attributed to those haunts of vice and ruin, the gin-shops.' Gin had produced in the men 'incurable laziness, sottishness, and fearful laxity of principle', and turned 'the lower female classes' into the 'wretched, blear-eyed, half-clad wretches which haunt those unhallowed temples, and are to be found staggering near their portals'.

The majority of gin shops had been driven out of business, but they were far from the only places where Londoners could continue to indulge their favourite habit. The city was packed with taverns, inns, alehouses and coffee shops, where a tempted Londoner could pick up a dram or two. One such place was the Grapes, a narrow pub tucked between the houses in Limehouse, east London. As Limehouse was a working-class dock area, the pub mainly catered for lightermen and watermen. There were unsavoury, but hopefully fanciful, stories of watermen dragging drunks from the Grapes to the river to drown them, so that they could sell their bodies to doctors for dissection.

The Grapes had the distinction of being immortalised in Dickens' last complete novel, *Our Mutual Friend*, even if it did not have a particularly flattering cameo role. Dickens used it as the inspiration for his fictional 'the Six Jolly Fellowship Porters' public house: 'A tavern of dropsical appearance . . . long settled down into a state of hale infirmity. It had outlasted many a sprucer public house, indeed the whole house impended over the water but seemed to have got into the condition of a faint-hearted diver, who has paused so long on the brink that he will never go in at all.' Since 2011, the Grapes has been owned by Russian magnate Evgeny Lebedev and actor Sir Ian McKellen, so its clientele are rather different to their Victorian counterparts, but its etched glass, wonky steps and wooden deck that juts out over the Thames are still in place.

Back in its less salubrious days, the Grapes was famous for serving excellent Dog's Noses, a mix of gin and beer, and Purl. Purl was made across the city in many variations and had been a popular drink long before gin arrived. For centuries, it had meant ale steeped for months with bitter herbs — such as wormwood, gentian and horseradish — then strained and heated, and served as a warming breakfast drink. Samuel

Pepys regularly took a mid-morning break from work at a tavern near the Admiralty to have breakfast and a pint of Purl. By the Dickensian era however, Purl usually had the added ingredients of gin, sugar and ginger, and was drunk at all hours of the day.

Even if the ingredients had been tweaked since Pepys' day, as Charles Dickens described it in *The Old Curiosity Shop,* it was still 'a rather strong and heady compound', relied on as a winter warmer: '. . . a great pot, filled with some very fragrant compound, which sent forth a grateful steam, and was indeed choice purl, made after a particular recipe which Mr Swiveller had imparted to the landlord.' Swiveller was extremely proud of his concoction. '"Next," said Dick, handing the Purl, "take a pull at that; but moderate your transports, you know, for you're not used to it."' The Dog's Nose was similar. It was a warm gin and ale-based drink, but with none of the frills.

Although there were fewer people drinking gin, the kind of drinker that it attracted had not yet improved a great deal. Gin's links with prostitution, for example, were as strong as ever. A girl only referred to as 'Watt' was found guilty by Sir Peter Laurie, a Westminster magistrate and later Lord Mayor of London, of stealing several sovereigns from a Mr Sergeant at 'a house of evil repute' in Shire Lane, a street that used to run behind Temple Bar, 'whither gin and love had seduced Mr Sergeant to follow her'. It was exactly the kind of scenario that had been replicated all over London seventy years earlier.

For Daniel Merritt, a clerk at the Custom House, 'gin and love' proved his undoing as well, one October night in 1813, when he alleged that Charlotte Holmes and Martha Nagle had stolen a £10 note from him while he was sleeping.

Merritt told the court that he was walking along the Strand, between 11 p.m. and midnight, when he met Nagle and Holmes on the street. He explained, without going into too much detail, that the three of them had adjourned to a private room together at the Rose Tavern on Ship Lane. He asked the landlady to change the note to pay Nagle and Holmes, but she did not have the money on her, so Merritt said that they would have to wait until the morning for payment. Merritt awoke in the night to find that Nagle had left the room to ask the landlady for more gin, but she did not return. An hour later, Holmes went on the hunt for snuff. It was then that Merritt realised that his money was gone, he said, but he could not find a constable to conduct the arrest. The prosecution asked Merritt if he had been sober at the time. Merritt admitted, 'I had been drinking to be sure,' and the jury sided with the women.

Had Nagle and Holmes been sentenced to a spell in prison, they would not have been short of a dram or two in any case. The scale of corruption meant that prisoners could spend their sentences in one prolonged stupor if they had the funds. Gaolers grew rich from an inventive range of rackets – whether it was selling male prisoners access to female prisoners, levying fees from prisoners to allow them to leave when they finished their sentences, or touting seats in the chapel to watch the ordinary tending to the souls of the condemned. The most organised form of selling gin was through the system of whistling shops, so called because of their code for entry, as Mr Pickwick learns in Dickens' *The Pickwick Papers*:

'"What is that, Sam? A bird-fancier's?" inquired Mr Pickwick.
'"Bless your heart, no, sir . . . a whistling-shop, sir, is where they sell spirits."'

Job Trotter explained that it involved prisoners 'retailing the favourite article of gin, for their own profit and advantage'.

In 1828 Sir Peter Laurie, the industrious magistrate who had sentenced 'Watt', set out to inspect Whitecross Street Prison near the Barbican, and to hear the complaints of its inmates. One of the many that Laurie noted was of all the gin racketeering. A disappointed candidate who had stood for the role of steward at the prison told Laurie that he had been unsuccessful because the winning candidate sold gin to the prisoners and permitted gambling. Laurie was sympathetic to the man's allegations and ordered a renewed effort to hunt down the suppliers.

William Smith reported in his book *State of the Gaols in London* that about 120 gallons of gin and eight butts of beer were drunk at the King's Bench Prison in Southwark every week. It was not until the 1840s with a much more rigorous new prison system, standards would eventually improve, and drinking became much more difficult after a body of prison inspectors was established. The whole prison ethos would change dramatically in the mid-Victorian era, with the introduction of draconian rules such as long periods of solitary confinement.

Stamping out gin and the web of corruption that surrounded it at the workhouses proved just as much of a headache as at the prisons. In 1828 the master of the Aldgate Workhouses raised the alarm that he had, for some time, 'perceived a spirit of insubordination among the paupers'. He must have appeared a sorry sight before the Lord Mayor, as he turned up with his head in a bandage, having been injured by a drunken rabble. The master said that measures had since been taken 'to suppress this rebellious spirit, which seemed to have pervaded the whole inmates of the workhouse, men, women, and children'. In the meantime, he had tracked the source of the gin to be 'Lamb, the messenger to the paupers', whom he found *in flagrante delicto* carrying seven small bottles of gin to the inmates. Explaining how matters had become so out-of-hand, the master insisted that he had 'repeatedly cautioned the messenger not to bring gin into the house'. In the hope of mitigating his crime, Lamb told the Lord Mayor that the inmates needed gin to ease the pain of their existence: 'When they are sick in the bowels, a'nt they to have no-thing to comfort 'em? If they gets a little tossicated, it's because their stomachs is empty [sic].' The Lord Mayor was not moved by Lamb's emotive excuse and sent him to the House of Correction.

Even if living standards in London were improving by the early nineteenth century, the most impoverished areas were hardly better than they were during the gin craze. The *Spectator* grumbled that London's absence of planning had resulted in a sprawling, unmanageable mess that could never be rectified: 'Many streets, as in Marylebone for instance, look like lines of brick wall with holes cut in them; while in Pimlico and Regent Street we walk amongst palaces.' The slum areas were still extensive and the conditions deplorable. For those living anywhere near the markets, on top of grim accommodation, they also had to cope with all the animal noises, the thundering carts and the reek of manure.

London was now the largest city in the world, with more than one million inhabitants. When the first census was taken in 1801, 20 per cent of the British population had lived in towns or cities and 80 per cent in the country. By 1911, this ratio would be reversed. Such rapid, unplanned growth over the nineteenth century exacerbated the crowding in poor areas, where migrants from the country tended to arrive as their first bolthole. St Giles in particular suffered, as labourers swarmed to its grotty lodgings. The parish council came up with all sorts of suggestions to accommodate the influx, including parish dormitories for the homeless 'to supersede the filthy lodging-houses' and to provide accommodation 'for the industrious and employed labourer and his family . . . with every regard to health, comfort, and cleanliness'. It was still a city where the most foetid dwellings stood side by side with its most impressive. As it always had been, Drury Lane was a byword for vice and filth, but now it was just a few hundred yards away from the Lowther Arcade – the most fashionable place in town to buy luxury goods. As the contemporary economist and journalist Walter Bagehot put it when reviewing Dickens, 'we pass a corner and we are in a changed world'.

The *Illustrated London News* complained, as the *Spectator* had, about the lack of planning to keep the city running smoothly. It listed 'the wants of London', which included insufficient sewers and drains, river crossings, decent infrastructure for the traffic and, most damningly, any plan to achieve it. Even in upmarket areas, keeping the city clean was an ongoing battle, particularly with all the unpaved roads that quickly turned to mud in the rain, as pedestrians and vehicles trampled through, churning it up with the horses' manure.

There were some improvements, however. Unlike the days of Judith Dufour, Thomas Tutty et al, the main routes around the city became properly lit. By the 1820s, 200 miles of road were lit by 40,000 gas lamps. With the establishment of the

Metropolitan Board of Works in 1855, the naming of streets became properly documented. For all Londoners' complaints, these initiatives were gradually helping the city to become more modern and ordered.

Although better-quality gin brands were becoming more widespread in the early nineteenth century, the poor continued to knock back their improvised rot gut versions of the spirit. This was feared by their social superiors, even if the scale of pandemonium was no longer so drastic. Melodrama surrounded the drink, in verses such as this one, written by Thomas Hood (1799–1845):

> *Gin! Gin! a Drop of Gin!*
> *The dram of Satan! the liquor of Sin!—*
> *Distill'd from the fell*
> *Alembics of Hell.*

Cartoons such as Thomas Rowlandson's *The Dram Shop* in 1816, part of his ominously named *The English Dance of Death* series, presented a grotesque vision of the poor. At Rowlandson's dram shop a skeleton is pouring 'oil of vitriol' into a vat, to make the innocent-sounding Old Tom and Brady's Best Cordial. Building on its reputation for promoting immorality, groups of men and women in the cartoon are pictured canoodling as they drain their gin glasses, and the sickliest-looking wretches are sprawled on the floor by the bar.

More sinister was George Cruikshank's *The Gin Shop*, from 1829, in which a whole family were the customers in a brightly lit, elaborate bar. Despite the superficially pleasant surroundings, the scene is a sordid one. The wizened mother pours gin into her baby's mouth, while the older daughter drains her glass. A hag behind the father represents what awaits the family if they make it into old age. Behind the warm glow of the lights, there are little symbols of death encircling them. In a pleasing play on words, they are all encircled by a gin trap on the floor. Although an early Cruikshank cartoon, it was already very characteristically his style, with threats of damnation conveying his outrage at easy access to alcohol in Georgian London.

Increasingly despairing, Cruikshank channeled his fear for society into a very widely reproduced series of bleak etchings called *The Bottle*, which warned of alcohol's capacity to ruin lives. One picture showed a despondent, alcoholic father slumped by an empty fireplace, with his young family in distress around him. Underneath, the description read: 'He is discharged from his employment for drunkenness: they pawn their clothes to supply the bottle.' Another showed the man attacking his wife, all their furniture sold or broken, with the stern caption: 'Fearful quarrels and brutal violence are the natural consequences of the frequent use of the bottle.'

The series was so successful that it became a novel, a play and a collection of cautionary waxworks. It was followed up by *The Drunkard's Children*, showing life after the death of the alcoholic father in *The Bottle*. In the last of the drawings, the daughter throws herself from a bridge over the Thames, with an eerie full moon behind her illuminating the Port of London. She is just another tragic girl in an uncaring city. The caption underneath read: 'The maniac father and the convict brother are gone – The poor girl, homeless, friendless, deserted, destitute, and gin-mad, commits self-murder.'

Cruikshank's own father, Isaac, had died after a drinking competition, and George himself had been a heavy drinker. After *The Bottle*, however, he took the oath of abstinence and became a zealous champion of the Temperance Movement.

Back on the real streets of London, the profile of gin-drinkers was not much improved, with poster boys such as the freed slave Black Billy Waters, with his peg leg and feathered hat. He had arrived in London after fighting for the British in the American War of Independence and became one of London's most famous beggars, playing his fiddle at his regular patch outside the Adelphi Theatre in the Strand. He died in 1823, at the St Giles workhouse. Tongue-in-cheek advice to his son was printed in the broadsheet *The Death, Funeral and Last Will of Black Billy*:

> *Now, I do advise my little son,*
> *If he should live to be a man,*
> *To do just as his daddy's done,*
> *And drink good gin whene'er he can.*

Gin was still commonly used as a shorthand for poverty at the time. As the *Spectator* mentioned when explaining the concept of advertising:

> *An advertiser does not look merely to the sale of a*
> *newspaper – he takes its character also into*
> *account. It must be plain that a journal which lies*
> *on the table of 500 opulent persons . . . is a better*
> *medium for advertising . . . than one of which*
> *5000 copies are distributed among ladies' maids,*
> *gentlemen's valets, and gin-drinkers.*

The *Spectator* clarified gin's social position: 'A gentleman may drink gin and beer, but they are not the usual beverage of the caste.' In 1833, when it was calculating the average tax for each class, in the middling-class expenses bracket it put 'brandy and Geneva' but for gin, on the other hand: 'It will be observed, that we only considered home-made spirits (gin and whisky) as falling upon the Poor. Foreign Spirits we estimated as paid wholly by the Middling class.'

As ever, women were singled out as being particularly badly behaved when given free rein to consume gin. Whenever there was a perceived increase in what we now call anti-social behaviour among women, gin was suggested as the cause or, at the very least, a hallmark of such a woman. Magistrates had no hesitation in sending women to prison for drinking offences, and gave the wife of a naval captain a month in the House of Correction to be punished through hard labour, after she was thrown out of the captain's house 'in consequence of her inveterate addiction to gin'. When Eliza Cook was convicted at the Old Bailey in 1832 for murdering a Mrs Walsh, the *Observer* summed up her repugnant character in one line, as 'a woman of violent passions, given to swearing, thieving, drinking of gin, and cat-skinning'.

It was still strongly associated with brawling hags. A few months after Eliza Cook was hanged, the *Spectator* featured an in-depth portrait of a whole life of nuisance behaviour committed by a 'female pauper, nearly sixty years of age, named Sarah Stokes'. In the article, entitled 'Old women – the plagues of the police', Mrs Stokes demonstrated that there was 'no more formidable person than a spiteful old woman at a police office'. Her most recent incident was when she was charged before the future Lord Mayor, Sir Chapman Marshall, at the Mansion House, with having 'frequently insulted Kinnersley, the Beadle of Aldgate, and threatened to beat him'.

Stokes stood accused not only of subjecting Kinnersley and his family to the 'grossest abuse', but also of being a benefits tourist. As each parish was in charge of its own poor relief, Stokes was able to pocket thirty shillings a week by pleading for money in four London parishes. The Beadle of an adjoining parish who, like the unfortunate Kinnersley, had to deal with her requests, said that Stokes 'was the terror of that part of the city'. In another recent incident, she was noted to have 'a strong fancy for gin, which she drank when she could get it, until it stretched her in the mud; and on Monday last she was dragged out of the puddle to the watchhouse'.

Passing out in puddles aside, Stokes was, in fact, at the Mansion House on this occasion to answer the accusation that she had hit Kinnersley's son. She protested that she only did it in response to being 'dragged along the street for no offence'. She did, however, concede: 'It's all true about the gin. I was "mops and brooms" Sunday, sure enough; but that's no reason I'm to be keelhauled and floored like a bullock agoing to be slaughtered. Blessed if I don't give it your son, Kinnersley, for that ere whopping. I'll fetch him a right down jolly good topper.'

Stokes did not help her case when she then went on to call Kinnersley a 'dung-cock' in the witness box and challenged him to a fight once she had served her sentence: 'I'll tell you what, Kinnersley, keep your body up till I comes out, and then we'll see which is the best man, you or me.' The *Spectator* concluded that she was indeed 'the hyena of the East of London'.

More tragic was the story of Mary Ann Pearce a few months
later. In a court report, she was also accused of being for
many years 'the terror' not only of Beadles, but of watchmen,
publicans and police officers. She reportedly would often
smash the glasses and windows at public houses 'unless they
gave her as much gin as she desired'. Rumoured to be the
mistress of Lord Barrymore, Pearce died one Monday night in
October at her lodging, 'a miserable attic' off Drury Lane.
She had been found drunk and disorderly around Covent
Garden twice that night and been marched to the police
station on both occasions. There she was sent home by
Thomas, the superintendent, for 'at least the hundredth time'
according to him. She promised to follow Thomas's advice to
go home to bed. However, the 'ruling passion of her life, the
love of gin' led her astray once more. Incorrigible to the last,
it appeared that instead of returning home as promised, 'she
found out some of her favourite haunts, and became again
intoxicated'. At around midnight, her landlord arrived back at
the police station to say that Pearce was 'either dead or
dying'. The cautionary conclusion of Pearce's death came
from Thomas, who went with the landlord to inspect her
body. Although Thomas was unlikely to have had any medical
training, he pronounced that she had 'expired from a general
decay of nature, brought on by her addiction to gin'.

WHILE MOST OF the middling and upper classes were still
wringing their hands over the lower orders' thirst for gin, it
emerged as a bohemian drink for a new wave of artists who
wanted to challenge bourgeois mores. The Romantics were
fascinated by using drugs and alcohol's ability to create an
altered state of consciousness and stimulate the imagination.
The fact that gin was disreputable made it all the more
appealing as their drink of choice. If we take sociologist

Bernice Martin's definition of Romanticism as seeking 'to destroy boundaries, reject conventions, undermine structures', then gin's appeal becomes very clear.

Lord Byron, the archetypal Romantic, who was famously 'mad, bad and dangerous to know', claimed that all his inspiration came from gin and water. Ever since, it has been a fashionably disreputable drink in literary circles, with its air of seedy glamour imbued by Byron et al. Alexander Gordon, founder of Gordon's, was resoundingly proved right when he said at the time, 'I dare say some young bucks may follow his example,' on hearing that Byron was a gin drinker. In the twentieth century, T. S. Eliot would up the ante. When he was asked at a literary lunch what inspired his poetry, he replied, 'Gin and drugs, dear lady, gin and drugs.'

For all those who have postured their capacity for alcohol since, Byron is still remembered as one of the classic heavyweight literary drinkers. When the diplomat and politician Harold Nicolson was out in Italy during the Second World War, the first thought that came to him as he looked around Pisa was Byron's riotous sojourn there in 1821. Byron had stayed at the Palazzo Lanfranchi, described by fellow poet Percy Bysshe Shelley as 'one of those marble piles that seem built for eternity'. Byron had retired to Pisa for health reasons where he was joined by his friend Shelley, who brought his cousin, Thomas Medwin, in tow. Medwin went on to dedicate a whole book, *Conversations of Lord Byron: noted during a residence with His Lordship at Pisa*, to his time there. The image of Byron as a gin-swigging libertine was still very much alive in Harold Nicolson's mind over a century later. He fondly thought of all the times when 'a tipsy Thomas

Medwin would have paused to note down . . . the really terrible indiscretions in which Lord Byron had just indulged' just before 'the fumes of gin had obscured them'.

Like Byron, the artist George Morland was also surprisingly productive despite his hedonistic extracurricular activities, which often resulted in Morland being in debt or in prison – or both. One would never guess from his pastoral scenes of the British countryside that Morland's personal life was so debauched. Such was Morland's notoriety that an anecdote in the *Monthly Magazine* recounted that at his lodgings in Somers Town, north London, he was found in the 'following extraordinary circumstances': 'his infant child, which had been dead nearly three weeks, lay in its coffin at one corner of the room . . . and himself whistling over a beautiful picture that he was finishing at his easel, with a bottle of gin hung up on one side'. Whether Morland's life really was that grim, we may never know, but the fact that the magazine thought that was a plausible scenario hints at his level of infamy. A contemporary from the Royal Academy, portrait painter George Dawe, stuck up for his much-maligned friend: 'Although he had certainly done vast quantities of spirits, yet his feats in this respect have been exaggerated for no constitution could long have sustained the continual excesses which have been laid to his charge.'

However, it does seem as though Morland had a fairly good crack at it. In a letter to his brother, he listed his consumption for a day out in Brighton, when he had 'nothing to do'. Before breakfast, he had already polished off 'Hollands Gin and Rum and Milk'; then before dinner, 'Hollands and Hollands with water, along with port wine with ginger, ale and shrub'; then more 'gin and water, shrub, ale, punch, porter, and opium and water' after dinner. The list was indeed prodigious; it amounted to twenty drinks in all.

The dubious honour of being the heaviest drinker of London's artistic circles at the time went to essayist and writer Charles Lamb, whose vice of choice was gin and water, with a little ale on occasion for variety. He was a prolific writer of poems and plays, and the author of children's book *Tales from Shakespeare*. Given how tragic his personal life was, it was hardly surprising that he drowned his sorrows. In 1796, when he was twenty-one, his mentally ill sister, Mary, had stabbed their mother to death. Lamb, who never married, dedicated his life to looking after Mary at their house in Little Queen Street, near Drury Lane, to spare her from life in an asylum.

Lamb's *Confessions of a Drunkard*, originally published in the *Philanthropist* in 1813, was a reflection on his own excessive drinking. The historian Thomas Carlyle commented, after meeting him only once, that 'poor old Lamb' had an 'insuperable proclivity to gin', as he would drink 'till he is utterly mad'. Lamb's *Confessions* depicted habitual drinking as an urge profoundly ingrained at the centre of his personality. He claimed that 'the drinking man is never less himself than during his sober intervals'. He wrote of one night when he tried to abstain from 'the poisonous potion', and it caused him 'to scream out, to cry aloud, for the anguish and pain within him'.

Lamb's account is one of the earliest British examples of personal writing about alcoholism as an addiction. The eloquent, literary manner in which Lamb described his own battle with gin – and indeed any alcohol that he could find at the time – was an early example of imbuing spirit-drinking with creative connotations, the notion of the tortured artist, which is a cultural legacy that we recognise today. Lamb described the desperate sensation:

> *When a man shall feel himself going down a*
> *precipice with open eyes and a passive will, to see*
> *his destruction, and have no power to stop it, and*
> *yet to feel it all the way emanating from himself; to*
> *perceive all goodness emptied out of him, and yet*
> *not to be able to forget a time when it was other-*
> *wise; to bear about the piteous spectacle of his*
> *own-self ruins.*

One of Lamb's friends, the lawyer Basil Montagu, perhaps based on watching him in action, wrote *Some Enquiries into the Effects of Fermented Liquors* in 1814. Montague was a friend to many Romantic writers, including Samuel Taylor Coleridge, William Hazlitt and Shelley, whom he represented in court on one occasion. Although he enjoyed their company, he did not join in with his louche friends' drinking, instead arguing for total abstinence. From sober observation, he concluded that the daily pattern of 'dram drinkers' was 'in the morning, sullen, dejected, and silent; in an hour or two, however, they are all hilarity'. And so the cycle continued.

10: Gin's Other Powers

GIN AND CLOVES
*A dash of Phillips Pink Cloves cordial
and room-temperature gin*

❧

FOR ALL GIN's evils, the older belief that its characteristic juniper possessed medicinal qualities lived on, and the characters of Dickens showed how miscellaneous the conditions could be. Gin was still thought to be a remedy for all manner of complaints. The use of gin in cordial remedies continued well into the mid-Victorian era. In *The Pickwick Papers* gin and cloves was used as a hangover remedy by Sam Weller and Job Trotter; in *Bleak House* as a 'stomachic' to cure indigestion; and in *David Copperfield* 'Mrs C' likes to have a quarter of gin and cloves at the pub, as an all-purpose pick-me-up. Health-boosting variations included gin infused with splints of pine bark, which contains a very high concentration of vitamin C, and wormwood, which is used as a botanical in many modern gin recipes, to relieve stomach cramps. A more complex combination was lovage cordial, served to settle an upset stomach, containing gin with celery root, sweet fennel, cinnamon, caraway seeds and capillaire, a syrup made from the maidenhair fern.

The idea of giving gin on its own to the sick also carried on into the twentieth century. In the absence of proper medical understanding, it was used as a reviver for those feeling weak, in particular if they complained of stomach pain. It was used to comic effect in George Bernard Shaw's play *Pygmalion*, which opened in London in 1914. Now better known as the musical *My Fair Lady*, it explored the relationship between elocution teacher Professor Henry Higgins and Cockney flower girl Eliza Doolittle. With her newly acquired Received Pronunciation, in a moment intended to really hammer home how humble Doolittle's family is, she tells Higgins's house guests that when her aunt was dying of influenza, her father 'kept ladling gin down her throat' to rouse her. When Higgins' assembled guests express concern at the idea of pouring gin down the throat of a dying woman, Doolittle matter-of-factly explains, 'gin was mother's milk to her'. Besides, she says, her father 'poured so much down his own throat, he knew the good of it'.

Although Bernard Shaw's depiction of working-class life was hardly subtle, the medicinal use of gin was still a reality. Shortly before *Pygmalion* made its debut, Surrey County Council published a leaflet called 'Hints for the care of infants under 1 year old'. It reflected their concerns about the 'fitness' of working-class mothers, notably in the stern warning never to give babies 'gin or other spirits without the doctor's advice'.

This had certainly been common practice throughout the nineteenth century, with products such as Daffy's Elixir, a children's medicine that contained the laxative senna and was administered with gin. In *Oliver Twist* Mrs Mann, who runs the orphanage where Twist lives until he is nine, often gives the orphans the mixture to quiet them down and soothe their stomachs. 'Daffy' became a nickname for gin, and adults who wanted to administer themselves were known as daffiers. As one popular verse ran:

> To daffy shops for luscious drops
> Folks stalk in now so numerous,
> And soak their clay with sweet, sweet gin,
> And jest and joke so humorous.

Although juniper was used for a plethora of ailments, since the medieval ages it had most closely been associated with inducing abortions. This may have been another reason why gin became such a potent symbol of maternal neglect. For contemporaries, juniper's link to abortion made it a sinister ingredient for women to be ingesting recreationally. The archaic term for the variety of juniper used in abortions was *Juniperus sabina*, commonly known as savin. So the phrase 'giving birth under the savin tree' was a euphemism for inducing a miscarriage. Nicholas Culpeper had also warned in his *Complete Herbal*, in the seventeenth century, of the particular danger that juniper posed to pregnant women as it gave 'speedy delivery to women with child', whether they were ready to give birth or not. During the gin craze and beyond, drinkers would certainly have been aware of juniper's properties as a uterine stimulant.

There may even be a grain of truth in the idea that juniper really would help to induce a miscarriage as one recent American study found that the isocupressic acid in the needles can indeed reduce blood flow through the placenta and stimulate contractions. Rue plants and tansy were also believed to have this property, so they were often paired with gin in cordials. As ingesting either could make people extremely ill, it was a very risky approach to family planning.

Given juniper's connotations it is no coincidence that gin has always been the alcohol of choice for DIY abortions. Even now, people are familiar with the old wives' tale that drinking gin in a hot bath can stop an unwanted pregnancy, and this method was used by desperate women as late as the post Second World War period, as depicted in Alan Sillitoe's novel *Saturday Night and Sunday Morning* from 1958. It tells the story of factory worker Arthur Seaton, who embarks on an affair with his best friend's wife, Brenda. When Brenda becomes pregnant, Arthur turns to his Aunt Ada for help, who recommends that she should 'take a hot bath with hot gin. Tell her to stay there for two hours, as hot as she can bear it, and drink a pint of gin. That should bring it all off.' As a less brutal approach, women could also buy a brand of pill called the 'Lady's Friend' containing juniper, which was advertised in the back of magazines. Thankfully, these methods became decreasingly necessary after 1967, when a law was passed to give scope for legal abortions.

In keeping with gin's supposed abortive powers, it followed that bad nineteenth-century midwives should be depicted as gin-addled crones. Although the word 'midwife' can be traced back to Anglo Saxon times, it would not be until 1902 that the profession was finally defined and properly regulated. Until then, any unqualified person could practise. One verse described them 'Taking snuff, drinking gin and tea, and the midwife's half-crown fee', and the cartoon *A Midwife on Her Way to a Labour*, by Thomas Rowlandson from 1811 depicted the stereotypical, unmaternal midwife, sozzled and grotesque.

Dickens created the most famous monster of a midwife –
Mrs Gamp in *Martin Chuzzlewit*. Sairey Gamp was created in
a rich tradition of disreputable midwives enjoying far too
much 'mother's ruin'. In one scene Gamp and her gin-loving
crony Betsy Prig drain a teapot of gin before having an
acrimonious row. One of Gamp's most memorable character-
istics was her love of gin: '"Mrs Harris," I says, "leave the
bottle on the chimney-piece, and don't ask me to take none,
but let me put my lips to it when I am so disposed, and then
I'll do what I'm engaged to do."'

11: The Advent of the Gin Palaces

CREAM GIN

Served neat and at room temperature, at gin palaces gin would have been aged in a barrel with cream and sugar

A TEN-MINUTE WALK from the old Sipsmith distillery, on an unprepossessing strip of the Uxbridge Road, is a grand building that jars among the off-licences, council blocks and endless traffic. Having survived an ill-advised phase as a 'rock 'n' roll pub' in the 1980s, the Princess Victoria in Shepherd's Bush is one of the finest examples of a London gin palace that we can still see. Its first incarnation was as a very unregal, low-grade gin shop, but in 1829 it was given a costly makeover to become one of the city's earliest gin palaces. Its new-found popularity and imposing architecture turned it into a local landmark. When the tram began carrying 1,000 passengers a day between Acton Vale and Uxbridge Road, the Princess Victoria was ideally positioned next to the cobbled end of the line for a quick gin and water before heading home.

Most gin palaces fell out of fashion in the late Victorian period and it was then that the Princess Victoria was refitted as a pub. More unusually, it was given another makeover in the 1980s, this time by Richard Branson. As Branson then owned Virgin Records, he made it into a music venue. Phil Collins was one of Virgin's signings, so Collins reputedly had his music videos for 'Sussudio' and 'One More Night' filmed there. The pub became a little edgier than Collins and his ballads when it became the scene of a shooting, and shortly afterwards Branson sold up. In the following years the Princess Victoria suffered from under-investment and was known locally as a haunt for drug dealers. Happily though, much of its architectural splendour has now been restored. These days, it serves as a slick gastropub, but there are remnants of its gin palace past all over the three-storey building – from the sweeping mahogany counter that still dominates the main bar, to its vast double-height windows, high ceilings and the gas lights outside.

Georgian gin shops had been extremely basic affairs, but gin palaces like the Princess Victoria could not have been more determinedly different in appearance: immense windows, etched and frosted mirror-work, richly patterned wallpaper, heavy curtains, innovative gas lighting and ornate mouldings were all hallmarks of their style. Inspired by the new shop fronts of the West End, they stood out ostentatiously in streets of dark brick and wooden shutters, with their huge bow windows, colourful adverts and hanging signs above the door. Their long, gleaming mahogany bars were based on shop counters, designed for swift service and ideal for encouraging customers to drink fast while leaning against it. The high-Victorian public house, still a defining feature of the current London landscape, owes many of its features to this aesthetic.

The phrase 'gin palace' would come to be used for any pub, or indeed yacht, done up in the same style, but they were originally very different from a run-of-the-mill pub. These new drinking holes mushroomed around the West End and out in the poorer suburbs throughout the 1820s and 1830s. Like the explosion of distilling itself a century earlier, the whole gin-palace phenomenon resulted from a short-sighted legislative blunder. As a way to discourage smuggling, in 1825, duties on English spirits were reduced from 10s 6d to 6s a gallon, to make them more attractive than imported or smuggled ones. However, the tax was so low that it made English spirits more appealing than beer and porter once more, which were weak and expensive by comparison. The gin palace therefore gained huge popularity as an alluring place to drink all this newly cheap gin.

Having successfully forced the closure of the majority of gin shops and made gin too expensive for the very poorest, the 1825 budget undid much of that progress. It sent legal consumption shooting back up across the country, from just under 3.7 million gallons in 1825 to just over 7.4 million one year later. Modern drinkers are extremely moderate by comparison – both levels were far higher than today's average of just over half a gallon per head.

The 'gin palace' nickname for these new venues caught on early in newspapers and in the literature of anti-gin campaigners. Henry Fearon, the proprietor of the famous gin palace Thompson and Fearon's on Holborn Hill, was one of the first people to use the phrase in an article in 1830. He did not coin it though, as concerned readers of *The Times* had already been writing in to complain about these 'palaces' for the past year. After they exploded in popularity in the 1820s, the public houses would start to ape their features, in the hope of making as much money.

Thanks to a grumbling grocer who had to work opposite one of these thriving original gin palaces, we have a vivid idea of what customers could expect. George Wilson, who owned a shop on Tothill Street, near the Houses of Parliament, complained to the select committee set up to tackle 'the Prevailing Vice of Drunkenness' in 1834 about all the noise and inconvenience that it was causing. He explained how the 'low dirty public house' across the road had been converted into:

> *A splendid edifice, the front ornamental with pilasters, supporting a handsome cornice and entablature and balustrades, and the whole elevation remarkably striking and handsome . . . the doors and windows glazed with very large squares of plate glass, and the gas fittings of the most costly description . . . when this edifice was completed, notice was given by placards taken round the parish; a band of music was stationed in front . . . the street became almost impassable from the number of people collected; and when the doors were opened the rush was tremendous; it was instantly filled with customers, and continued so till midnight.*

Like the irritated Mr Wilson, the *Spectator* was not won over by these garish homages to glass and brass. It conceded that 'the number and splendour of the gin-palaces have made many dram-drinkers', but it could not fathom the attraction for the lowly clientele: 'One would think the squalid wretches who seek such transient relief from misery, would dislike this ostentatious contrast with their rags and filth: no, the show is associated with prosperity and abundance, and they like to be connected with them, however indirectly.'

Despite the apparent luxury of the surroundings, the gin palaces were still serving the urban poor. Social superiors considered their expensive decoration to be vulgar and still did not wish to be seen drinking gin in any case. Critics feared their insidious beauty was seducing the lower classes into excessive drinking. Once more the Society for the Diffusion of Useful Knowledge, founded to publish improving literature for the working classes, warned that the poor should not be lured in by the palaces' 'jumble of awkward, tawdry, meretricious finery'.

As part of the considerable investment in their appearance, several were designed by the most esteemed architects of the day. Thompson and Fearon's hired John Buonarotti Papworth, whose accomplishments included designing the Montpellier Pump Room in Cheltenham and furnishing the gentlemen's club Boodle's in St James's. Papworth's closest gin-palace rival was Stephen Geary, who later renounced alcohol after regretting his role in promoting gin. Sadly, none of Geary's gin-palace work survives, leaving as his most enduring legacy the beautiful Highgate Cemetery where he is buried.

When the gin palaces took off in earnest in 1829, they caused a flurry of complaints about increased drunkenness. From the poor's point of view, the excuse for all this continued gin-drinking was a simple one – the cold. It was the most innocent, emotive reason that gin sellers and drinkers could use with the authorities – and they did so liberally. By January 1830, gin sellers were being called before Westminster magistrates Sir Richard Birnie and Sir Peter Laurie to explain all the drunken people on the streets. One appealed to the magistrates by reiterating how much the poor needed gin, particularly in the winter:

> *At this season of the year, when the suffering poor,*
> *whose miserable pittance, whether obtained by their*
> *own labour or from the charity of the well-disposed,*
> *is insufficient to enable them to meet the increased*
> *expense of firing, and father, mother, and shivering*
> *children sit starving in a room presenting no means*
> *of warmth save a little straw, would you deprive*
> *them of the relief, how-ever temporary, which both*
> *the agonies of the mind and the sufferings of the*
> *body derive from the much-abused glass of spirits?*
> *They are too poor to purchase the materials for a*
> *fire: there is one mode of assistance open to them,*
> *which is the only one not beyond their reach, and*
> *they avail themselves of this. And would it not be*
> *cruelty indeed to deprive them of this last comfort.*

It is unlikely that Richard Birnie would have had much
sympathy for this appeal. He had already explained to a
gathering of London constables that year, in no uncertain
terms, that 'most of the charges that had lately occupied his
time originated in drunkenness; and if the lower orders did
not drink so much gin, there would be much less crime'. On
a note of self-congratulation, he mentioned that he himself
had 'never drunk a glass of gin in his life, and what was
more, never meant to drink one'.

As a fledgling writer in the 1830s Charles Dickens became
curious about the palaces' strong attraction for the poor. He
was already on his way to becoming a wealthy man, but he
had not lost his concern for London's most impoverished
inhabitants. After all, he had early experience of hardship
himself when he worked in a factory as a child after his
father had been imprisoned for debt. Like Hogarth before

him, whose father had also ended up in debtors' prison, Dickens felt a lifelong duty to convey the misery of London's poor to a wider audience.

Before he embarked on any of his novels, under a nom de plume Dickens wrote a collection of short pieces called *Sketches by Boz*, in which he depicted London life through a series of 'sketches'. He guided his educated middle-class readers inside the gin palaces – establishments they had probably only ever seen from the outside. He explained how they were 'perfectly dazzling when contrasted with the darkness and dirt' of the street, and remarked that the décor was 'even gayer than the exterior', describing how the bar 'of French-polished mahogany, elegantly carved' extended 'the whole width of the place'. However, all this grandeur was punctured by the people inside them. The staff were 'two showily-dressed damsels, with large necklaces' and the customers were two fat old washerwomen, drinking gin and peppermint, and two old men who had 'finished their third quartern'.

It is likely that Dickens, when he lived at 48 Doughty Street in Bloomsbury, visited many of the local gin palaces out of professional curiosity. The Lamb on Lamb's Conduit Street, which is still going and retains some gin-palace-era features, would have been very near his house. Inspired by what he saw, his novels would later be awash with gin-swigging characters – from Krook the rag-and-bottle merchant in *Bleak House*, to Mr Swiveller with his purl and gin and water in *The Old Curiosity Shop*, to just about everyone in *Oliver Twist*.

How very elaborate these buildings were made an impression on many of Dickens' contemporaries as well. While gin shops were inconspicuous as spare rooms in ordinary houses, gin palaces were designed to entice passing trade, and they worked to great effect. The prominent gaslights over the doors in particular became a beacon on the streets. One such dazzling example was on the Ratcliff Highway, a Roman road that runs through Wapping from East Smithfield, now renamed The Highway. It was a disreputable area, known for its slums, robberies and, most notoriously, the Ratcliff Murders of 1811. A temperance campaigner who was sent to investigate the gin palaces' popularity there must have approached with trepidation, but even he was grudgingly impressed when he recorded that one had a 'revolving light with many burners playing most beautifully' over the main door, and another door with 'no less than THREE enormous lamps with corresponding lights'.

In the hope of cultivating some customer loyalty in the crowded marketplace, gin palaces often served gin in their in-house style. Particularly popular was any variation on 'cream gin', made by infusing gin with cream and sugar in the barrel. It could be made on the premises or bought from a distillery, such as J. & J. Vickers and Co., who widely advertised the 'Celebrated Cream Gin' from their Victoria Street distillery near Westminster Abbey.

In this period, gin was transported and stored in large wooden barrels, to be served from jugs and smaller casks. By the time that the gin reached the drinker, it would often have been resting in the cask for weeks, giving the flavour an extra dimension that we do not experience these days. Held up by decorated gantries, florid barrels with appetising names such as 'Cream of the Valley', 'the celebrated Butter Gin', 'Best Cordial Gin', 'Choice Compounds' and, rather more alarmingly, 'the real Knock-me-down' lined the walls, creating the impression of bounty and hospitality. As Dickens described the layout in one that he visited in *Sketches by Boz*: 'There are two side-aisles of great casks, painted green and gold, enclosed within a tight brass rail and bearing such descriptions as "Old Tom 549"; "Young Tom, 360"; "Samson, 1421".' It would not be until 1861 that William Gladstone, then Chancellor of the Exchequer, would introduce the Single Bottle Act, which allowed spirits to be sold in bottles from grocers.

The success of these palaces caused considerable anxiety for owners of London's traditional drinking holes. When the palaces began flourishing in the east, the Association of Licensed Victuallers met at the Shadwell Dock Coffee House, to demand measures from local magistrates to protect them 'from the unfair competition of the numerous gin palaces which have arisen in that neighbourhood'. The old-fashioned publicans who addressed the meeting pleaded that the palaces were 'increasing to such an extent as to render it necessary' for them to 'adopt some measures to secure to themselves a remunerating profit for their trade'.

The publicans reminded the magistrates that both the government and the public feared gin palaces' 'encouragement of immoral habits', and that it was therefore the magistrates' duty to help them. The publicans threatened that they would be 'compelled in self-defence to convert their houses into gin palaces, and pull down the parlours and taprooms provided for the accommodation of travellers and labourers'. This was a significant threat, because it was widely acknowledged that public houses served a valuable role in providing some rare communal space for the poor. If publicans joined the

gin-palace trend, it would mean denying the public 'accommodation and refreshments after the labour of the day' and
somewhere to socialise in a civilised manner.

As anti-gin campaigners had a century before them, the publicans evoked the dichotomy between gin as a drink of wastrels
and the disenfranchised, while the beer that they sold was the
wholesome drink of workers. The gin palaces were not such
blatant hotbeds of crime and prostitution as their shadowy
Georgian predecessors, but they had made little progress in
other ways. Customers still had to stand at the bar, knocking
back acerbic, often adulterated, gin. They often sold other
drinks in smaller quantities, but still offered no food or comfortable meeting rooms for business, as the public houses did.

Public houses offered proper meals, seating and the chance of
company, and publicans felt that their cosy homes-from-home
deserved legal protection. As publicans never tired of pointing
out, as glamorous as these gin palaces were, they had no
seating at all. This came to symbolise the gap between
establishments where drinking was socially acceptable and
those where it was not. The palaces were supremely efficient
in moving drinkers in and out to maximise turnover with
separate entrances for different customers, including the 'jug
and bottle entrance', the 'wholesale bar' and the 'retail bar'.
As well as having no tables and chairs, gin palaces did not
offer any newspapers, nor any private meeting rooms for
societies and groups, as the pubs did. There was nothing else
customers could do there other than drink.

At their peak, there were 5,000 gin palaces around the city
but the *Spectator* continued to be baffled as to their appeal: 'At
present a person goes in . . . takes his glass at the counter, and

moves off. Suppose he were furnished with a seat at a table, would he take less gin? It is not credible. How then can the addition of "sufficient accommodation and refreshments after the labour of the day", lessen the sale of gin?' One petition to magistrates in 1835 wanted to prevent any more palaces winning licences 'unless they afforded the usual accommodation found in public-houses, and which is required by the statute and the ancient law and customs of the realm'.

The *Spectator* waded in on the publicans' side and suggested refusing licences to all spirit retailers who did not also provide food. The fact that people had to drink standing up and were offered nothing to eat was taken as a disturbing sign that people were just drinking to get drunk rather than socialising. As one observer put it in 1831: 'Every minute the door opens, and some slide in, and some slide out, without saying a word to each other.' Fearon, one of the more outspoken proprietors, boasted that at Thompson and Fearon's, eight out of ten customers would spend 'less than a minute' drinking a pennyworth of gin there before leaving. This style of serving gin proved extremely efficient. At their peak, the fourteen largest palaces in London together served more than half a million customers a week.

This was borne out by the experience of American lawyer Theodore Sedgwick II, who wrote in 1836 that he visited three palaces in Holborn Hill, where he marvelled at 'men, women, and children, who generally went in at one door and out at another'. He noted that none of them 'stayed long, as far as we could see; they came in, drank, and went off'. On Friday and Saturday nights a gin palace in a well-chosen spot could earn a guinea a minute, historian Jessica Warner has calculated.

As the publicans in Shadwell had feared, with their cheap drinks and alluring surroundings, the palaces were poised to drive other drinking holes out of business. The journalist and judge Henry Chapman lamented in *Pamphlets for the People* in 1835 that the more money that was splashed out on the new palaces, the more 'publican after publican was compelled to embellish expensively or lose the trade'. When public houses were transformed into gin palaces, the first thing the builders would be certain to do was remove any chairs and low tables that might cause people to linger.

Tavern and alehouse owners stood to make vast profits by converting their sleepy watering holes, or selling them to investors to do the same. However, looking at the valuation records from bankruptcies, many came unstuck after spending ruinous amounts on the decoration. Although the potential profits were undoubtedly attractive, the cost of converting one 'common public-house' in Southwark into a 'splendid gin-palace' with all the trimmings was in the region of £3,000 – a vast sum for the time. The *Temperance Journal* estimated that £2,000 was needed to establish an 'ordinary class' of gin palace, but £10,000 or more would be needed to achieve one of the grandest.

London magistrates had swiftly cottoned on to the danger of public houses receiving these gin-palace makeovers. As early as 1829, the magistrates who controlled licences across north London were trying to withhold them from the speculators. The *Spectator* bemoaned the number of public houses being sacrificed for the trend, such as the Lomac, which was currently 'a common public-house', but money had been put forward for its renovation, so 'another splendid gin-palace is about to raise its unsightly head on the Surrey side of Blackfriars Bridge'. However, it did identify a sympathetic reason for their allure, describing how the poor 'work as hard as ever, or harder; but they come home to a reduced, scanty meal. There is discontent where there should be happiness, want where plenty has been. Home becomes uncomfortable, and the "gin-palace" is at hand.'

Realising that allowing gin to be comparatively cheap was encouraging the wrong kind of drinking again, parliament removed duty on British beer in 1830 and allowed any ratepayer to sell it in return for a licence costing only two guineas. In the first six months alone 25,000 new licences were taken out. This tax cut meant that public houses offering beer and comfortable seating would eventually end the brief reign of gin palaces by winning back working-class drinkers. Counteracting the evil of gin with beer created its own problems but the idea was to wean people off gradually – beer was morphine to gin's heroin.

A poem of the time, 'Heavy Wet', showed how happy the ordinary man apparently was to be able to afford his beer once more:

> *King William and Reform, I say,*
> *In such a case who can be neuter?*
> *Just let me blow the froth away,*
> *And see how I will drain the pewter*
>
> *Another tankard, landlord, fill*
> *And let us drink to that ere chap, Broom;*
> *And then we'll chaunt God save King Bill,*
> *And send the echoes thro' the tap-room.*

12: The National Gallery Versus the Gin Palaces

GIN AND PINE
After infusing a cask of gin with pine trees splints for a week, serve neat and at room temperature

FRIGHTENED BY THE popularity of the gin palaces, it was in the 1830s that parliament started to tackle the causes of drinking in a much broader, more recognisably modern way. As Dickens suggested, they needed to find the impulse behind this mass drunkenness, not just clamp down on sales. Four years after the Beer Act, the 1834 select committee, established 'to inquire into the causes and consequences of the increasing evil of drunkenness', was an admission of many failed policies thus far.

The committee came up with some progressive ideas, which it hoped would end the gin-palace trend and rein in the worst excesses of heavy-drinking Londoners. MP James Silk Buckingham, who led the committee, had first-hand experience of the evils of drink from his Sheffield constituency as gin palaces had sprung up in northern industrial cities as well. The committee believed that 'the higher and middle classes are not so intemperate as in the days of our forefathers, but that

the labouring classes are much more so'. They therefore
focused once more on the problem that politicians had
grappled with a hundred years ago – how to stop the urban
poor drinking to excess.

The committee offered two explanations for the poor's
penchant for alcohol. The long-term cause was the bad
example set by the upper classes, whereby drinking to mark
all social occasions was socially acceptable. As the committee
pointed out, it was not only rites of passage that were celebrated with liberal amounts of alcohol, but 'even in the
commercial transactions of bargain and sale'. Against this
cultural backdrop, the short-term problem was how cheap
and readily available gin was, with the gin palaces' 'additional
allurements presented by every new competitor, who seeks to
present more powerful attraction, to visitors'.

The committee called many experts in to help it formulate some
fresh solutions, one of whom was Robert Edwards Broughton, a
police magistrate at the Worship Street court in Shoreditch. He
gave an impassioned statement about his work dealing with the
'terrible' cases of drunkenness that he saw every week. He said
that, over the past seven years, the people charged with drunkenness were 'much more numerous now'. He was particularly
concerned about the 'great number of women', as it led to 'more
pernicious disease, than when it takes possession of men: it leads
to more evil consequences in the family'.

Edwards Broughton painted a grim picture, whereby 'when
the mother takes to drinking, she drinks in the day, and the
children are left to beat about; and if the girls are good-
looking and smart, they are picked up and become prostitutes, and the young boys beat about in the streets, and are

picked up by the thieves, and instructed as young thieves'. He also picked up the concern of public houses being killed off, lamenting that because of the competition, 'the old public-houses, where a man could have his steak dressed, and sit down and take his ale, are extinct: they are obliged to convert them into splendid houses, and sell gin at the bar'. Edwards Broughton was suspicious of gin adulteration, especially in gin palaces with 'lower character', because of the price discrepancies. He told the committee: 'I have known . . . that whilst gin was selling at 4d a quarter at respectable houses, it was selling at 2½d at other sorts of houses'. The Lord Mayor of London, Henry Winchester, offered a simple explanation for their great financial success: 'Either the gin must be very bad, or the glasses very small, to afford any profit.'

Distillers themselves protested that their casks were often on display, but refilled with cheaper or diluted spirit. Henry Fearon of Thompson and Fearon's made no secret of watering down the gin, even though customers were ostensibly paying for the neat spirit. American visitor Theodore Sedgwick tried a halfpenny's worth of gin at a different establishment and found it 'undoubtedly adulterated; it seemed to be sweetened, and certainly had not the flavour of pure gin'. However, Edwards Broughton was concerned that there was something more sinister going on: 'If the adulteration were what Messrs Thompson and Fearon say it is, sugar and water, I should say it was for the benefit of the public; but I am inclined to think it is not the case.'

As the first wave of anti-gin campaigners had a century before, the 1834 committee explained that drinking was undermining the poor's ability to contribute to society, and in that sense should be a concern to everyone. It made an estimate of the loss sustained by the nation through drinking and declared it to be 'little short of fifty millions' a year.

To ease the problem, the committee made a selection of suggestions. One of them was public policing, with all 'spirit-shops as open to public view as other shops, where wholesome provisions are sold – such as those of the baker, the butcher, and the fishmonger'. This was a throwback to Lord Bathurst's very similar argument back in 1743 – by opening up these shops to inspection from passers-by, it was hoped that drinkers would be embarrassed into moderation. The practice of paying workmen their wages at places where alcohol was sold had been outlawed in 1831, but the committee wanted further action. It advised that wages should be paid on the mornings of market days, so that wives had the chance to buy necessary provisions, instead of finding all too often that it had been squandered by their husbands the night before. The committee also suggested replacing the reliance on gin not with beer this time, but with tea and coffee.

The most ambitious of the committee's recommendations is an approach that British society has since embraced. It was a programme of civic improvement, with free public parks and gardens to encourage healthy outdoor activity, and museums and parish libraries charging the lowest possible admission fees. The committee clarified that all intoxicating drinks should be banned from these places. The notion of providing wholesome recreational activities to combat drink problems would become a mainstream part of policy only later in the nineteenth century.

The early frontline of this cultural approach would become the National Gallery. The meeting of that 1834 committee marked ten years since the gallery had been founded in a Pall Mall townhouse to showcase art. Now it was going to take on a much broader role, that of diverting poor Londoners from their more unsavoury leisure activities. This notion of 'Rational Recreations' would, it was hoped, lure the working man away from drinking and gambling and provide a place in which he could enjoy refined pastimes in the company of his family. A parliamentary bill in 1834 expressed the hope that museums could 'draw off by innocent pleasurable recreation and instruction, all who can be weaned from the habits of drinking'. Four years later the National Gallery would be unveiled by the newly crowned Queen Victoria in its current location where it could hold huge numbers of visitors, unlike the townhouse where it began life.

Coaxing the masses out of their gin palaces with the watercolours of J. M. W. Turner had its setbacks. Thomas Uwins, keeper of the National Gallery in the 1840s, became concerned with the behaviour of visitors who were unaccustomed to art appreciation. He complained in an official report that one family was found using the gallery as a picnicking area. They came in with a 'basket of provisions' and 'sat down and seemed to make themselves very comfortable'. When Uwins went over to explain 'the impropriety of such proceeding in such a place', the family was unruffled. They were 'very good-humoured and a lady offered me a glass of gin and wished me to partake of what they had provided'.

Although this softer approach to tackling drinking gained sympathy among some MPs, parliament as a whole was not yet quite convinced. When the press reported the committee's suggestions, it mockingly referred to it as 'Mr Buckingham's Drunken Committee'. The *Spectator* was particularly scathing:

It is impossible to read a single paragraph of this document without laughing – it is so rich in absurdity. The most commonplace and hacknied ideas are decked out in such pompous phraseology – the political economy is so superlatively bad – and the remedies for gin and beer-drinking are so fantastical and impracticable – that had some facetious 'licensed victualler' laboured with all his might to throw ridicule on the Committee and the subject of their investigations, he could not have done it more effectually than by getting some Member of the House to draw up such a report as this.

MPs in the House of Commons were not much more respectful than the commentators. They reportedly 'roared with laughter during the reading of some parts of the Report' and began to regard all its recommendations as 'merely as a lengthy jeu d'esprit'.

Although Silk Buckingham and his select committee did not make a great deal of headway at the time, the idea of using places such as the National Gallery and the British Museum to 'civilise' the poor remained a hope in some quarters. The belief that high culture may save the working man from a life of drunkenness proved resilient despite a majority of naysayers. A further select committee in 1836 recommended opening the British Museum later into the evening and on national holidays to keep Londoners away from their less edifying activities. The committee had called in experts, who advised Sunday openings 'as one of the best modes of counteracting the effect of gin palaces'.

For all the committees', the publicans' and the public's worries, the reign of gin palaces would eventually pass. After their mid-century heyday, they were bought up by breweries to be converted into pubs – as was the fate of the Princess Victoria. Because many pubs had already imitated their architecture and decoration, aesthetically it would become very difficult to distinguish the two. Despite the superficial similarity in appearance, however, the pubs' style of socialising had in fact won the battle. They had used their comfort and sense of community as their chief selling point to triumph over the gin palaces' conveyor-belt approach.

13: *Moderation Versus Teetotalism*

SUMMER GIN PUNCH

'Summer gin punch is thus made at the Garrick Club. Pour half a pint of gin on the outer peel of a lemon, then a little lemon juice, a glass of maraschino, about a pint and a quarter of water, and two bottles of iced soda-water; and the result will be three pints of the punch in question.'

'Hints for the table; or, The economy of good living'
by J. Timbs, 1866

The Victorians would bring us the gin palace, the gin and tonic and the cocktail – the legacies of which we are still very much enjoying today. Pushing back against these frivolous innovations, however, were those pleading for moderation, or even abstinence. The gin palaces that the 1830s select committees had tried so earnestly to tackle had mobilised a militantly anti-alcohol group, the nascent Temperance Movement. In fact, Silk Buckingham, who had led the 1834 committee, was one of their supporters. The British and Foreign Temperance Society, which was officially founded in 1836, can of course be judged a straightforward failure as prohibition was never established. While the society fell far short of its ultimate goal it did, however, manage to encourage much debate over the decades. This tussle ended up in the moderate set of measures that has framed British drinking laws ever since, so it was not an entirely fruitless exercise.

For all the anxiety over poor Londoners' drinking habits, very few British people believed that a total alcohol ban was the answer. Dickens proved an eloquent spokesman for the moderate majority. He was deeply concerned about alcohol abuse, but disagreed entirely with the teetotal approach. He was not at all convinced that it would result in a nation of sobriety. In an article of 1848, he accused teetotalers of only concerning themselves with the symptoms of alcoholism, not the social decay that lay behind it. He had been arguing for a different approach as early as *Sketches by Boz*, in which he had written:

> *Gin drinking is a great vice in England, but wretchedness and dirt are greater; and until you improve the homes of the poor, or persuade a half-famished wretch not to seek relief in temporary oblivion of his own misery, with the pittance which, divided among his family, would furnish a morsel of bread for each, gin shops will increase in number and splendour.*

Dickens wrote at length about the evils of gin, but that did not put him off enjoying a little himself. He was no puritan and drew the critical distinction between use and abuse. He was particularly partial to the Summer Gin Punch at the Garrick Club in Covent Garden, made with lemon peel and juice, gin, maraschino, water and soda water. He served a similar punch, and Gin Slings, to guests at his country house, Gad's Hill Place in Kent, where in between mixing drinks he found the time to write *Great Expectations*.

He liked to create an air of theatricality for his punch-making, often wearing a velvet smoking jacket for the occasion. It would then be kept on ice for the rest of the evening, a great luxury at the time. When the contents of his cellar were auctioned off on his death in 1870, they included a very decent stock of sixteen bottles of 'Old Geneva' and thirty-six bottles of 'London cordial gin'.

Before moving to Gad's Hill Dickens spent the summer at Broadstairs in Kent every year, where he liked to invite his friends down from London. 'We have been in the house two hours,' wrote Dickens invitingly to his best friend, the journalist Thomas Beard, 'and the dining-parlour closet already displays a good array of bottles, duly arranged by the writer hereof – the spirits labelled 'Gin', 'Brandy', 'Hollands'.' Back in London, like his own characters, Dickens often enjoyed gin and water at the Jack Straw's Castle or the Spaniard's Inn after a walk up to Hampstead Heath. The Spaniard's, which was mentioned in *The Pickwick Papers,* is still one of London's most charming pubs and well worth a visit.

If even Dickens and his friends were keen drinkers then teetotalers had quite a battle on their hands. A newspaper as upright as *The Times* dismissed the teetotalers as 'intolerant brooding theorists'. However, the 'brooding theorists' did have some important successes on points of policy. Their first victory was stopping seven-days-a-week access to alcohol.

This was certainly a move in the right direction. When Captain Frederick Marryat, author of *The Children of the New Forest* and a friend of Dickens, moved to London, he was absolutely horrified by how little regulation there was on access to drink. He reflected anxiously that the gin palaces were 'like hell, ever open to a customer . . . there must be something wrong in all this'. Even respectable people could be found drinking at all hours. The auctioneers at Billingsgate Market used to meet at the Darkhorse Tavern, for example, to start the day at 4 a.m. with their morning drinks of gin and milk while they discussed prices. Dickens himself was partial to two tablespoons of rum with fresh cream first thing in the morning.

In the summer of 1839 one of the first tasks of the newly formed Metropolitan Police, which had jurisdiction over the fifteen miles around Charing Cross, was to crack down on Sunday drinking before 1 p.m. On the first Sunday that selling alcohol was banned, it was remarked that the city was not quite as rowdy as usual. However, in the panic for supplies on Saturday night, 'the rush to the gin-shops and public-houses to procure a supply for the next morning's consumption, created some disturbance. The shops were cleared at midnight with difficulty.'

To make sure that they did not lose out on custom, publicans and gin-palace proprietors hung signs in the windows to remind customers to stock up for Sundays, Christmas Day and Good Friday by bringing their jugs and bottles along the night before. The only condition on which they could now open before 1 p.m. on Sundays was to offer 'refreshment for travellers'. The police also tried to restrict how much alcohol children were able to order, although the law was too vague to prevent it altogether. It applied to anyone found 'know-ingly' supplying alcohol to under-sixteens 'to be drunk upon the premises'. It gave owners plenty of scope to plead ignorance or to simply give children the alcohol to take away.

Even these modest restrictions caused anger. Tensions began to arise over the new rules being unfair to poorer Londoners. Curbing drinking was still fundamentally treated as a question of order, rather than health, as the upper classes were given free rein to drink away. As the *Spectator* put it, 'the conservation of order' required 'what may be called sumptuary laws – that "licensed victuallers" and gin-sellers in Holborn and Whitechapel must be restrained from acts permitted at the Athenaeum or the Carlton and Bellamy's – that a gentleman and MP may enjoy what to the swinish herd is prohibited.' As the distillers had protested to parliament, even back in 1729, 'the Brewing Trade, and the Wine Trade, are liable to the same Objections' and yet they did not 'find it argued by any body that therefore we must have no Beer, nor Wine'.

In 1855 there was a bolder attempt to restrict Sunday drinking for the entire day in 'places of amusement'. This was more than poor Londoners could bear and they rioted in Hyde Park after Lord Robert Grosvenor's bill was debated in the House of Commons. It was widely seen as one law for the rich, whose private clubs remained open on Sundays, and another for the poor who could not face a drink ban on their one day off of the week. Even *The Times* sided with them, calling the proposed law 'one-sided' for interfering 'with the comforts and recreations of the working classes'.

14: The Gentlemen Distillers

OLD TOM

A sweet gin, Old Tom would need nothing more than a squeeze of lemon and a dash of soda water

WHILE ALL THESE wranglings had been going on about the parameters of drinking, at the top end of the market gin itself had been quietly improving. By the mid-nineteenth century, Clerkenwell was a bustling hub of London Dry gin, as the Gordon's, Tanqueray, Nicholson's, Booth's and Langdale's distilleries all clustered together to take advantage of the springs of the Clerks' Well, Finsbury and Goswell. Clerkenwell was well-placed to receive grain from the mills, which meant that it was also home to many breweries, such as Whitbread's on Chiswell Street and Cannon's on St John Street.

Pure water was still a commodity in London, and a position near the best springs gave these emerging gin brands cachet, distinctly setting them apart from the rot gin that was still swilling around the city. These family businesses would go on to be famous all over the world, and many were still in operation until the Second World War. A trade directory of 1794 for London, Westminster and Southwark had listed only forty distillers and rectifiers, which showed the extent to which it was only the big players left after the gin craze.

Of the London distilleries that survived all the way into the twentieth century, the earliest was J. & W. Nicholson & Co., founded in the 1730s, in the thick of the craze, by brothers James and William. Their first distillery was on St John Street, Clerkenwell, and they later acquired Three Mills in Bromley-by-Bow, where they made their Lamplighter gin and neutral spirit for other companies. As with so many redundant London buildings, their Clerkenwell distillery has now been converted into a block of upmarket flats.

With the drastic reduction in numbers of gin shops and gin palaces, gin itself could start to gain a little prestige. A strong indication of its improving reputation in the mid-nineteenth century would come when the Nicholson company horses had the honour of pulling the Duke of Wellington's funeral carriage in 1852. It seems highly likely, although the evidence is circumstantial, that William Nicholson, owner of the distillery, also had the distinction of choosing the Marylebone Cricket Club's much-loved 'Bacon and Eggs' colour scheme. The MCC had played in light blue until the 1866. However, after Nicholson, a county-level cricketer himself, lent it the money to buy the Lord's cricket ground freehold, the club colours changed to the red and yellow of Nicholson's gin, probably in acknowledgement of all that he had done to secure the club's future.

A few years after the Nicholsons, the Booth family started their gin business in Clerkenwell too. Like many distillers of the period, they came from a wine-merchant background. In fact, the Booths may have been involved in the wine trade as early as 1569. In 1740 they expanded their business to jump on the new gin bandwagon. Philip Booth commissioned a sprawling distillery at 55 Cowcross Street, next to where Farringdon Station is now. By 1778, Philip Booth and Company were officially listed in the Directory of Merchants, along with sister company Boord's, with its distinctive cat-and-barrel label.

Philip eventually passed the Cowcross distillery on to his three sons, William, Felix and John. As business was booming, the brothers built another, even larger, distillery at Brentford, near their homes in the genteel west London suburbs of Ealing and Gunnersbury, which made Booth's the largest distilling company in England. Eventually, in 1830, Felix took sole control and began using his money for philanthropic interests.

Like the Nicholsons, the Booths hit new heights of respect-ability at this time. Their moment came when Felix was made a baronet in 1835 for financing the British attempt at Arctic exploration by his friend naval officer Sir John Ross. Ross's mission to find a navigable channel between the North Atlantic and the Pacific ultimately failed. However, he did succeed in locating the north magnetic pole, and named Cape Felix, Felix Harbour, the Gulf of Boothia and the Boothia Peninsula in Canada after his patron. The expedition had nearly proved disastrous when Ross's ship, the *Victory*, became trapped in ice. Eventually, the men had to abandon ship and set up camp on an island, where they awaited rescue by a whaling boat. After four years in the Arctic, no one has perhaps ever been so overjoyed to arrive in Hull as Captain

Ross and his men, in October 1833, when they sailed up the Humber Estuary.

The Booth family managed to hang on to the business until Felix's nephew, Sir Charles Booth, died in 1897. Two years later, the new directors had the Cowcross distillery rebuilt as a Renaissance-style palazzo, reflecting the company's self-confidence at the turn of the century. The grandeur of the six-bay façade, heavy keystones and pediments over the windows were offset by the pièce de résistance – the Classical-style frieze designed by F. W. Pomeroy, which rendered gin manufacture in Portland stone. As a condition of the building's demolition, you can still see the panels, which were carefully re-erected around the corner, on Britton Street. The site itself is now occupied by shoe designer Kurt Geiger's British headquarters.

A few minutes away, a distillery of the same vintage came to an unusually sudden end. Edward Langdale had built his Black Swan distillery on Holborn Hill in 1745 on the site of an old coaching inn, but it did not survive beyond the Gordon Riots in the summer of 1780. Langdale's distillery, where Captain Bradstreet had spend his last £13 on gin, was razed to the ground when Lord George Gordon led a mob of 10,000 people through the city in an orgy of destruction of property owned by Catholics, in which 200 people died. Langdale's distillery burned down with dozens of drunk rioters inside. With some poetic licence perhaps, Londoners were said to have been desperately scooping up gin that was flowing all down the street as flames engulfed the building.

The event was so frightening that Dickens evoked it graphically sixty years later as the backdrop for his novel *Barnaby*

Rudge. Dickens described how 'the streets were now a dreadful spectacle. The shouts of the rabble, the shrieks of women, the cries of the wounded, and the constant firing, formed a deafening and an awful accompaniment to the sights which every corner presented.' Luckily by the time that the mob had made it up Holborn Hill, Langdale himself had escaped through the back of the building, but the damage amounted to £50,000 – an eye-watering sum for the time. Although there is now no Langdale's gin, the recipe for Essence of Cinnamon, which has been made since 1745, is still in production. The site of the old distillery is only a few streets away from where the City of London Distillery has recently opened on Bride Lane.

The Gordon Riots captured the imagination of those who had witnessed it, and those who grew up in its shadow, alike. With characteristic flair, Lord Macaulay evoked the scene half a century later in his speech on universal education when he asked MPs to 'count up all the wretches who were shot, who were hanged, who were crushed, who drank themselves to death at the rivers of gin which ran down Holborn Hill.' He referred to the gin-guzzling mob as being 'as rude and stupid as any tribe of tattooed cannibals in New Zealand, I might say as any drove of beasts in Smithfield Market'.

A less alarming Gordon to arrive in Clerkenwell was Alexander Gordon, who had originally opened his Gordon & Co. distillery in Southwark in 1769. Clerkenwell became such a gin hub that Gordon moved his distillery there in 1786 to take advantage of the famed fresh water. The family bought a mansion on Charterhouse Square, by their new distillery at 67–8 Goswell Street, just off Old Street. During the riots,

Gordon had feared that his distillery may be next and armed senior employees with muskets, and his watchmen with cudgels in case hand-to-hand combat became necessary.

Another, now-forgotten, gin brand made by Israel Wilkes also moved from Southwark to Clerkenwell for the same reason. The Wilkes too lived near their new distillery, in a grand house on St John's Square. Wilkes had been a big enough distiller at one time to have the honour of being master of the Worshipful Company of Distillers. Keen to flaunt his riches, Wilkes was conveyed around town at all times in a six-horse carriage. His son, also named Israel, grew extremely wealthy from buying up tenements in nearby Spitalfields, where a street is named after him.

While the Wilkes family would fall by the wayside as gin-makers, by 1814, Gordon's was so successful that it was using premises at both Goswell Street, always referred to as 'the House', and at Pear Tree Street, around the corner. In 1823 Alexander Gordon died but the connection to him has lived on until today in a small way thanks to the boar's head on the bottle lid. Gordon, who was born in Wapping but was of Scottish descent, proudly displayed his roots with the boar from his crest. Legend had it that one of the Gordon clan rescued the king of Scotland from a boar when out hunting, who then bestowed upon them the right to use the boar's head as a family symbol.

Just downriver from Gordon's former home in Southwark was Sir Robert Burnett's grand distillery on the waterfront in Vauxhall. Burnett chose to not follow the crowd to Clerkenwell. Instead, he took over a distillery that had been established in 1767 by Sir Joseph Mawbey, which included a luxurious residence with three stables and a bowling green. Although we now associate 'energy efficiency' with modern developments, such as Bombay Sapphire's new hi-tech eco-friendly distillery in Hampshire, Burnett had his own, more rudimentary methods. He used the waste botanicals and grain from his gin-making to keep 2,000 pigs in the grounds, and had a sideline selling their meat.

Burnett's distillery must have stood very near what is now Vauxhall Station because the approach to Vauxhall Bridge was built across his property. On the site of an old inn by the distillery, Burnett used his considerable wealth to build a new house, 'replete with every Office and Convenience fitting for a genteel Family'. This house stood at 85 Albert Embankment, now the MI6 building that dominates that side of the river. The company remained in the family until 1928, when, as happened to so many, it was bought up by the Distillers Company, which was created by the merger of six firms in 1877.

To the east of Burnett's empire, Mark Beaufoy had set up another lucrative business. He established Beaufoy, James and Co. in 1741, on the site of Cuper's Bridge in Lambeth, where the National Theatre is now. Full of enterprising spirit, Beaufoy made not only gin but vinegar and 'fruit wine'. However, the original Beaufoy recipe for gin did not sound much better than the stuff on the street: 'Oil of vitriol, Oil of almonds, Oil of turpentine, Spirits of wine, Lump sugar, Lime water, Rose water, Alum, Salt of Tartar'. The fact that even a professional, registered company such as Beaufoy's was using all these substitutes for the proper ingredients showed how widespread the practice must have been. Family legend has it that seeing Hogarth's *Gin Lane* ten years later made such an impression on Beaufoy that he decided to abandon the gin and stick to his more innocent products.

The Beaufoy distillery remained there until 1810–13, when the works were relocated to 87 South Lambeth Road to make way for Waterloo Bridge. The family lived on the new premises in their elegant house, Caron Place, and remained there into the Second World War, until George Beaufoy died in 1941 during an aerial raid that destroyed most of the house and its ballroom. Walking past on the South Lambeth Road, you can still just catch sight of the clock tower and cupola of the old vat house.

Dozens of other distillers set up shop south of the river, where land was cheaper, but the other family names did not survive into the twentieth century: George and Charles Orme made gin on Blackfriars Road; J. Sinclair on what is now Black Prince Street in Lambeth; the Hodges' distillery was on Church Street by Lambeth Palace; John Gaitskell in Dock Head, a street that runs off Jamaica Road in Bermondsey; G. W. Gray on Tooley Street; Vincent and Pugh just by Borough Market; H. and A. S. Pigeon on Borough High Street. Stephen Child and Son's distillery in Trinity Church Square, behind Borough High Street, sounded particularly impressive. The counting house and the family's residence were built in classical Italian style, with stables, warehouses and the distillery on the same site. Boord and Son, who owned a distillery on Tooley Street, near the current London Bridge Station, were the only ones still making gin in the twentieth century.

The new status of the distillers by the mid-nineteenth century hinted that gin was gradually moving up the class system, even if the cheaper end of the market meant it still had a disreputable air. To protect their interests and elevate their craft, a refined group of London distillers set up an exclusive club. Just as the Worshipful Company of Distillers had originally grouped together to secure a royal charter from Charles I, so an elite of gin-makers came together once more. They formed the Rectifiers' Club, which met as an unofficial guild at the City of London Tavern every month. The members were the crème de la crème of distilling, including Messrs Booth, Gordon, Nicholson, Burnett, Seager and Evans, and newly established Tanqueray.

By 1837, a crafty match was agreed at one of these meetings between Alexander Gordon's granddaughter Susan, and Edward Tanqueray, Charles's elder brother. Gordon was so delighted that he immediately went out to buy six bottles of champagne. This match would lay the ground for a merger between the two great distilling families at the end of the century. The club would achieve its greatest coup in 1850, however, when it lobbied successfully to avoid paying duty on all export spirits by introducing a private bill in parliament. It was this vital exemption that would propel British distillers to become household names in the furthest corners of the world.

15: London Dry

GORDON'S AND WATER

A room temperature shot of Gordon's gin with a dash of water

UNTIL 1832, ALL of these distillers would have been making sweet Old Tom gin. Then a more subtle style would come along to push Old Tom to near-extinction – London Dry. A technical advance called the Coffey still, patented in that year, made this new style possible. Aeneas Coffey, an excise officer from Dublin, had been wily enough to patent his simple but revolutionary design, even though it was uncannily similar to one developed by Scottish inventor Robert Stein a few years earlier. A second wave of enduring, big-name distilleries then opened, which were able to take advantage of this still that created a more consistent product, on a much more efficient scale than the old copper pot ones.

The new ability to create a purer base spirit meant that sweeteners like licorice, which masked low-quality ingredients, were no longer necessary, allowing a variety of more delicate botanicals to come to the fore. As production methods grew more sophisticated, so the gin recipes could become increasingly nuanced and artful.

Until this leap forward, even large-scale professional distillers had been stuck using the basic pot still. Although it may have certain advantages in terms of flavour, it was an inefficient way of making gin. Because the pot created alcohol of a lower proof than the Coffey still, it was a comparatively expensive, labour-intensive process. The alcohol also needed to be distilled two or three separate times to achieve a similar effect to its new competitor. The Coffey still was very efficient at stripping away the raw spirit's flavour to create more of a blank canvas for the rest of the gin.

The company that Coffey established in London in 1835 is now the oldest distillery equipment-maker in the world, and is still in private hands. In 1872, Aeneas Coffey & Sons changed its name to John Dore & Co. after Coffey's sons made the company over to their foreman, John Dore. Dore and his family then operated the works out of their garden on Bromley High Street until they were forced to move by the local council, who built a tower block of flats on the site in the 1960s. Many stills that the company made over a hundred years ago are in active service today. The one used to make Martin Miller's gin was manufactured in 1903, for example, and Beefeater's number seven still was made by them in 1898.

The main variation on the Coffey still is the Carter head, which involves the alcohol vapours passing through a copper basket layered with botanicals to give a lighter, more delicate flavour. The last Carter heads by John Dore were made in the 1960s for Beefeater, but many distilleries still use the older Carter heads, such as Hendrick's, who bought a 1948 model at auction and Bombay Sapphire uses one made in 1834. Even if these stills are expensive, they do seem to last several lifetimes.

Before the term 'London Dry' was coined, it was referred to simply as 'unsweetened gin', but its classic notes, such as orange peel, cardamom and coriander, were already taking root in this era. Master distillers of all these rival gins had to vie with each other to create unique flavours, leading to a much more inventive use of botanicals. By the mid-nineteenth century, a typical dry gin could require more than a dozen exotic botanicals. Even by the time of John Rack's *The French Wine and Liquor Manufacturer*, in 1868, which advertised itself as a 'practical guide' for the liquor merchant, the term 'London Dry gin' was not yet in common parlance, but he suggested many ingredients that we would recognise now, such as orange peel, orange flower water, coriander seeds, angelica root, calamus root, cassia buds, lemon peel, cardamom, oil of cedar, sweet almonds, nutmeg, mace, caraway seeds and honey.

In making their gins, distillers of this period took maximum advantage of all the resources that London had to offer. The delicate herbal and floral notes that characterise London Dry gin were possible thanks to the ingredients that came in on the Thames from around the ever-expanding British Empire. Since the end of the Seven Years' War in 1763, Britain had control over most of North America, India and much of the Caribbean, the produce of which could be used to flavour gin. Between the springs of Bloomsbury and Clerkenwell, the botanicals coming in from the Thames and the grain coming in on barges by canal from the fields of Hertfordshire, the city was an ideal gin hub.

The Isle of Dogs became a vital part of the industry, as several docks opened up over the century to accommodate imperial trade. Herbs, spices and sugar had begun arriving

at the West India Docks from 1802. At the time they were
the largest in the world and vast warehouses were built on
reclaimed land nearby to be filled with goods from the
West Indies. Four years later, the East India Docks at
Blackwall opened, which were in use all the way up until
1967 when they became the first of the docks to close.
Once London distilleries had worked their magic on the
botanicals, thousands of cases of gin were sent to the
Millwall or Royal Victoria Docks to be exported around the
world.

As gin's popularity snowballed thanks to the fresher London
Dry style, more distilleries set up shop around Clerkenwell,
Bloomsbury and Southwark. It was such a thriving industry
that it was rare for a gin business not to make a lot of
money, very quickly. Tanqueray opened for business in 1830,
Boodles in 1845, Gilbey's in 1857, and Beefeater in 1863.
These family businesses created gin that was in demand all
over the world, but of all those distilleries only Beefeater has
managed to stay in London to this day.

Beefeater's first master distiller, James Burrough, started the
company by buying up John Taylor & Son, a gin and
liqueur company which had been going since 1820, for
£400. He renamed it James Burrough, Distiller and
Importer of Foreign Liqueurs and took over the premises at
56 Cale Street in Chelsea. Like the Gordons and the
Wilkes, he and his family lived around the corner from his
business, in a townhouse on Marlborough Square. A trained
chemist, Burrough had been daydreaming about his gin
empire for some time before he gathered the necessary
funds. His recipe book from 1849 included several spirit
ideas, such as a blackcurrant, an apple, and a raspberry gin,

and various liqueurs. His tabletop experimental retort still from Cale Street is used at the present Beefeater distillery, where it sits surrounded by the towering stills that make the normal Beefeater gin. It is currently used to make Burrough's Reserve, the present master distiller Desmond Payne's premium oak-aged gin.

Burrough's original London Dry-style gin recipe, which formed the gin now called Beefeater, contained juniper, coriander, Seville orange peel, lemon peel, and angelica root and seed. The recipe has only varied slightly since then, with the additions of almond, liquorice and orris root. Burrough was particularly keen to secure the sweetest oranges that he could, which was tricky in the 1860s, and he was delighted to find a reliable supplier of Seville oranges at Covent Garden by the name of Mrs Isaacs. He had to use what was available at London's markets, which inspired Payne to set himself the same challenge a few years ago to make Beefeater London Market gin as a limited edition. They offer much more now, of course, so Payne could experiment with kaffir lime leaves and pomegranates. James Burrough could only have dreamed of such botanicals for his original recipe.

Burrough's gin, which had been years in the planning, was clearly a winning formula nevertheless, as one of his first customers was Fortnum & Mason. The *ne plus ultra* of food shops considered gin a respectable-enough drink to sell from 1849, when they first listed a Dutch gin and a 'Fine Cordial Gin' in their catalogue. The gin that Fortnum & Mason sold was made by Burrough, but he was yet to adopt the Beefeater brand name. It was only in 1876 that it would start to appear in company papers. Fortnum's would eventually stop selling the Dutch gin, as London Dry's popularity took hold.

Beefeater flourished in the Victorian gin boom and Burrough created an array of liqueurs and other gins, such as his Ye Old Chelsey gin, a punch liqueur called Punchetta, Chelsey Sloe Gin and Ye Old Chelsey Peppermint, as well as exporting to North America, with great success. When he died in 1897, his sons Frederick, Frank and Ernest took over a humming distillery, but one that was outgrowing its home. With only two years left on their Chelsea lease, in 1904 the Burrough family began the unenviable task of relocating all of their operations to the other side of the river.

Sentimental about the Chelsea days, they named the new site just off Black Prince Road in Lambeth the Cale Distillery. They used the two remaining years on the old lease to stock the new premises with the latest stills from John Dore & Sons. Beefeater hung on to the same suppliers, including distillers' chemist Sparks White, which they continued to use until it closed down in the 1990s. In Lambeth they found themselves next door to the Royal Doulton factory, which they then commissioned to make Beefeater's stoneware flasks and liqueur decanters. In 1958 Beefeater would move to an even larger site, by the Oval cricket ground, which it took over from Hayward's Military Pickles, who abandoned it after it suffered extensive damage during the Blitz. This is still Beefeater's home, where the public can now look around for the first time in its history.

For all their undoubted success, the Burrough family had a great deal of local competition. Over the river, two men in their twenties, James Lys Seager and William Evans, had established Seager Evans and Co. in 1805. Their first base was the Millbank Distillery, also known as the Thames Bank

Distillery, on Grosvenor Road in Pimlico. Seager Evans began as a wine and spirits company, but spotting a trend, started to make their most famous product, Seagers Gin. Among its notable fans was Charles Dickens, although he was not always a happy customer.

In May 1868, Dickens was anxious enough about his gin supply to write them a letter of complaint from his country house, addressed to the Millbank Distillery:

> *Mr Charles Dickens sends his compliments to Messers. Seager Evans and Co. and begs them to test the accompanying bottle of gin drawn from their cask this morning. It appears to Mr Dickens to have neither the right strength nor flavour, and he thinks it must have been tampered with at the Railway. When the cask was tapped at Gad's Hill on Saturday, it was observed to be particularly full.*

Luckily for Dickens he had Gilbey's, another favourite gin, to fall back on when his Seagers reached him in poor condition. Gilbey's was so proud of its famous customer that it had Dickens' cheques framed on the wall of its headquarters until it closed down. Sir Walter Gilbey had also started off as a wine merchant. After volunteering in the Crimean War as a 22-year-old in 1853 with his brother Albert, he arrived back in London four years later, unsure of what to do. After several months of indecision, he and Albert decided to set up a business together, importing wine from South Africa with money borrowed from their elder brother Henry.

The Gilbeys started working from a rented basement at the corner of Berwick Street and Oxford Street, and managed to attract 20,000 customers within the year. Less than three years later, W. & A. Gilbey's was the third largest wine importer in the country. When he had gathered enough profit from his supremely successful business, Gilbey invested it in building a distillery at Camden Lock in 1869. What is now the Roundhouse music venue was originally a steam-engine repair shed, which he converted into a vast gin warehouse.

As this second wave of distillers became wealthier, they too were inclined to spend on philanthropic pursuits and aggrandising projects. To mark his success, in 1868 Gilbey leased Hargrave House in Hertfordshire, which came with 950 acres of land. Although he was involved with the business until his retirement in 1905, he became primarily a man of leisure. By 1874 he had bought a lord of the manor title and upgraded to Elsenham Hall, a Georgian mansion with an 8,000-acre estate in Essex. There he enjoyed breeding shire horses, and writing books and articles on agriculture. He did keep his eye on the business though, maintaining Cambridge House in Regent's Park as his London residence.

The Tanqueray family had the distinction of being granted a crest in 1838, only a few years after brothers Edward and Charles had founded their distillery on Vine Street in Bloomsbury. The crest somewhat incongruously featured a pair of battleaxes and a pineapple. The battleaxes were said to commemorate their illustrious but distant Tanqueray antecedents' part in The Crusades while fighting in Palestine under Richard I. The pineapple, a sign of hospitality, came from the coat-of-arms bestowed on the French Willaume family in 1767, from whom the Tanquerays were also descended.

They had arrived in Britain as Huguenot refugees in the seventeenth century. The mother, Anne, came from the Willaume family and married David Tanqueray, a goldsmith, in 1717 and had three sons. Thereafter three generations of Tanquerays became clergymen in the parish of Tingrith in Bedfordshire, where the elegant rectory is now named Tanqueray House.

Young Charles Tanqueray broke away from his father's ecclesiastical interests. The advent of large-scale, quality distillers meant that the profession was just about respectable for the privately educated son of a clergyman, without causing too many raised eyebrows. Alexander Gordon had died in 1823 a highly regarded Londoner, and Tanqueray was embarking on his career a good seven years later. With considerable foresight, the Tanquerays quickly formed an alliance with the Gordon family when Charles' brother Edward married Susan, the granddaughter of Alexander Gordon.

Circumstantial evidence suggests that Tanqueray took over a distillery that had been running since 1757. None of the buildings from the original Tanqueray distillery on Vine Street have survived, but the street itself is still there. Renamed Grape Street, it runs between High Holborn and New Oxford Street. Although Tanqueray's legacy has proved to be its London Dry, initially it also made Old Tom, and the ever-industrious Charles released another recipe, a spiced gin called Malacca, named after the Straits of Malacca.

A few years later Tanqueray started to make inroads abroad, as suggested by a large ceramic crock inscribed with 'Tanqueray Gin' that was recovered off the coast of Jamaica in a trading-boat shipwreck in 1847. Tanqueray's use of crocks was a very useful way of elevating the brand above the rest. While other distillers complained that their casks were on display at taverns, public houses and gin palaces, often in a diluted or adulterated state, Tanqueray would not sell in bulk. Instead it was sold in distinctive crocks through merchants and grocers, and they would carry on using stone crocks until the turn of the century. In that sense, it was perhaps the first self-consciously premium gin.

In 1868 Charles Tanqueray died, leaving the family business in the hands of his son Charles Waugh Tanqueray. At twenty, Charles Waugh was the same age that his father had been when he founded the business. Luckily, Charles Waugh proved every bit as energetic. Remaining at the helm for the rest of the century, his final act would be the merger with Gordon's. In 1878, Gordon's had been bought out by John Currie & Co., a distillery in Bromley. By 1897, Charles Tanqueray was talking to them about a possible merger, and a year later, the two companies came together to create Tanqueray, Gordon and Co. and production was centralised to the House on Goswell Road. The Tanquerays carried on but Charles Gordon retired, severing the last link with the Gordon family.

16: Gin is the Tonic

GIMLET

*50ml of London Dry gin, with 35ml of Rose's Lime Cordial,
served cold*

ON A QUIET street by the Thames is an enchanting walled
garden, which has stood there since 1673. Cosseted inside the
Chelsea Physic Garden's high walls, Britain's first cinchona
tree was tentatively grown in 1685 – the first known to
survive outside its native South America. The specimen now
standing in the tropical glasshouse does not look especially
remarkable, particularly among the 5,000 other plants.
However, it was the cinchona tree that facilitated the growth
of the British Empire, and indeed of all European empires. It
became urgently sought-after in the nineteenth century, as
countries seeking expansion in far-flung places realised that
they would all need access to their own cinchonas. For the
bark provided the original prevention against malaria –
quinine.

As soon as the garden was founded by the Worshipful Society
of Apothecaries to train its apprentices, it became a plant-
growing hub for species from around the world. Its head

gardener, John Watts, pioneered Europe's first heated green-house, which enabled him to nurture the cinchona, most likely to have arrived as seeds from South America. This early triumph would have been lost to history were it not for the diary of Sir John Evelyn, a writer, keen horticulturalist, and founder member of the Royal Society. He wrote that on going to visit Watts's new greenhouse he found 'a collection of innumerable rarities . . . Particularly, besides many rare annuals the Tree bearing the Jesuits bark'. Evelyn's use of the phrase 'Jesuits bark' referred to the Spanish Jesuits in South America, who had first sent cinchona samples from Peru back to headquarters in Rome in 1631. They had been the first westerners to discover its antimalarial properties, and by the 1650s regular shipments of the bark were arriving in Spain.

By the time of *The Gardeners Dictionary*, written in 1731, it seems that the fledgling British cinchona tree had died, as it was not mentioned even though the book was written by Watts's successor at the garden, Philip Miller. The cinchona currently growing at the garden is still producing quinine. So along with the juniper, coriander, cardamom, orris root and liquorice that also grow there, you could make a classic London Dry gin and tonic out of the four-acre garden. Desmond Payne from Beefeater was so impressed by a visit there recently that it inspired him to create a special edition London Garden Gin in 2014 – a London Dry with verbena and thyme.

Although quinine was vital for Western imperialism, it took the British centuries to get a reliable source. Cinchona is indigenous to the forests of the Andes, stretching across Bolivia, Peru and Ecuador. As those countries formed part of the Spanish Empire, it was the Spanish who controlled shipments into Europe, and to protect their lucrative position, in 1751 they had declared a monopoly on cinchona imports.

Other European imperial nations became frustrated with the expensive and unreliable supply. As it arrived at the London docks, pharmacists had to judge the bark's quality by colour and taste, and much of it turned out to be unusable or adulterated with useless bark from other trees. As British scientific investigation into cinchona was so patchy, it was not yet totally understood just how vital it was for soldiers being dispatched to malarial areas. It was only in 1768 that James Lind, a Scottish naval doctor, insisted that 'every man receive a daily ration of cinchona powder' when anchored at a tropical port.

Even then not all politicians and doctors were convinced by Lind – until a series of military campaigns were plagued by malarial deaths. In the early 1800s naval forces manning a blockade of the West African coast were decimated by malaria, and during the Napoleonic Wars, it crippled the Walcheren Expedition of 1809. There, an army of 40,000 men was struck down in the Netherlands, where the expeditionary force was attempting to destroy the French fleet. Only 106 men were killed in combat but 4,066 died from illness, and thousands more were so weakened by disease that they could not fight. The expedition was such a debacle that a parliamentary inquiry was held afterwards. Contemporaries referred to the disease from which the soldiers died as 'Walcheren Fever'. It seems now that this was an umbrella term for malaria, typhoid and typhus.

Once it was widely accepted that quinine was necessary for the occupation of marshland and tropical colonies, energy was finally channelled towards the pursuit of quinine. By the 1840s, soldiers and colonialists in India were consuming 700 tonnes of cinchona bark every year, and this only increased during the time of the Raj. As the hunt for quinine moved up the national agenda, the Royal Botanic Gardens at Kew was charged with the task of getting cinchona to grow out in the colonies by germinating the seeds in London and sending them out to the plantations. Kew and the newly formed India Office organised the widespread planting in India, Sri Lanka, Jamaica and East Africa.

However, the whole endeavour was very hit and miss. A British expedition in 1860, led by Sir Clements Markham of the India Office, did manage to procure cinchona seeds and plants from the Andes. The plants that Markham himself collected did not fare well on the long journey to India, however, and had all died by the time they arrived. Fortunately Dr Richard Spruce, an intrepid botanical explorer of the Amazon, who knew the area far better, collected healthier seeds and plants from the forests of Ecuador to send to India. The expedition had been gruelling and Spruce had suffered from paralysis in his back and legs. Nevertheless, six weeks later, he had recovered enough to complete the mission. Spruce had been exploring South America from 1849, when he had arrived at the age of thirty-one, but after fifteen years ill health brought him back to England in 1864. Markham managed to secure a small pension for Spruce to eke out his final, sickly years at a cottage in Coneysthorpe, North Yorkshire, near where he was born.

Spruce's seeds were widely planted in India and Ceylon, but the enterprise began only as a qualified success. The particular species was not as rich in quinine as hoped, but it did ease the supply problem. Frustratingly for the British, of all the places that cinchona was cultivated, it was most successful in Dutch-occupied Java. The Dutch had ended up with such incredibly productive cinchona trees thanks to the bad luck of a British trader, and sometime alpaca breeder, by the name of Charles Ledger. Ledger bought a sample of cinchona seeds from a Bolivian in 1865, which he managed to illicitly smuggle out and send back to his brother George in London. None of the experts who George showed them to realised that they were anything exceptional so after a while George sold the seemingly unremarkable seeds on to the Dutch. They proved to have an exceptionally high quinine content that was well-suited to Java's climate. These trees, named *Cinchona ledgeriana* after Ledger, shifted the centuries-old South American monopoly into Dutch hands instead. The *Cinchona ledgeriana* is still considered to produce the purest quinine and is now used by premium tonic brands such as Fever Tree.

Despite this misfortune, the British ended up with a reasonable supply of quinine out in India. Now there was one thing missing – the tonic. So far, the daily dose of quinine had been bitter and very unpalatable. The cinchona bark was dried and crushed into small pieces to be dissolved in various tinctures as cinchona alkaloids are highly soluble in alcohol. To make the medicine go down more easily, colonialists occasionally mixed the powder with sugar, water and gin. This bittersweet combination would eventually evolve into that classic colonial drink – Schweppes Indian Tonic Water and gin.

The first popular brand of tonic water was not Schweppes however. In 1858 Erasmus Bond, owner of the W. Pitt & Co. drinks company back in London, patented his unappetisingly named 'improved aerated tonic liquid'. Bond marketed it as a health product, but it was so delicious with gin that it spent little time in the medicine cabinet and moved swiftly to the drinks cabinet.

Soon rival brands of tonic water emerged, including the eventual winner of the scrum, Schweppes. Swiss amateur scientist Johann Schweppe had founded his company back in 1783, after he discovered a way to produce carbonated water on a commercial scale. Five years later he brought the Schweppes brand to London, opening his first factory on Drury Lane, where he made soda water. J. Schweppe & Co.'s great commercial success was celebrated by its inclusion at the Great Exhibition of 1851, hosted to celebrate the wonders of industry from around the world. At the centre of the exhibition at the Crystal Palace in Hyde Park stood a 27-foot-high fountain made from four tons of pink glass, which flowed with Schweppes soda water, and the fountain has been the company trademark ever since. As gin and tonic became increasingly popular back in London, Schweppes experimented with a mixture of oranges, sugar, and quinine, and in 1870 it finally launched its Indian Tonic Water.

Quinine would retain its primacy well into the twentieth century. When Sir William Osler, regius professor of medicine at Oxford University from 1909 to 1917, was asked about malaria treatment, he simply said, 'this is comprised in three words: quinine, quinine, quinine'. Winston Churchill, with typical exuberance, would attribute it with saving 'more Englishmen's lives than all the doctors in the Empire'. After all, until the technological developments of the 1940s there were no viable alternatives.

However, there were downsides. Too much of it induced a syndrome known as cinchonism, the first reported case of which was in 1857, the year that the British Crown took over the government of India from the East India Company. The condition caused loss of sight, tinnitus and nausea. The only person to complain of such side effects recently was the late TV chef Clarissa Dickson Wright. According to Dickson Wright, doctors thought that she had malaria in the 1970s, but it turned out to be quinine poisoning. She said that washing down two bottles of a gin a day with four pints of tonic water for twelve years had given her this antiquated condition.

Like tonic water, many drinking innovations were born of medical necessity. The navy's gin-based remedies in particular added a great deal to drinking culture. Both Pink Gins and Gimlets were responses to staying healthy at sea, and the gin of choice for these drinks at the time was Plymouth. By 1850, Plymouth was supplying the navy with over 1,000 barrels a year of its Navy Strength gin at 57 per cent ABV, which Plymouth continues to make in a copper pot still that was installed in 1855.

The 57 per cent strength was important not only to make a peppy Pink Gin after a long day on deck – it also meant that, in the days of rudimentary storage, the gunpowder would still ignite even if the gin spilled on it. This is the origin of the term 'proofed' alcohol. To check that alcohol was the right strength before storing it aboard ship, one method was to mix it with gunpowder to check if it still caught alight. If there was not enough alcohol in the gin, then it would not be 'proofed'.

The other main gin to supply thirsty officers was Senior Service gin, 'senior service' being a nickname for the Royal Navy. It was made by the Burrough family from 1863 who delivered it to the navy's Royal Victoria Dock, its food and drink headquarters in Deptford. Again, Senior Service gin was made at the required 57 per cent ABV, so that it could be stowed away below deck. The Hayman family, who are part of the Burrough dynasty, now make their own Royal Dock gin from their Burrough family recipe under their own label.

Whether Burrough's or Plymouth, much of this gin would end up being used for Pink Gin, also known as gin and bitters, which started as a treatment for seasickness. Bitters were invented by Dr Johann Siegert, who concocted a mixture of spices and herbs as a stomach medicine in Venezuela in 1824, in a town then called Angostura. By the late nineteenth century, the two most popular manufacturers were Peychaud and Angostura, both of which are still in production. Angostura aromatic bitters are now made in Port of Spain in Trinidad, after the Siegert family moved there in 1875. Peychaud was sold all over the world, but the British tended to plump for Angostura, after officers discovered it while visiting Venezuela in the 1830s. Bitters can be any drink made from gentian, herbs and spices, but those two brands are still the most successful.

When the navy began putting a few drops in their glasses of gin, the trend caught on around the Empire and became popular back in the gentlemen's clubs of St James's. One of the earliest known mentions of the drink is from an article in the *Reading Mercury* on 7 August 1780, in a recollection from the navy: 'The Captain told me I was welcome on board, and asked me if would have a glass of gin and bitters'. A few drops of Angostura were making their way into other drinks back in London as well. American author Mark Twain wrote to his wife Olivia in 1874:

> I want you to be sure to have in the bathroom, when I arrive, a bottle of scotch whisky, a lemon, some crushed sugar and a bottle of Angostura Bitters. Ever since I have been in London, I have taken in a wine glass what is a so-called cock-tail (made with these ingredients) before breakfast, before dinner, and just before going to bed . . . To this I attribute the fact that up to this day my digestion has been wonderful, simply perfect . . .

Whether the few drops of Angostura really did improve Twain's digestion or not, it certainly proved a popular daily ritual at home and abroad, with a few variations in serving styles. The Angostura packaging was distinctive in cocktail cabinets thanks to its paper label, which was too large for the bottle and apparently began as an ordering mistake. Officials in the Indian civil service liked to add onions pickled with chilli to theirs, known as a Gin Piaj. In Malaya, it was known as a Gin Pahit as 'pahit' is Malay for bitter. Whether a Gin Pahit, Gin Piaj or Pink Gin, it acquired a suave aura.

As a drink with strong colonial connotations, the Pink Gin continued to have cameo roles in literature set in the Empire well into the twentieth century. It was a fitting drink for W. Somerset Maugham to use in his 1926 short story 'P. & O.' for example. The protagonist is a rubber planter named Mr Gallagher, who is returning from Malaya to Galway on a P&O liner after twenty-five years of working on a plantation. On the boat home, he buys a drink for a woman he has just met: 'the Irishman ordered a dry Martini for her and a gin pahit for himself. He had lived too long in the East to drink anything else.' Somerset Maugham himself would have sympathised with Gallagher's longing for a Pahit. He revealed his own fondness for it on his travels through what was then Burma and Siam in *The Gentleman in the Parlour*.

Another superb twentieth century novelist, Graham Greene, revealed his penchant for a soothing gin abroad. In *Journey Without Maps*, Greene described his travels around Liberia in 1935. To alleviate boredom on board ship, Greene and his fellow travellers were 'drunk on bad Madeira and the pink gin they call Coasters' by dinner time. It was Greene's first experience of Africa and he identified 'the need in a strange place of some point of support, of one or two things scattered around which are familiar and understandable, even if they are only Sydney Horler's novels, a gin and tonic.'

Alongside the Pink Gin, the other enduring naval drink, the Gimlet, was also introduced for medical reasons. Its dose of Rose's Lime Juice was vital to ward off scurvy. Scurvy was a debilitating disease that had killed innumerable sailors, who we now know were suffering from a lack of vitamin C, which is needed to build tissue all over the body. The painful symptoms included bleeding gums, swollen legs, heavy bruising and haemorrhages. In 1867 the Merchant Shipping Act finally made it compulsory to carry lime or lemon juice rations, although the fight against scurvy had started over a century earlier.

James Lind, the far-sighted Scottish doctor who had prescribed quinine for sailors in 1768, had begun to search for a scurvy remedy back in 1747. While serving as surgeon on HMS *Salisbury*, Lind worked out that citrus fruits were the key to it.

To gather his evidence, he had divided twelve sufferers into six pairs, giving each pair a different addition to their diet. Some were given cider, others seawater, others a mixture of garlic, mustard and horseradish, another pair was given spoonfuls of vinegar, and the last two oranges and lemons. As we would now guess, the pair fed citrus fruit recovered. The importance of Lind's findings on scurvy were recognised at the time, and Thomas Trotter, the naval physician who had pioneered the understanding of alcoholism, took up Lind's campaign after witnessing the horrifying effects of scurvy at sea himself. However, it was not until 1795 that an Admiralty order was issued on the supply of citrus fruit to the navy.

In the 1860s Scottish entrepreneur Lauchlan Rose devised the world's first concentrated fruit drink using lime juice from the West Indies. Trade for Rose absolutely boomed because citrus fruit rations were now compulsory on merchant ships as well. By 1893, Rose had bought his own estates on which to grow lime trees, so he made even more money. Rose's cordial made the Gimlet extremely easy to rustle up aboard ship, but who first put the gin and Rose's together is uncertain. Although there is no written evidence to support the story, there was a Surgeon Rear-Admiral Sir Thomas Desmond Gimlette (1857–1943) in the Royal Navy when the cocktail became popular. He may have given his name to the Gimlet, but his obituary in *The Times* made no mention of any particular deftness with a cocktail shaker. The likely alternative is that it was named after the device used to bore holes in lime-juice casks before Rose's cordial came along.

Not all army and navy drinking could be claimed as medicinal, however. Lord Kitchener's forces at Khartoum and Omdurman in the Sudan had shipments of Pimm's sent up the Nile in 1898. Pimm's used this as a canny marketing coup for their bottles, which thereafter read: 'Supplied to the officers' mess in Cairo and Khartoum during the Egyptian Campaign'.

Officers stationed out there dutifully wrote telegrams of thanks for the shipments to assure that they had arrived safely. It could actually be rather tricky to get hold of the bottles once they had arrived in Egypt, as it was such an unfamiliar product to customs. Major H. P. Shekleton of the 14th Soudanese in Khartoum sent a telegram addressed to the manager of Pimm's at the Poultry branch in July 1898: 'Many thanks and good luck to you. Pimm's has already caused a good deal of excitement and is refused registration but hope for the best.'

Shekleton, who had been promoted to colonel by November, wrote of another hiccup in getting the Pimm's through Europe:

> We are nearing Brindisi in an Austrian Lloyd Steamer and I thought you would like to know how Pimm's No. 1 got on. It has been an object of the greatest suspicion. Nobody would register it and every custom house wanted to charge enormous duty. It was only by a display of calmness that it ever arrived, and it gave the custom house much more amusement than all the rest of the baggage put together. It has been sealed and resealed, stamped, labelled and tied up in all sorts of ways with tape and coloured string, but has survived it all and is now reposing in my cabin looking well after its many vicissitudes.

Once it became familiar cargo, the soldiers had an easier time getting to actually drink it. Colonel Rogers, the director of supplies at the army headquarters in Cairo, wrote: 'It is really very kind of Messrs Pimm to be so thoughtful about poor fellows sweltering out in these regions. It is nice to know that people at home take practical interest in our welfare.'

17: Fancy Drinks

GIN FIZZ

'Put into a tumbler the juice of half a lemon and one wine-glass of gin. Fill with shaved ice, shake well, and strain into a glass. Add a teaspoonful of icing sugar in which is placed a pinch of carbonate of soda. Stir again and drink while it effervesces.'

'Convivial Dickens' by Hewett and Axton

FOR MODERN DRINKERS, cocktails evoke images of streamlined Art Deco bars, slick bartenders and spotless silver shakers. In fact cocktails have much older, more rudimentary beginnings. Their forerunner, 'mixed drinks', had been evolving for over a century before the cocktail golden age of the 1920s and 1930s. Because the British rarely used the word 'cocktail' itself before the late nineteenth century, their contribution to early cocktail-making is often overlooked. British recipes and manuals usually referred to specific cocktails without using the collective word itself. For under the umbrella of 'cocktail' are many drink styles – from smashes and cups, to slings and fizzes – and the British tended to use those terms instead.

The earliest known British reference to a 'cocktail' dates back to a 1798 London newspaper, the *Morning Post and*

Gazetteer. It reported that the landlord of the Axe and Gate tavern next to Downing Street had been so ecstatic to win on a lottery that he had erased all his customers' tabs as an act of generosity. The newspaper imagined, as a satirical feature, what politicians of the day might have had on their tabs at the tavern. Among the drinks listed, Prime Minister William Pitt the Younger owed for 'L'huile de Venus', 'perfait [sic] amour', and a less exotic drink: '"cock-tail" (vulgarly called ginger)'. In the piece there was no description of what this 'cock-tail' itself was like, other than the mention of ginger, but it is a valuable link between what we drink today and the very earliest understanding of the word.

This reference also suggests that cocktails are not as American as Americans would like to think, even if they were indeed early adopters. The oldest printed definition of a cocktail in an American publication came from a magazine eight years later; it was described as 'a stimulating liquor, composed of spirits of any kind, sugar, water and bitters'. As with so much etymology, theories abound as to the provenance of 'cocktail'. One of the most plausible is a nod to a seventeenth-century custom of docking horses that had mixed blood, turning them into 'cocktailed' horses. The act of mixing a drink therefore created a cocktailed spirit.

Although the definition of exactly what a cocktail was then, or even is now, is a moveable feast, the groundwork for the twentieth-century cocktail boom was laid in London as early as the mid-seventeenth century, when punch houses became a feature of the landscape. The name 'punch' is thought to be a nod to its Indian origins because in Sanskrit pancha means five, the usual number of ingredients. Initially, when sailors popularised the drink, punch had been made from rum but London punch-makers adapted it with gin. At the time it would have been the Old Tom style, which was sweet like rum in any case. The practice of drinking punch in shared bowls was an uplifting step away from the depressing solitary shots of the gin shop. Punch houses were known for their lively, party atmosphere.

London's most celebrated punch house was run on Ludgate Hill from 1731 to 1776 by James Ashley, who would prepare his concoctions at customers' tables, so that they could be satisfied that they were not being shortchanged. Over his 45-year tenure Ashley earned many happy customers. One obituary claimed that 'he was the first to introduce the selling of punch in small quantities', by which he made 'a large fortune'.

Punch would remain a fixture for jovial communal gatherings well into the nineteenth century. The elaborate accoutrements with which it could be served at home suggest that it was very much a feature of upmarket entertaining. Porcelain punch bowls were often given as fashionable wedding presents and Dickens owned an enviable collection of punch-making trinkets, including a silver nutmeg grater, engraved ladles and an engraved tankard.

However, punches, like gin itself, did not become the preserve of the wealthy because the quality and expense varied enormously. The aptly named satirical magazine *Punch* published a cartoon poking fun at how cheap gin could be masked by punch's many ingredients: '"Did you speak to Taplino about the gin, Fanny, my dear? . . . The last was turpentine, and even your brewing didn't make good punch of it."'

Even Bob Cratchit, the impoverished hero of *A Christmas Carol*, managed to put together a festive one for his family, with touching relish: 'Turning up his cuffs – as if, poor fellow, they were capable of being made any more shabby – [he] compounded some hot mixture in a jug with gin and lemons and stirred it round and round and put it on the hob to simmer.' A similarly hearty punch turns up to warm the cockles in *David Copperfield*, thanks to jolly Mr Micawber:

> *I never saw a man so thoroughly enjoy himself*
> *amid the fragrance of lemon-peel and sugar, the*
> *odour of burning spirit, and the steam of boiling*
> *water, as Mr Micawber did that afternoon. It was*
> *wonderful to see his face shining at us out of a thin*
> *cloud of these delicate fumes, as he stirred, and*
> *mixed, and tasted, and looked as if he were*
> *making, instead of a punch, a fortune for his*
> *family down to the latest posterity.*

Following on from punches, a very simple cocktail called the Gin Twist became the latest intoxicating way to keep warm. It was easy to throw together, with just gin, lemon juice, sugar and boiling water. It seemed a fairly respectable drink in Sir Walter Scott's 1823 novel *St Ronan's Well*, as Captain MacTurk requests: 'Sir Binco, I will beg the favour of your company to the smoking-room, where we may have a cigar and a glass of gin-twist.'

A more venerable drink was the Gin Flip, made with egg, sugar, gin, nutmeg and heated beer. It was adapted from the late–seventeenth-century 'flips', which had a frothy top that came from stirring the mixture with a hot iron. By the mid-nineteenth century this had evolved into a cold drink, with the froth effect achieved by whisking eggs.

Even when recipes were written down, the nomenclature was very slippery. Mr Venus sums up the difficulty of pinning down exactly what cocktails mean to different people in Dickens' *Our Mutual Friend*. When Silas Wegg asks him, 'What do you call a cobblers' punch?' It elicits the response: 'It's difficult to impart the receipt for it, sir . . . because, however particular you may be in allotting your materials, so much will still depend upon the individual gifts, and there being a feeling thrown into it. But the groundwork is gin.' Although Venus was not entirely sure, a Cobblers' Punch indeed did have gin as the base and was usually made with treacle, vinegar and water.

Unless cocktails were recorded as being made by a particular bartender, it is difficult to pinpoint exactly who created them either. As cocktails evolved, many rival claims were made. One that seems fairly certain is that John Collins, the head waiter at Limmer's Hotel and Coffee House on Hanover Square during the 1820s and 1830s, was responsible for what we now call a Tom Collins. The earliest written reference to the John Collins is from 1865: 'that most angelic of drinks for hot weather – a John Collins (a mixture of soda water, gin, sugar, lemon and ice)'. Luckily because the ingredients are listed, we know that this is now a Tom Collins, perhaps because of the Old Tom gin used to make it.

It would seem that the bar at Limmer's was still going strong decades later. In 1878's *Old and New London* by Edward Walford, Limmer's was given the backhanded compliment of being 'the most dirty hotel in London; but in the gloomy, comfortless coffee-room might be seen many members of the rich squirearchy, who visited London during the sporting season . . . you could always get a good plain English dinner, an excellent bottle of port, and some famous gin-punch.'

The most enduring success story of the early mixed drinks began in 1823, when Pimm's Oyster Bar opened on the site of an old tavern on Poultry, near to where Bank Station is now. It was here that James Pimm created his winning mixture of gin, liqueurs and fruit – a kind of drink called a cup – which he sold in pints from pewter tankards to aid digestion after his oysters. This concoction went on to become the Pimm's No. 1 Cup that we drink today.

By 1851, Pimm had perfected another two variations – the No. 2, with Scotch, and the No. 3, with brandy. His chain flourished across the City, with well-located restaurants in Gresham Street, Bishopsgate, Threadneedle Street and the Old Bailey. Thanks to its snowballing popularity, he started bottling No. 1 for sale at bars and restaurants outside the Pimm's chain in 1859.

At this time, Londoners still had rather an embarrassing reputation for drinking sweet, low-quality gin in horrifying quantities, not for serving drinks of sophistication. However, with these early mixed drinks, we can see how London prepared the way for New York to introduce many of the more elaborate classic cocktails that we know so well today. Along with the gin and tonic, the popularity of Pimm's helped gin to progress to being a respectable long drink – not a spirit to be hocked back as a neat shot.

Although the word 'cocktail' was not in common usage yet in London, as early as the 1850s, what we now call cocktails were becoming widely available. They made for a spectacular showcase at London's first cocktail bar, when Alexis Soyer, a Frenchman who made his career at the Reform Club on Pall Mall, opened the Victorian equivalent of a pop-up bar in 1851. At his bar he offered a wondrous choice of forty cocktails to the six million visitors who attended the Great Exhibition in Hyde Park. Because he was asked to make his drinks non-alcoholic, rather than take part in the exhibition itself, Soyer set up shop in a rented building by the gates. There he could make his drinks as punchy as he wanted. The scale of his ambition for the venture was reflected in the name – his Gastronomic Symposium of All Nations. Around 1,000 visitors a day came to his gastronomic symposium for food, cocktails, music and fireworks. Although a spectacular achievement it proved financially ruinous, and left Soyer profoundly in debt. Soyer took a hit personally because of the sheer extravagance of his bar, but it did show that Londoners were keen to experiment with these new drinks.

The two big contributions that American bartenders then made to cocktails were showmanship and the use of ice. Although Dickens was a keen drinker, who was aware of the latest trends, in his 1842 travelogue *American Notes* he marvelled at the modernity of cool drinks. 'Hark! To the clinking sound of hammers breaking lumps of ice, and to the cool gurgling of the pounded bits as . . . they are poured from glass to glass.' In 1863, in the drinks guide *Cups and their Customs* by Henry Porter and George Edwin Roberts, it still had to be patiently explained to British readers that ice was a welcome addition to a drink: 'when a cool cup is to be made, its greatest adjunct is ice, in lumps'. All of Porter and Roberts' descriptions assumed a lack of familiarity with ice. They included the new fashion for cold drinks in their Gin Punch recipe:

> *As a mild summer drink, and one readily made,*
> *we recommend Gin Punch, according to the*
> *following recipe: Stir the rind of a lemon, and the*
> *juice of half a one, in half a pint of gin; add a*
> *glass of Maraschino, half a pint of water, and two*
> *tablespoonfuls of pounded white sugar, and,*
> *immediately before serving, pour in two bottles of*
> *iced soda-water.*

Perhaps spurred on by their more flashy American bartending cousins, Porter and Roberts felt emboldened to elevate their craft too: 'As in this age of progress, most things are raised to the position of a science, we see no reason why Bacchanology (if the term please our readers) should not hold a respectable place,' although it never seemed to catch on as they hoped. Porter and Roberts still did not refer to 'cocktails', but explained their book as 'a collection of recipes for the brewing of compound drinks, technically termed "Cups"'. Although the recipes are certainly what we would now call cocktails, they demurred from the word itself.

Porter and Roberts happily went along with the fashion for ice, but they had no time for the new-fangled American cocktails, which they referred to as 'sensation-drinks'. They sniped that they had 'no friendly feeling' for these drinks 'which have lately travelled across the Atlantic . . . so we will express our gratification at the slight success which "Pick-me-up", "Corpse-reviver", "Chain-lightning" and the like, have had in this country.' They dismissed the new American bars with their 'bad brandies and fiery wine'. As we know in hindsight, Porter and Edwards were, of course, wrong to dismiss both 'sensation-drinks' and the new American bars.

The next major British bartending work was William Terrington's delightful *Cooling Cups and Dainty Drinks* in 1869. In his guide, the 'cocktail' was only a subsection of the list of punches, cups, juleps, cobblers, smashes, possets and toddies; it was still yet to be a catch-all term. As Porter and Roberts did, Terrington tended to refer to them as 'compounded drinks'. He did use the word 'cocktail' to describe one particular recipe though, his 'Gin Cocktail', which contained a splash of water, ginger syrup and bitters.

It was in this period that drinks started being widely served in glassware, as opposed to heavy, opaque tankards. This transition helped the cocktail business as it then became relevant how attractive the drink looked in the glass, and this elevated the barman's skill. The new sophistication of cocktails helped to make gin respectable, endearing it to a more genteel sort of drinker.

Although the taste for warm drinks was certainly fading, the notion of refrigeration was still a novelty even for the most affluent. A particularly clear example of how cocktails changed in temperature over the nineteenth century comes from two editions of *Oxford Night Caps: Being a Collection of Receipts for Making Various Beverages Used in the University* by Richard Cook, a drinks guide popular with the undergraduates. In the 1835 edition of *Oxford Night Caps,* Cook mentioned the occasional use of ice tubs, but most of the drinks were served hot or at room temperature. Typical drinks would be ones like Rumfustian – a warm pint of gin mixed with egg yolks, strong beer, white wine, grated nutmeg, lemon juice, cinnamon, sugar and sherry. The recipe boasted 'such is the intoxicating property of this liquor, that none but hard drinkers will venture to regale themselves with it a second time'. Also recommended by Cook as a party drink was the Gin Punch, made hot with two bottles of gin mixed with boiling water, the juice and rind of lemons and oranges, liquid calves' feet jelly, white wine and capillaire. He in fact reminded drinkers, 'Care must be taken that the ice water does not get in to the jug which contains the Punch' because iced water was still so unsafe to drink.

The idea of actually putting ice in a drink was virtually unheard of earlier in the century, as it would have been such a health risk. It would take decades for English bars to secure a safe, affordable supply of ice. By the time of the 1871 edition of *Oxford Night Caps*, ice in drinks was now possible with the development of reliable refrigeration. When the Cobbler was first introduced Cook explained, 'Ice was procured from the confectioners and fishmongers, which had been taken from stagnant ponds and noisome ditches; consequently those who partook of it imbibed the filthy impurities which it contained.'

For this later edition, as an instance of smart opportunism, the Wenham Lake Ice Company took out a page advertising recipes for a Mint Julep, and Champagne Cup that required the ingredient *du jour* – ice. *Oxford Night Caps* showed how much drinks had changed. When it came to the fashion for cooler cocktails, London bartenders were left imitating the Americans, but eventually they did catch up. As opposed to the heavy hot punches of the earlier century, the cooler temperature allowed for the more subtle flavours of the drier, unsweetened gins coming on to the market to come to the fore.

Although mixed drinks did have a long London heritage, they were certainly given a big, bright American makeover, and this is where American showmanship played an important role too. The notion of a glitzy bar where the barman took centre stage, serving his signature drinks with an air of theatricality was an American development, acknowledged by cocktail bars being widely referred to as 'American bars'. The *Spectator* described, in bewilderment, how elevated their approach to bartending was, with all their careful techniques and flamboyant artistry. It described to its readers how the Americans made the cocktail spout 'from one glass and descend into another, in a great parabolic curve, as well defined and calculated as a planet's orbit' while it was mixed.

London bartenders took their lead from the legendary Jerry Thomas, who showed off his expertise when he toured London, Southampton and Liverpool in 1859. He exhibited his flair with the aid of a solid silver bar utensils set worth £1,000. A master self-publicist, before his guest stint at the new American Bar at the Cremorne Pleasure Gardens in Chelsea, Thomas had leaflets dropped over west London from a hot air balloon, to announce his arrival. The leaflets promised 'The real genuine iced American beverages, prepared by genuine Yankee professor'.

At his bar visitors were treated to a choice of gin, brandy or port wine juleps, punches made with milk, whiskey, brandy, rum or gin, as well as 'nectars and liqueurs of every variety'. From the 'fancy' section of the menu, Thomas rustled up Gin Slings, Ladies' Blushes, Private Smiles, Sherry Snips and Brandy Smashes.

Three years later Thomas brought out the most influential cocktail book of the nineteenth century, the *Bartender's Manual*. These cocktails would enter the British cocktail canon, and Porter and Edwards' dismissiveness of 'sensation-drinks' looked increasingly like wishful thinking on their

part. The Ladies' Blush made by Thomas at the Cremorne
Pleasure Gardens became the signature drink of Leo Engel's
bar at the Criterion restaurant, one of London's earliest
permanent cocktail bars, at Piccadilly Circus. Engel had the
grace to doff his cap to the Americans for their 'ingenious
inventions that have greatly added to the comfort of the
human race'. The recipe for Ladies' Blush was included in
Engel's *American and Other Drinks* collection from 1878: 'To
a wine glass of Old Tom gin add one tea-spoonful of Noyau
and five drops of Absinthe; sweeten to taste, about one
teaspoonful of sugar. Shake up well with shaven ice, strain,
and pour into a coloured glass, the rim of which has already
been damped with lemon juice and dipped in white sugar.'

One sad casualty of the cocktail's new popularity was that it set
Old Tom on the path to near extinction. Hot, sweet drinks were
out, and cool, dry drinks were in. Old Tom's sweetness made it
difficult to mix in cocktails, which tipped sales overwhelmingly
in London Dry's favour. During the twentieth century Old
Toms, which typically contained between 2 and 6 per cent
sugar, practically died out. The little that continued to be made
in Britain was mainly exported to Finland, Japan and the USA.

By the end of the century, a deluge of recipe books had been
printed to help home entertaining match the new level of
sophistication in London bars. Somewhat surprisingly, two of
these came from women. In 1891 Harriet Anne de Salis, who
also wrote *Kissing; its origin and species,* also released *Drinks à
la mode: Cups and drinks of every kind for every season.* Gin
even made it into that epitome of domestic propriety, Mrs
Beeton's *Book of Household Management.* In her 1906 posthu-
mous edition, it was listed under 'American Drinks' – gin
finally had the seal of respectablity.

18: Grime and Grandeur

KUBLA KHAN No. 2
Gin, vermouth, and a few drops of laudanum

THANKS TO THE popularity of cocktails, the gin and tonic, and the exclusive American-style bars of the West End, gin was becoming ever more acceptable in polite society. The gin bottle had finally earned its place in the most elegant bars and private houses. However, for all this change, it did not mean that successive Victorian parliaments were any less afraid of cheap gin in lower-class hands. The public and politicians fretted that the working poor were still squandering their time and money on drink. It fell to Victorian, and later Edwardian, policy-makers to face the problem once more.

When music halls first opened, they were dreaded as yet another venue where the urban poor could indulge in their unsavoury, socially corrosive drinking habits. This image was not helped by popular music-hall entertainers, who sang as debauched characters, such as Gin-and-Water Bill, who would 'drink to myself I fill', and Alfred Vance, with his hit songs *I Do Like a Little Drop of Gin* and, more simply, *Rum, Rum,*

Rum – the second cheapest spirit of the time. When the Ealing Studios made the musical *Champagne Charlie*, about the rivalry between music-hall stars in the 1860s, it opened the film with Alfred Vance leading a singalong, baying for 'gin, gin, gin' at a pub in Elephant and Castle. This reminded *Champagne Charlie*'s 1940s audience of the days when gin had been the drink of Victorian London's poor, rather than the stylish spirit they now knew.

The opening of *Champagne Charlie* may not have been as much of a caricature as it sounds in the early days of music hall as the venues grew out of rowdy entertainments called penny gaffs. For one penny, drinkers could jostle into the back room of a pub to watch amateurish entertainers while getting extremely drunk. The social researcher and journalist Henry Mayhew described the scene: 'There a raucous singer delighted the audience with a repertoire of crude ballads, competing with shouts for more gin.' However, Mayhew explained that, by the late 1860s, these were starting to give way to 'more respectable, and comfortable' music halls. Just as the gin shop was upgraded to the gin palace, so the basic penny gaff moved aside for the more elaborate music hall.

Even if the music halls were not quite the dens of vice that the middle and upper classes feared, for many the idea of the working classes spending any of their money on alcohol still rankled. The *Spectator* argued indignantly that they had no right to resent upper-class extravagance because in relative terms they were in fact the more wasteful. It grumbled about: 'The man on ten shillings a week abusing his landlord for drinking Lafitte [sic], while he himself sips gin, at perhaps three times the proportionate waste of means. A great deal of their bitterness is due to the want of the faculty of keeping a pecuniary perspective.'

Sniping about pecuniary perspectives aside, the mood of concern about drinking and its effect on public order was back. Parliament was compelled to curb the country's excesses – not just in gin now, but also in rum and porter. The Temperance Movement had formed an organised pressure group, the UK Alliance, that had many powerful political supporters, and they wanted action. A series of acts scaled back public-house opening hours in the mid-nineteenth century, and these passed without much comment. Then Prime Minister William Gladstone upped the ante by pushing through the 1872 Licensing Act, which outraged public opinion. The act was a watered-down version of a bill that he had proposed the year before, which would have halved the number of licensed public houses across Britain.

During the debate in the House of Lords, the Archbishop of York huffily declared that he would prefer to see 'England free than England compulsorily sober' – not a sentiment that endeared him to his pro-temperance peers. Despite the Archbishop's protestations, the controversial act was passed. It regulated the alcohol content of beer, ordered fines at a maximum of forty shillings for anyone drunk in charge of any carriage, horse, cattle or steam engine, or indeed for anyone who was just 'drunk in any highway or other public place'. It even gave boroughs the option of banning alcohol altogether.

The act did work in the most basic terms of limiting the number of places where people could drink. The ratio became one public house for every 300 people in Britain by 1901, rather than one to every 200 in 1872, but this heavy-handed clampdown remained widely resented. Gladstone would later claim that the Licensing Act was responsible for the thudding Liberal defeat of 1874. 'Borne down', he lamented, 'in a torrent of gin and beer'.

Still politicians were not satisfied, and in 1893 parliament redoubled its efforts. New chancellor Sir William Harcourt's Liquor Bill was widely criticised as his blow was aimed squarely at gin palaces, public houses and beer houses, where the poor went to drink. Meanwhile, drinking establishments with good reputations, such as inns, private clubs, restaurants and hotels, were free to carry on. Whenever Victorian parliaments sought to tackle drinking, they left elite drinkers in peace. This selectiveness caused ill-feeling among the public and left temperance campaigners unenthusiastic, as it was not comprehensive enough.

Even the *Spectator*, whose readership was not at all affected by the new regulations, weighed in to support the gin-drinkers against the temperance politicians. To rally its readers to the cause, it put them in the poor's position: 'Suppose a league of gin and whisky drinkers were organised for the purpose of putting down the drinkers of Lafite and Château Margaux, on the ground that these fine clarets were injurious and costly stimulants, the sale of which was publicly and privately harmful.' It asked its readers to imagine that if gin-drinkers took on claret-drinkers in the same way, 'people would surely retort, "How about gin? What right have you to deprive your neighbours of a pleasure which you contentedly enjoy yourselves? What can be said against claret which cannot with more force be said against gin and whisky?"' The passionately argued conclusion was that alcohol must be dealt with equally, or that the gin-drinkers should be left alone. It argued that Harcourt's bill would not cut the consumption of beer and gin, but merely move it from the public house into the home or the working men's club.

As the Establishment had so long been grappling to contain gin, it became its point of reference for dealing with a problem that was taking hold far from home. The British East India Company was selling opium to the Chinese, and its sale was helping to balance the books of imperial adventure. For all the evils of opium, in parliamentary debates, some politicians tried to argue that gin was still the more evil. When parliament was soul-searching over the lucrative trade, Sir Mountstuart Grant Duff, the Undersecretary of State for India until 1874, thought that the best way to make his point was to argue that profiting from opium was 'rather more moral than the revenue derived from gin'. As he pointed out, parliament could suppress the sale of gin altogether, and was therefore 'in some sort responsible for the consequences of its sale'.

There was ostensibly medical evidence to back Grant Duff up. A parliamentary commission that reported on the effects of opium and hemp declared that neither was as harmful as the 'temptation to overmuch gin', because 'a small dose produces the result which the Asiatic opium-eater is desiring. His happiness consists not in self-forgetfulness or unconsciousness, but in calm.' So even if opium-eaters were addicts, they were at least docile. This perception of the two substances had a fairly mainstream medical underpinning, as a Dr Eteson advised, during a debate between doctors as to whether they should carry on prescribing alcohol, that opium was 'less deleterious than gin . . . producing rather inertia than vice'. The critical difference, the *Spectator* argued, was simply that 'while alcohol generates crime, opium does not', rendering it less socially harmful because at least it 'destroys energy instead of stimulating it in unlawful directions'.

Opium and its variants also became widely abused back in London, where they were easily obtainable from apothecaries and pharmacists. It became a fashionable, bohemian drug that attracted writers such as Wilkie Collins, Thomas de Quincey and Lewis Carroll. While the debates continued as to which was worse – opium or gin – some very much enjoyed mixing the two. One such dabbler was influential occultist Aleister Crowley, who claimed to have created the Kubla Khan No. 2 at the Fitzroy Tavern off Charlotte Street in Soho. It was a cocktail of gin and vermouth topped with laudanum – a tincture of powdered opium that was flavoured with spices and sold cheaply in little glass bottles. The name of the cocktail was borrowed from the Samuel Taylor Coleridge poem, which he wrote following a feverish laudanum-induced dream. It was only in the twentieth century that opiates were really understood to be toxic. After the Victorians, laudanum's recreational and medical use became virtually non-existent, and it certainly did not feature as a cocktail ingredient thereafter.

The death of Queen Victoria in 1901 heralded a new age. It was a moment for contemporaries to take stock of all that had happened during the longest reign in British history. Few Londoners had lived long enough to remember her accession as an eighteen-year-old in 1837 first-hand, but it was clear that much had changed over her 63-year reign. For London, one of the most vital developments was in public order. The justice system had become infinitely more professional and consistent, with greater efficiency in court, a regularised police force, the building of many new prisons, and the overhaul of old ones.

Alongside this rigour in law and order, there were many civic improvements that had made London a pleasanter, more recognisably modern city. By the end of Victoria's reign, the British Empire extended over a fifth of the earth, and the centre of that empire was growing prodigiously as well. With over seven million inhabitants, there were more people thronging around London than Paris, Berlin, Moscow and St Petersburg put together. London had a bustling self-confidence. All its major train stations had been built in the Victorian era, starting with Euston in 1837, then Waterloo Station a year later, Paddington in 1854, Victoria in 1860 and St Pancras Station in 1868. More innovative still was the underground train running from Paddington to Farringdon that became known as the Tube, which opened in 1863 and kept the city cohesive as it expanded. Places for 'civilised' leisure sprang up: the present National Gallery building was completed the year after Victoria became queen, followed by the Victoria and Albert Museum in 1857 and the Natural History Museum in 1881. New wealth found expression in the pursuit of shopping at the elegant department stores such as Harvey Nichols, completed in 1880, and Harrods in 1883, and the opening of Whiteley's in 1863 and Liberty in 1875.

The lot of the urban poor was slowly but surely improving as well. There was a more widespread willingness to help the poor, rather than vilifying them. In the 1860s alone, four major charitable trusts were founded in London – the Peabody Trust, Barnardo's, the Society for the Relief of Distress and the Charity Organisation Society. The central slums were redeveloped into more sanitary, quieter places to live, although progress could be painfully slow. The clearing of the Clare Market slum, which had provided cheap accommodation because of the stench and noise from the animals slaughtered there, took sixty years of negotiations. The clearing was needed to build a main road between Holborn and the Strand, but it involved the eviction of over 3,700 people. In all around 120,000 Londoners had to leave their homes between 1840 and 1900, to make way for the city's modernisation.

However, for all these changes swirling around them, in many pockets of London the corner pubs still provided transient solace. At the turn of the century, gin sold at 4½d a quartern and beer at 1d for a half-pint, but however cheap the alcohol was, it was too much for disapproving temperance activists. To them, any spending on alcohol was unacceptable, not only for the sake of the individual, but for all of society. To drive this point home, they began to publish an annual National Drink Bill, which they made into posters and leaflets. In 1903 they calculated total expenditure to be £174,445,271, with the 'RESULT: Poverty, Over-Crowding, Under-Feeding, Disease, Sickness, & a high rate of Mortality' printed underneath.

By the time of chancellor Austen Chamberlain's 1905 budget, the fight against lower-class drinking seemed to be going the government's way. There had been two further acts in 1902 and 1904, making licences even harder to obtain. However, when the Liberals won a landslide victory in 1906, they were determined to finish the job. Their battle suffered a setback when their next chancellor, Herbert Asquith, introduced the Licensing Bill which attempted to reduce the number of licences by one third again, and increase tax on publicans. This resulted in demonstrations in Hyde Park as 130 trains full of protestors arrived in London, organised by the brewing trade. The wording of the Bill even described itself as 'of a drastic nature', and in the end the House of Lords scuppered it.

Undaunted, Herbert Asquith, who became prime minister in 1908, tried again, with his new chancellor David Lloyd George to support him. Lloyd George was from a Welsh Baptist family and was himself a zealous temperance campaigner. He unveiled a landmark budget in 1909, known as the People's Budget, with even higher licensing and tobacco duties. However, the House of Lords blocked this as well. It was after this humiliation that the Lords lost its power of veto over public legislation, and eventually the budget was passed.

Lloyd George's perseverance would eventually pay off and the First World War provided his big chance to hit the drinks trade with strong regulation. It was a watershed moment in the nation's drinking habits. Instead of 5 a.m. until midnight, opening hours were cut to noon until 2.30 p.m. and then 6.30 p.m. to 9.30 p.m.; the strength of beer was weakened; the manufacture of spirits was limited; and a 'No Treating Order', with a maximum penalty of six months in prison, meant that drinks could only be bought by drinkers themselves.

In the hope of inspiring the people to embrace sobriety, Lloyd George even managed to persuade King George V to take 'the King's Pledge' to ban alcohol from the royal household for the duration of the war. He could not, however, coax prime minister Herbert Asquith into following suit. In fact, Asquith blustered that Lloyd George had 'completely lost his head on drink'. A leader in *The Times* similarly suggested that he was becoming preoccupied with his quest. When he declared that not only was Britain fighting three enemies 'Germany, Austria and drink', but that 'the greatest of these deadly foes' was drink, *The Times* concluded that he was getting matters 'a little out of perspective'.

Whether it was due to the efforts of the new Central Control Board, which curtailed the drinks trade during the war, economic hardship or demographic changes, alcohol consumption of all kinds plummeted and barely recovered when the war ended. In 1914 Britain had been guzzling through eighty-nine million gallons a year; by 1918 it was down to thirty-seven million. It was a resounding result.

Despite alcohol consumption overall going into decline, gin benefitted from a bit of legislative luck. It was given a lift over whisky thanks to the Immature Spirits Act, which stated that whisky had to spend three years maturing before it could be sold. This not only made it into a more expensive product, but also instantly cut off much of the supply while it matured for the requisite time. Duty on whisky had already been raised in 1915, making gin, once again, a very attractive choice for poorer drinkers.

After vexing politicians for nearly 200 years, drinking was finally pushed to the margins of the political agenda in the interwar years and the Temperance Movement was no longer a powerful pressure group. The number of convictions for drunkenness fell by two-thirds between 1910 and 1930; the old anxieties about public order seemed to be ebbing away. As a result of all the wartime clampdowns, the number of pubs declined from 99,500 before 1914 to 77,500 by 1935

– a downward trend that has continued to this day. The pubs that did remain were changing too. Brewers embarked on costly improvements to draw custom from the expanding middle class. Huge premises with new-fangled frills such as loggias, smart dining rooms, and bowling greens appeared across the country. They were promoted by brewers as the future of the English pub. However, even if these new drinking places were more expensively decorated, like the gin palaces before them, they were not always considered tasteful by their target audience. In general the new modern pubs proved very popular, although the more discerning would have agreed with George Orwell, who sniffily dismissed them as 'dismal sham-Tudor places' in *The Road to Wigan Pier*.

The whole culture of drinking was changing, as the new pubs that were opening tended to be clean and fashionable establishments that focused on selling food and encouraging people to sit down and drink slowly. They were seen as respectable places that men and women could visit as couples, which helped to break down the pubs' traditional heavy-drinking culture. This was exactly the sort of cultural change that William Gladstone had tried to encourage as chancellor in 1860, when he had presented a bill that would exempt restaurateurs from needing a licence to sell wine and beer. In choosing those drinks, Gladstone sought to encourage people to drink weaker alcohol, ideally replacing the habit of swigging gin on its own with sipping wine with dinner instead.

As well as changing fashions in drinking, Britain's collective alcohol dependency was also eased through the rise of alternative leisure pursuits. The 1834 select committee had been mocked for suggesting such measures, but a hundred years later it seems that they were vindicated. The 1920s saw the rise of rival attractions to the pub, such as cinemas, dance halls and larger football stadiums. The introduction of paid holidays for workers in the 1930s and the boom in holiday camps provided an additional wholesome diversion.

Just as drinking was coming under control through moderation in Britain, in the United States they decided to take the most extreme action possible – prohibition. However, it soon became apparent that clamping down to that extent in America from 1920 to 1933 was as difficult as it had been in 1730s London.

The term that the Americans coined for their own illicit, ersatz spirit was 'bathtub gin', to evoke the ramshackle, domestic nature of its creation. Like London's rot-gut gin before it, bathtub gin was lacking many of the right ingredients, hence the development of so many gin-based cocktails in the Prohibition era to make it vaguely passable for the real thing. Martinis became particularly unpalatable, as there was nowhere to disguise rough gin in a Martini glass. This led to variations such as the Knockout Martini, which added mint and aniseed to take the edge off. As a location to enjoy alcohol sociably, speakeasies emerged to fill the gap left by bars. These illegal drinking dens were selling bootleg, low-quality liquor, some of them in surroundings so basic that they could almost be mistaken for Georgian gin shops. Mobsters and organised crime gangs who were much more vicious and professional than Dudley Bradstreet made millions from selling alcohol in those thirteen years that drinking was pushed underground.

There was very little chance of Britain following suit, particularly as it did not seem to going particularly well across the

Atlantic. By now successive British governments had tried offering more wholesome leisure pursuits, encouraging drinking at home and with food, and restricting opening hours and the number of public houses. Finally, a mixture of those policies, as well as organic cultural changes, had created the longed-for moderation. England was not to be made completely sober.

19: How are the Martinis? Dry as a Bone

(Noël Coward, Blithe Spirit)

One quarter French vermouth, one quarter Italian vermouth, to one half gin

Martini from 'The Savoy Cocktail Book' by Harry Craddock

PROHIBITION HAD A very lucky, if unexpected, outcome for Londoners – an influx of America's most talented barmen. Far from being inspired by the mood of abstinence across the pond, Londoners were simply thrilled to have the extra cocktail experts. The most famous of these out-of-work barmen was Harry Craddock, who went on to compile *The Savoy Cocktail Book,* the world's most famous cocktail compendiums. Craddock is often thought of as American, but he was actually born in Gloucestershire. In 1897, at the age of twenty-one, he had sailed to New York to make his fortune, but returned in April 1920, as soon as Prohibition began. He arrived at the Liverpool docks at the age of forty-four, with his wife and daughter, and made for London hoping for the best.

If Craddock had any anxieties about leaving New York, he need not have. He found a job at the Savoy's American Bar, which he ran with great flair, making it a haunt for old-money Londoners and Hollywood stars such as Ava Gardner, Errol Flynn and Vivien Leigh. Like Jerry Thomas before him, he knew how to self-publicise. He even used to advertise his return from holidays in *The Times'* announcements. In 1930 he published his collection of 750 recipes from the Savoy, predominantly of gin-based cocktails, with Plymouth as his preferred brand. It has been a hugely influential book both in Britain and America ever since.

Craddock thought it 'a great necessity of the age' to develop effective 'Anti-Fogmatics'. These were alcoholic drinks that were designed to clear the head in the morning, which Craddock did not believe to be a contradiction in terms. Indeed for centuries it had not been uncommon in Britain to drink in the morning. Historically it was usually nothing stronger than ale but some did have a similar attitude to Craddock. Lord Henry Hastings, a notorious nineteenth-century rake who lived only to the age of twenty-six, liked to begin the day by tucking into mackerel poached in gin, with claret to drink, for his breakfast. One obituary bluntly summarised his brief but destructive life: 'He had destroyed a fine fortune, ruined his health, and by associating with low characters, on the turf and elsewhere, considerably damaged his reputation.'

Perhaps unaware of the untimely death of Lord Hastings, Craddock insisted that drinking in the morning was an excellent way to rouse oneself. He recommended that his cocktails be drunk 'before 11 a.m., or whenever steam and energy are needed'. One of his enduring anti-fogmatics was the unappetisingly named Corpse Reviver No. 2, although one would be hard-pressed these days to find anyone who knocks them back before lunchtime. With a dash of absinthe on top of the gin, Cointreau and Kina Lillet, Craddock did offer the health warning, 'Four of these taken in swift succession will unrevive the corpse again.' He was well-aware of the potency of his own concoctions and advised for the Bunny Hug, a mix of whisky, gin and absinthe, 'This cocktail should immediately be poured down the sink before it is too late.'

Craddock also mixed more delicate drinks, such as the ever-popular White Lady, a light combination of gin, egg white, Cointreau and lemon juice; the Bentley, to celebrate Bentley Motors' Le Mans rally victory, made from Calvados, Dubonnet and Peychaud's bitters; and the Mayfair Cocktail, a delicious spiced mix of cloves, gin, apricot brandy, orange juice and syrup. Many of the libations were adaptations of classics, such as his Casino Cocktail, made from gin, maraschino liqueur, fresh lemon juice and orange bitters, which was akin to the Aviation from New York. Craddock also championed the Dry Martini in London, for which the British have been grateful ever since.

Craddock is considered one of the finest barmen to have ever lived. Largely forgotten, however, is his predecessor, the Savoy's first and only female bartender, Ada Coleman, who mentored him when he arrived. Many of the cocktails that Craddock compiled were already favourites at the Savoy, which suggests that she created many of the drinks for which he has since been credited. Coleman mixed her first cocktail while working at Claridge's, back in 1899. She told the *Daily Express*, 'I remember it was a Manhattan that I made first, and that it was Fisher, the wine butler, who gave me my first lesson.' Four years later, she secured one of the most prestigious jobs in London when she joined the American Bar.

Coleman's signature drink was the Hanky Panky, which bears a passing resemblance to a Negroni. She explained how she made it for one of her regular customers, the comedy actor Sir Charles Hawtrey: 'Some years ago, when [Hawtrey] was over-working, he used to come into the bar and say "Coley, I am tired. Give me something with a bit of punch in it."' She claimed that the moment Hawtrey sipped her creation, he said, 'By Jove! That is the real hanky-panky!' These days, it is generally made with gin, sweet vermouth and Fernet Branca, but for the original she used Cognac. When she retired in 1925, the *Daily Express* effusively paid tribute to her: '"Coley" is known to thousands of men all over the world, Britons who are now roughing it in various parts of the Empire, Americans who think of her every time they remember their own country's dryness.'

The Savoy faced stiff competition around London, particularly after 1929, when construction began on a big new rival on Park Lane. The Dorchester's owner Sir Robert McAlpine promised a hotel that would 'rank as the finest in Europe', and he clearly meant business. What had been a makeshift hospital during the First World War became a temple of 1930s luxury, with every impressive innovation of the time – telephones in every room, draught-proof windows, and sound-proof walls lined with compressed seaweed. When its bar was completed, there was one obvious candidate to make the glittering Art Deco room the place to be seen, and in 1938 they managed to poach him.

True to form, Craddock's new venture attracted the glitterati of the day from Elizabeth Taylor and Danny Kaye, to Sir Ralph Richardson and Alfred Hitchcock. In honour of this flying start, one of the present Dorchester Bar's signature cocktails is Craddock's Dorchester of London. Its base is, naturally, London Dry Gin with Bacardi and Forbidden Fruit, an American brandy-based liqueur flavoured with pomelo and honey. Forbidden Fruit is no longer made, so the Dorchester went to tortuous lengths to create its own version. One of the hotel pastry chefs, Robert Petrie, recreated the formula at home in Essex, using Courvoisier, pomelo skins, Seville oranges and vanilla pods.

For posterity, Craddock buried shakers filled with cocktails that he thought epitomised the roaring twenties in the walls of both the Savoy and the Dorchester. His selection of the White Lady, Dry Martini, Sidecar, Bronx and Manhattan were very popular on both sides of the Atlantic. Jay Gatsby, F. Scott Fitzgerald's most enduring character, memorably sent his staff into overdrive in *The Great Gatsby*, to keep up with his demand for the Bronx: 'There was a machine in the kitchen which could extract the juice of two hundred oranges in half an hour if a little button was pressed two hundred times by a butler's thumb.' Craddock's alcoholic time capsules were uncovered during building work at the Dorchester. Although the Savoy shakers are yet to be found there are photographs of Craddock putting them in the wall, so they are still in there somewhere.

The other star of post-war London was Scottish bartender Harry MacElhone. His big break came in 1911 at the New York Bar on the Rue Daunou in Paris. The New York Bar is long forgotten but when MacElhone acquired the site and turned it into Harry's New York Bar, it became one of the most iconic watering holes in history – as beloved by F. Scott Fitzgerald, Ernest Hemingway and Coco Chanel. James Bond gave it more cachet still when he proclaimed it the best place in town to get a 'solid drink' in *Casino Royale*, Ian Fleming's first Bond novel. The bar, which is still owned by MacElhone's family, claims to be the birthplace of such classics as the French 75, a wonderful gin and champagne cocktail named after a First World War gun, the Bloody Mary, and the Monkey Gland, made from gin, orange juice, grenadine and absinthe. Embracing the bar's louche reputation, MacElhone thoughtfully had luggage tags made for regulars that read, 'Return me to Harry's Bar, 5 Daunou.'

When the war ended Harry, flushed with success, took up a role in London at Ciro's Club, behind the National Gallery, where he compiled *Harry of Ciro's ABC of Mixing Cocktails* in 1921. It was here that MacElhone worked on the earliest version of a White Lady, which he made with gin, crème de menthe, triple sec and lemon juice. Ciro's was already famous during the First World War as one of the first London venues to host an all-black house band. Its nightly performances made it extremely fashionable as a place to drink excellent cocktails in a more informal setting than the hotel bars. Edward VIII, then Prince of Wales, and his brother Prince George loved visiting clubs like Ciro's, where they could indulge their passion for gin and jazz. Edward was such a jazz devotee that he went to see one of his favourite artists, American singer Florence Mills, twenty-five times.

A British Pathé clip that was filmed inside the club in 1932 opened with the reverential introduction: 'Everybody has heard of "Ciro's", the famous London rendezvous of Smart Society. Today, Pathetone glances inside.' The footage showed off the grandeur of the club, which was converted from the old Westminster Public Baths, with its pillared dining room set around a stage and dance floor. Despite its popularity, Ciro's closed in 1939 because of financial problems.

Unlike the other Harry, MacElhone's magnum opus has not stood the test of time. His signature drinks, such as his take on the Turf Cocktail, with gin, bitters, absinthe and maraschino liqueur, are rarely featured on menus these days. He produced another book, *Barflies and Cocktails*, which included drinks such as the Scofflaw, a bittersweet mixture of rye whiskey, vermouth, lemon juice, bitters and grenadine, named after a Prohibition term for someone who managed to procure alcohol. Again, such drinks are known to few modern drinkers. Not all of the 1920s and 1930s cocktails would go on to be future classics, but one of the real joys of this golden age of cocktails was its restless experimentation.

In much the same way that successful chefs and restaurateurs these days all have their own cookbooks to show off their specialities, so too did the celebrity bartenders of the jazz age, and they all had to bring something new to the cocktail cannon. Robert Vermeire, of the Embassy Club on Old Bond Street, was one of the first to release his own collection when he wrote *Cocktails: How to Mix Them* in 1922. In it he included the first printed recipe for the Sidecar and now-obscure cocktails such as the Fairbank, a mix of gin, dry vermouth, orange bitters and crème de noyaux. Vermeire was in demand all over the world thereafter, and eventually moved back to his native France to live out his days mixing drinks on the Riviera.

Hopping on the bandwagon on nearby Regent Street, William Tarling brought out one of the most famous collections of the period. The exhaustive *Café Royal Cocktail Book* in 1937 involved Tarling trawling through over 4,000 recipes. His concoctions had wonderfully evocative names, such as Bachelor's Downfall, Empire Glory, Kill or Cure, and Eastern Sin. Tarling attempted to explain the provenance of some cocktails, but acknowledged that 'most of the history is a matter of conjecture'. He did have a highbrow theory about the etymology of the word 'cocktail' itself though. He believed that the association between strong, delectable drinks and the cock may have come from the poetry of Horace:

> *Be joyous, Dellius, I pray,*
> *The bird of morn, with feathers gay,*
> *Gives us his rearwards plume;*
> *For mingle draughts drive care away*
> *And scatter every gloom.*

Although Tarling followed suit with gusto, it seems to have been Craddock who set the rule in *The Savoy Cocktail Book* in 1930 that any cocktail made for the British monarchy should contain gin. For him, the word 'royal' in the name of any cocktail indicated that it contained gin. His Royal cocktails Nos. 1, 2 and 3 all had gin as their common denominator. It became an unwritten bartending rule that any self-respecting royal-themed cocktail should have a gin base and Tarling did not dare disappoint. To celebrate the milestone of George VI's 1937 coronation, he made a concoction of apple gin, syrup, lemon juice, kirsch and egg white. His King Edward cocktail was gin with Grand Marnier and old liqueur rum, while the Prince Edward was Booth's dry gin, Calvados, Lillet and Forbidden Fruit. His homage to Princess Mary was a dainty London Dry with a little crème de cacao.

After a facelift in the 1920s, Tarling's Café Royal had become an exclusive haunt that was ideal for people-watching as it drew a mix of notables from D. H. Lawrence, Virginia Woolf and Graham Greene to Winston Churchill and Noël Coward. It had started off life as the modest Café Restaurant Nicols in Glasshouse Street, opened by wine merchant Daniel Nicols Thévenon who had arrived in London in 1864, fleeing bankruptcy in France. Because of its location, even as a small café, it attracted an upmarket, if badly behaved, clientele. Tarling wrote extravagantly of the café's history: 'The staff had to be confidants, friends and diplomats at times of need, experts in the straightening of curious complications and disputes, hierophants of the genius of conviviality.'

Cottoning on to gin's new glossy image, household brands such as Gordon's and Pimm's used the cocktail boom to pitch themselves as high-end, luxury drinks, fit for the most elaborate of occasions. Pimm's now set their adverts in smart locations such as tennis clubs, where one woman coaxed from the pages of the *Evening Standard*, 'Having enjoyed getting hot with a racquet, enjoy getting cool with a glass of Pimm's No. 1. . . Why not drop a hint about Pimm's No. 1 to your Club Committee?' Another advert featuring a man with a monocle and luxuriant moustache told readers of the *Standard*, 'For over 70 years Pimm's No. 1 has been famous in the City; to-day it is fashionable wherever there is a thirst, civil or military.'

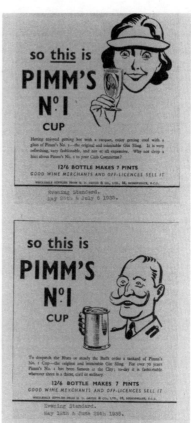

Riding the zeitgeist, distillers became energetic in angling theirs as the perfect cocktail gin. Gordon's took out adverts to explain why 'Drinks never taste thin with Gordon's Gin', playing up its 'richer flavour' and 'velvety smoothness'. Another advert encouraged drinkers to make 'A Gordon Gin Daisy For Hot Days', and explained how to put the ingredients of ice, aerated water, a slice of orange, lime juice, raspberry syrup and, of course, Gordon's dry gin together.

Gordon's also paid several aristocrats to convince drinkers that theirs was the most upmarket brand. In a series of adverts called 'cocktail confessions', Gordon's had Countess Howe as their poster girl, pictured in sepia in the *Tatler*. Beneath her photograph it read: '"The cocktail is often the first introduction to a delightful evening – therefore it must be beyond reproach," says Countess Howe, "and this includes my insistence on Gordon's".' Alongside her is a recipe for a Paradise cocktail of Gordon's, apricot brandy and orange juice, so that readers could take a leaf out of the countess's entertaining tips. Countess Howe was followed by another society beauty, Lady Moira Combe, who was pictured with her hair pin-curled to perfection, declaring that 'Gordon's Gin makes all the difference to a cocktail'.

Booth's gin went in for an upper-class angle on its adverts as well, with a full-length portrait of its illustrious founder, Sir Felix Booth, and an elegant scroll across the top that read, 'Unequalled for nearly 200 years'. Booth's even published a whole book of 'celebrity endorsements', the un-snappily titled *An Anthology of Cocktails: Together with Selected Observations by a Distinguished Gathering, and Diverse Thoughts for Great Occasions*, which featured the favourite cocktails of leading society figures. On its pages the Earl of Westmorland, Lady Mount Temple and the Earl of Northesk mingled with Shakespearean actress Dame Sybil Thorndike, motor-racing driver the Hon. Brian Lewis, chanteuse Yvonne Arnaud and champion golfer Archie Compston. Ivor Novello's cocktail, The Star, sounded particularly appetising: Booth's gin, Calvados, vermouth and a little fresh grapefruit juice. Photographs of celebrated barmen such as Fred of Quaglino's, Carlo of the Lansdowne, Frank of Claridge's and Dick of the Berkeley alongside their creations raised them to the rank of celebrity. The anthology thoughtfully came with a map of twenty-two West End drinking establishments for an upmarket bar crawl.

Clamouring for a piece of the cocktail action, the most traditional of brands invented products for the first time in decades. The Gordon's distillery was a hive of activity, with its new orange gin, and lemon gin. They were sold for cocktail mixing and as a warm nightcap with hot water. The two were popular, although the orange gin's claim to be 'rich in health-giving properties' seemed a little dubious. The new 'Ready-to-Serve' Shaker Cocktail range was so successful that Gordon's expanded the range from nine to twelve in 1930 with the introduction of the Rose, Paradise and Gimlet. Consumers seemed not to be so snobbish about pre-made cocktails as they are now – Beefeater also developed its own range and even that mecca of good taste, Fortnum & Mason, stocked gin cocktails by the bottle. Fortnum's made their own-brand bottled 'Ready-to Serve' range of Martinis, Mayforts, Manhattans and a Dry Gin cocktail. Encouraged by the success of all these products, Pimm's brought out more cups – No. 2 was based on Scotch, No. 3 was brandy and No. 4 was rum.

Another sign of how optimistic the distillers were about the future was their eager overseas expansion. Having moved their distillery to a larger site in Deptford, Seager Evans then built their Strathclyde distillery on the River Clyde to make whisky, and opened gin operations in Chile and Brazil, while Gilbey's set up shop in the Commonwealth markets of Australia and Canada. When Prohibition was repealed in America, British gin-makers jostled to establish themselves as soon as they could over there. Tanqueray Gordon & Co. had been bought up by the Distillers Company in 1922, and rapidly expanded into America only a year after Prohibition ended with a six-acre site in New Jersey. They were swiftly followed by Gilbey's.

This was gin's moment to shine and, as distillers had hoped, it became synonymous with the Bright Young Things – young, affluent Londoners who made having a good time an art form. Newspaper gossip columns recounted the minutiae of their lives, showing the first glimmerings of the modern obsession with celebrity. These flighty aristocrats and their coteries of middle-class hangers-on entertained at clubs, bars and grand private mansions all over London. One Bright Young Thing, Alec Waugh, Evelyn's older brother, claimed to have invented the cocktail party as a way to kill time before dinner. Waugh may not necessarily have invented them, but he was one of the first people to host one in London, and they quickly became a popular alternative to the formal Edwardian dinner party.

Gin was the fuel for the whirl of balls, dinners and dances in the 1920s and into the 1930s. In Noël Coward's play *Words and Music*, with characteristic mischievousness he expressed the world of the Bright Young Things by using a chorus of debutantes to sing:

> *The Gin is lasting out,*
> *No matter whose,*
> *We're merely casting out*
> *The Blues,*
> *For Gin, in cruel*
> *Sober truth*
> *Supplies the fuel*
> *For Flaming Youth,*
> *We can't refuse,*
> *The Gin is lasting out,*
> *We're merely casting out*
> *The Blues!*

An archetypal Bright Young Thing drink at such gatherings, particularly for young women, was a Gin and It. Easily thrown together at busy parties, it was simply equal measures of gin with sweet vermouth. It was through young aristocrats' forays into London nightlife that gin cocktails entered the stately home and really permeated the upper class's drinking habits. A few decades earlier, gin would not have been appropriate for the Flyte family in Evelyn Waugh's *Brideshead Revisited*, set in interwar Britain, but when the bell is rung for 6 o'clock cocktails at Brideshead, it is gin and vermouth that automatically arrives. Charles Ryder, and Sebastian and Julia Flyte are all Gin and It drinkers.

The Gin and It did not remain the 'it' drink unchallenged. The competition to serve the latest cocktail of the season was fierce, and many proved to be a flash in the pan. An Old Etonian was the toast of 1925 – gin, Kina Lillet, orange bitters and a dash of crème de noyaux – but was rarely heard of again.

Whatever the new heights of artistry at a professional level, Ambrose Hoopington, author of *A Letter to a Young Lady on Her Approaching Marriage*, complained that cocktails served at private parties could fall far short of expectations. He wrote of the misery of 'cocktail parties at which the drinks were principally compounded of lemonade and water'. Expectations of cocktails' potency were raised so high, Hoopington thought, because 'newspapers have thought fit to regale their readers with the subject, illustrated with the tragic fates of young women who left home and adopted the habit'.

However, despite any 'tragic fates' reported in the press, it was becoming acceptable for well-brought-up girls to have an elegant gin cocktail or two in public. Well-bred female drinkers of this vintage included Elizabeth Bowes-Lyon, later to become the Queen Mother. She was born in 1900 and remained faithful to the custom of her 1920s youth, drinking gin into her old age.

Although the British Empire was not to last much longer, it remained a strong influence on interwar cocktail fashions back in London. Inspiration came from all corners of the colonies. The Raffles hotel, whose Gin Slings were effusively complimented in Noël Coward's diary, became famous among expats for the Singapore Sling made by the barman Ngiam Tong Boon, with gin, cherry brandy, triple sec, Benedictine, pineapple and lemon. Over in Rangoon, Burma – now Yangon in Myanmar – the Pegu Club was a Victorian-style gentlemen's club built in the 1880s for officers and administrators. Its eponymous house cocktail was a refreshing mix of gin, lime juice, Angostura bitters, orange bitters and Cointreau, and the globetrotting regulars spread its fame far and wide. As with most cocktails, it is unclear who actually invented it, but it was certainly being made in London by 1927 when MacElhone included it in his *Barflies and Cocktails*. It was popular enough to crop up again in the *Savoy Cocktail Book*. As Craddock explained, it was a cocktail that 'has travelled, and is asked for, around the world'.

The great majority of these colonial clubs stuck to the classics though, and served run-of-the-mill cocktails. As George Orwell put it in *Burmese Days* from 1934, 'in any town in India the European Club is the spiritual citadel', whether it was innovative cocktails or tepid gin and tonics that they were serving. Veteran foreign correspondent Ann Leslie, who was born in India, remembers her mother sipping 'many a pink gin' and playing bridge with her friends at the Ootacamund Club in the Nilgiri Hills, one of the places where the cinchona trees from Kew Gardens had been planted for quinine.

Elsewhere in the Empire, expats' extracurricular activities were nowhere near as wholesome as Mrs Leslie's bridge and Pink Gins. Scottish historian Lord Kinross remarked in the 1930s that gin was a spirit 'which rose from the gutter to become the respected companion of civilised man'. It had indeed risen from the gutter but some of its new, upmarket drinkers were anything but civilised.

One particular group of upper-class settlers, the Happy Valley set, became notorious for their gin-fuelled misde-meanours in the Wanjohi Valley in Kenya. The social hub revolved around the Cholmondeley family and Josslyn Hay, Earl of Erroll, and his first wife Lady Idina Sackville, who settled in the 'White Highlands' in 1924. The scene for their escapades of drink, drugs and orgies was the Muthaiga Country Club in nearby Nairobi, with after-parties at each other's palatial lodges. These colonial playboys' seemingly endless whirl of soirées continued from the 1920s to the early 1940s. Frank Greswolde-Williams, who lived nearby but was not attractive enough to be invited to the orgies, supplied them with cocaine, and the drinks were easy to come by. Gin was particularly associated with the women, who glugged their way through the fashionable drinks of the day – John Collinses, White Ladies, Bronxes and Pink Gins, along with the odd Whisky Sour for variety. It was said of Lady June Carbery, the promiscous third wife of Irish peer Lord Carbery, 'Cut her in half, you'd find mostly gin.' Lady Idina Sackville, writer Frances Osborne's great-grandmother, usually stuck to her favourite – gin with orange bitters.

The most sought-after invitation in Kenya was to Lady Idina's lodge, Clouds. Her well-choreographed welcome, which involved greeting guests from her onyx bath before putting her clothes on in front of them, set the tone for their stay. After-dinner entertainment at Clouds would include the 'sheet game' in which the women could choose a sexual partner for the evening, or at least the next few minutes, by peeking through strategic holes in a sheet hung across the drawing room.

None of this would have been public knowledge were it not for the White Mischief trial that revealed details of their outlandish private lives to the press. The party finished abruptly when the Earl of Erroll was murdered in 1941 and his mistress Diana and her cuckolded husband Sir Jock Delves Broughton died soon after. Having been acquitted of Erroll's murder at the trial in Kenya, Delves Broughton returned to England, where he died from an overdose.

The Happy Valley set's old haunt, the Muthaiga Country Club, has not seemingly changed much since it opened in 1913. Even now, members are not allowed to wear flip-flops, T-shirts or hats 'other than those integral to national costume', although you are unlikely to find any coked-up aristocrats planning an orgy there these days.

Of course, for all the attention given to the Bright Young Things, the cocktails and the new bars, it passed some older Londoners by completely. Ambrose Hoopington grumbled that a great deal of 'unjustified criticism' was directed at the legal profession for its ignorance of 'modern affairs'. Judges were mocked in the press for asking questions in trials such as 'What is a White Lady?', needing to have the counsel explain to them that it was a cocktail. Hoopington argued that they should not be criticised for being oblivious to such things: 'There is no reason why the judge should not, like other elderly gentlemen, belong to a respectable club, where he can and does drink much better and purer spirit at a more reasonable price and under its proper name of gin, and neither he nor any other member need be concerned with the fancy names applied to curious mixtures.' The golden age of cocktails did not reach every watering hole.

20: Survival

PINK GIN
A few drops of Angostura Bitters, topped up with gin and ice

> *Her father's euonymus shines as we walk,*
> *And swing past the summer-house, buried in talk,*
> *And cool the verandah that welcomes us in*
> *To the six-o'clock news and a lime-juice and gin.*

'A SUBALTERN'S LOVE SONG', published in 1941, was John Betjeman's homage to middle England as much as it was to his muse Joan Hunter Dunn, a colleague with whom he fell in love at the Ministry of Information. The poem captured a certain vision of England, revelling in a world of Home Counties refinement and cosiness, in which Miss Hunter Dunn 'furnish'd and burnish'd by Aldershot sun' enchants Betjeman during a game of tennis.

When the Bright Young Things' party was abruptly ended by the Second World War, it was this quaint world of village halls, tennis matches and golf club dances with which gin would become principally associated. During the war and the decades that followed, gin came to encapsulate a nostalgic kind of 'Englishness'. The war suspended the days of a civilised daily lime juice and gin at 6 p.m., and gin took on a new, poignant significance for those who cherished such rituals.

For the next few years, bomb damage to distilleries, the requisitioning of grain, loss of workers to military service, and a drastic shortage of quinine all conspired to make a gin and tonic a sorely missed luxury. In pubs and shops empty shelves of spirits were a common sight as government control over all areas of the economy grew ever more restrictive. So sadly not everyone could live like Noël Coward, who described his approach to London air raids: 'When the warning sounds I gather up some pillows, a pack of cards and a bottle of gin, tuck myself beneath the stairs and do very nicely . . . until "all clear" sounds.'

Even with the most fastidious preparations, distilleries had not anticipated the level of civilian bombing to come. When war had broken out in September 1939, it put even the most successful and well-prepared under unprecedented strain, though some proved far more resilient than others. With a great deal of ingenuity, some of the larger distilleries managed to keep going remarkably well. Tanqueray Gordon & Co., for example, had set their emergency plans into action immediately, evacuating most staff to a mansion in Weedon, Buckinghamshire. From there, the company was run for the next six years in safety, with lofts over the stables used as warehouses to store the sacks of juniper and other botanicals. Even before the war started, staff had planned an Air Raid Precautions Scheme and routinely practised 'blacking out' the distillery and hiding safely.

When the Blitz began in September 1940, the seventy-six consecutive nights of bombing reduced buildings all over

London to rubble, and the city's distilleries were particularly vulnerable as they were so central – and flammable. Several direct hits on Tanqueray Gordon & Co. tore down the roof and the doors, and one of the bombs injured the distillery director, Mr Perry. At the time Perry was telephoning John Connell, the chairman of the company, to report the damage when another bomb fell just outside the window. Connell barked down the phone from Buckinghamshire that Perry should 'get the hell out of it at once'. Perry turned to the staff and told them, 'I suppose we had better go. We shall get into a deuce of a row if we get killed.'

Far worse was to come. On the night of 10 May 1941, the Luftwaffe's attack reached its terrifying climax – 1,436 people were killed, as 711 tons of bombs and 86,173 incendiaries rained down on the city from 11 p.m. until 6 a.m. When the sun rose on Sunday morning, there was little of Tanqueray Gordon & Co.'s offices, warehouses or distillery left. Perry had driven over to The House in the middle of the night to find it burning down. He and other members of staff started fighting the fire and rescuing equipment, dragging what they could out through the windows into the street. Staff who went to investigate the damage over at the warehouses found little that could be salvaged. The only Tanqueray still that survived the war was Old Tom. It was built in the reign of King George III (1760–1820) and remains in use at the distillery up in Scotland today.

As part of its wartime preparations, the company had dispersed its stocks of raw materials, bottling equipment and paperwork around London, Buckinghamshire, and some, as an extra precaution, up in Scotland. Using spare parts from their other bases, within a week of the House being destroyed, Gordon's and Tanqueray were distilling a small amount again. They then found temporary premises at the Watney Distillery in Wandsworth. Apart from that one interlude, they managed to keep production going while they waited until 1948 for new distillery plans to be approved. Renovation plans had in fact started back in 1937 because by then seven reigns had been and gone at the House with little modernisation, but the war had put them on hold.

Pimm's did not fare so well. It struggled to cope with neat alcohol being requisitioned for the war effort. To battle the loss in revenue the company undertook various cost-cutting initiatives, starting with the directors reducing their own pensions and salaries. Pimm's also suffered direct hits at the hotels and restaurants that it owned around London throughout 1940 and 1941. The London Tavern was destroyed in 1941, as was The Imperial by Fenchurch Street Station. The buildings could not be salvaged and the staff there lost their jobs as a result. Pimm's was luckier with the Cavendish Hotel on Jermyn Street, where a bomb landed but failed to actually explode. Most sadly for the heritage of the company, James Pimm's original Poultry restaurant, where he created the drink, was hit in an air raid in September 1940.

For more precarious companies, the war signaled the end altogether. J. & W. Nicholson had branched out in 1872, when business was booming, to buy the beautiful Three Mills distillery on the River Lea in east London. Since the *Domesday Book* there had been a working mill on the site, but when grain shortages hit and the mills were severely damaged by an aerial raid in 1941, production ceased altogether. The buildings are still clearly visible from the Tube between Bromley-by-Bow and West Ham, but they are now a museum. Outside London, Plymouth Gin suffered the most, as the Black Friars Distillery was damaged in the Blitz on Plymouth. The Admiralty sent a reassuring message to all ships afterwards, to let them know that although the city had been attacked, the distillery was thankfully in working order.

Even if companies were not physically hit during the war, they faced the considerable obstacle of a grain shortage. As food was the natural priority, a Ministry of Agriculture committee had established grain quotas for spirits, and this affected distilleries across Britain. At G&J Greenall in Warrington, one of the country's largest, they halted gin production altogether, and did not resume until the 1950s. Had the government not allowed some grain to be used for alcohol, it would have slowed post-war recovery even further. For Scotch, in particular, it was necessary to keep the grain supply going, as it takes so long to mature. Some gins did keep production going by using a molasses substitute base, which is still used by some cheaper brands today, but even with that and the grain allowance, it took many companies into the 1950s to get back up to speed.

Although ordinary pubs and shops were always running short, there were enclaves where the old luxuries were readily available. Despite the chaos around them, London's finest hotels maintained their rarefied atmosphere. They became havens for exiled European royalty, military leaders, journalists and politicians. Lady Diana Cooper, Viscountess Norwich fondly described the Savoy: 'You are certain to always find bits of the Cabinet there . . . actors, writers, the Press, Mayfair's hostesses who have abandoned their private houses and still want to entertain – they are all grazing at the Savoy Grill.' With considerable determination, the big four – the Dorchester, the Savoy, the Ritz and Claridge's – kept their standards up, although this did not sit well with the public. Readers of the wartime press, suffering shortages of all sorts of essentials, were angered by details of London hotels' plentiful food and warmth. The restaurants were exempt from rationing and the one curb on their service was only being able to offer meals of three courses or fewer. One satirist dubbed this bubble of opulence the 'Ritzkrieg'.

Victor Gower, who began working at the Savoy in 1946, explained that the bar 'had stocked up before the war' so that they 'never really ran out of anything'. The only problem for cocktail-making, he said, had been a shortage of lemons. There was, however, one nod to the war going on outside from the Savoy's head barman, Eddie Clark. The American Bar was a haunt for high-ranking officers from the armed forces and, in their honour, he created three cocktails. Wings was for the RAF men, the New Contemptible for the army and Eight Bells for the Royal Navy. By 1942, Clark himself had been called up. Fortunately he survived and went on to write the cocktail book *Shaking in the 60's*.

The idea of the upper classes enjoying three courses at the Savoy Grill and White Ladies at the American Bar proved too much for some. The resentment culminated in a group of seventy East End socialists invading the Savoy's air-raid shelter in protest. A rather tame affair in the end, the rabble spent twenty minutes inside before leaving without incident. However, to rein in the most obvious excesses the government did put a new restriction in place for restaurants, which were no longer allowed to charge more than five shillings a meal by 1942.

London's safest hotel was generally believed to be the Dorchester, due to its cutting-edge construction around a steel frame. Aristocratic cabinet ministers such as Lord Halifax and Duff Cooper used it as a home from home. While he lived there, Winston Churchill had the pleasure of planning his next moves over extremely Dry Martinis made by Harry Craddock himself. A physical remnant of Churchill's sojourn is to be seen as he had a wall built, which is still standing, to add privacy to his balcony. He frequently lunched with his cabinet at the Savoy as well, and continued to attend his dining club there until his death.

Those fighting overseas were just as keen as those on the home front to maintain their old drinking rituals. In the theatre of war, a familiar drink brought a welcome sense of normality. For men serving in the armed forces, a few hours spent trying to hunt down gin, or even make their own, was a welcome diversion from the grim drudgery of war. Sir Denis Thatcher, later to become the first male consort to a British prime minister, was serving as an officer in France when he and his men ran out of gin. At the time, they were holed up in what Thatcher called a 'very pukka' château outside Marseilles, so they had plenty of room to rectify the situation by rustling up their own. In one of the château's baths, they mixed the oil pressed from juniper berries into alcohol and hoped for the best. Thatcher recalled that 'a mouthful of this stuff nearly blew our heads off'. Indeed, it must have been an experience similar to drinking gin during the gin craze. Like the drinkers of that period, Thatcher too acknowledged that it was 'terrible stuff and tasted like hell', but drank it anyway. He and his friends did not quite manage the tonic, but made do with fruit juice, calling their concoction 'gin and jungle juice'. When Thatcher turned seventy, he would attribute his lifelong good health to his much-loved diet of gin and cigarettes.

Rather than face the war without gin, many officers also turned to the black market. Edmund Poland, who later rose to become rear-admiral, recalled that his best friend, Martin Solomon, had managed to make a little extra money by getting hold of some duty-free in Egypt, which he sold when they were on the destroyer HMS *Petard*, travelling from Britain to Turkey. Poland and Solomon sold the remainder to other ships when they arrived at Alexandria. Because of the difficulty of getting the right ingredients in wartime, however, the gin was not always up to scratch. 'There was a terrible row,' Poland recalled, 'because we were accused of having put paraffin into the gin. Of course it wasn't us. It was the extraordinary occasion when Plymouth Gin had been contaminated and we happened to have a tremendous amount of Plymouth Gin. There was some problem with the juniper juice or something from North America. I don't think Plymouth ever recovered from the episode.'

Commander Ronald Hay nearly came unstuck while getting his hands on cut-price gin as well. Having survived the Battle of Britain in 1941, Hay was out serving as a Royal Marine fighter pilot in Ceylon, modern-day Sri Lanka, from 1943 to 1944. There he found a town where he could buy Parry's gin in a huge four-gallon jar called a demijohn. Thrilled to find such a quantity, Hay was determined to bring it back with him to the capital Colombo, and managed to wedge it into the cockpit of his rickety Vought Corsair one-man fighter plane. Looking back, Hay said, 'I didn't know if I was ever going to get away with it . . . I couldn't do any manoeuvres.' However, it turned out to be particularly fortuitous cargo. When he showed his girlfriend Barbara the demijohn, he asked her what they were going to do with all of it. Barbara cannily went straight in for 'We could celebrate our engagement?' Hay took her up on the suggestion and proposed. They had a 'tremendous party at the Columbo Club' and married that summer.

Particularly in naval circles, the offer of gin was the height of hospitality, and it was a matter of honour to maintain the supply on board ship. As a friendly gesture, ships flew the green and white 'gin pennant' flag if they were inviting other guests in the harbour over for a Gimlet or gin and tonic. The pennants were not officially issued, but were roughly fashioned on board. Although their provenance is uncertain, they were certainly used in the 1940s.

When F. D. Ommanney, zoologist and author of *South Latitude*, was welcomed aboard in 1941 by a friend who had just joined the navy, he recalled that the first thing he was offered was a gin in the wardroom. Ommanney then whiled away the hours on board, as did the officers themselves, 'sipping my gin out of smeared glasses in that little cubbyhole, inhaling smoke-laden air'. Anthony Hogg, a naval officer who retired in 1956 to become a drinks writer, made certain that a level of civility was maintained on his cruiser *Black Prince*. When the ship was stationed off Normandy's Utah beach on D-day, Hogg ensured that the wardroom bar opened at six o'clock promptly every day.

At Christmas, gin became a particularly poignant reminder of home. A rare film taken in northern Burma, showed preparations by the 36th Division in 1944. The treats that the soldiers proudly displayed to the camera were 'Xmas Plum Cake', cigars, and one bottle of whisky and one of Crystal Court gin, which they had managed to procure from Australia. Although it was not from home, the now-discontinued Crystal Court's advert promised that it retained 'all the virtues of the finest London type Dry Gin'.

Quinine was still vital, not only for the officers' G&Ts in the evening, but for the practical purpose of staving off malaria for all the men out in tropical warzones. Until the Second World War, Indonesia had provided 95 per cent of the world's supply as Dutch colonialists had so successfully been growing cinchona trees there since the 1850s. However, in March 1942, the Japanese occupied the Dutch East Indies, cutting off supplies to Europe and North America. With the Allies in urgent need of anti-malarial medicine, scientists were charged with finding an alternative quinine source. In 1944 Robert Burns Woodward, still only a 27-year-old assistant professor at Harvard, discovered a substitute. Thanks to that breakthrough, quinine has been eclipsed ever since by synthetic antimalarials such as atrabine and chloroquinine.

A year later, on 8 May 1945, Churchill announced from the Cabinet Room at Downing Street that the war in Europe was over. Rapturous street celebrations marked the end of an agonising period in British history. Crowds gathered around London's great monuments and outside Buckingham Palace, where King George IV, the Queen, and Princesses Elizabeth and Margaret came out on to the balcony to share the joy.

21: Advance Britannia!

SILVER BULLET

Two shots of London Dry Gin, one shot of kummel, one shot of fresh lemon juice, one quarter shot of syrup

CHURCHILL HAD CLOSED his speech from the Cabinet Room with the rousing call of 'Advance Britannia!' This was to prove years of work, even just to clear and reconstruct the scarred London landscape, let alone to get a real sense of normality and optimism back. Pockets of the city had been so heavily bombed that they resembled lunar landscapes. Eventually distillers began building up their businesses once again and the purchase of consumer goods tentatively improved – although it would only be in 1954 that fourteen years of food rationing would finally end.

Over the course of the war, the British had lost their thirst for alcohol again, as they had during the First World War. Consumption in the late 1940s was at its lowest for the entire century, at an abstemious 3.9 litres of pure alcohol per capita per annum. This is less than half what the British drink now, and even further behind their Victorian forebears, who in 1900 managed to plough through 11 litres each on average.

It was a rocky post-war climb back up. When the blackouts and power shortages returned in the winter of 1947, one of the most severe of the twentieth century, recovery must have felt very remote. There was, however, a mood change on the horizon that year. On 20 November, the 21-year-old heiress to the throne, Princess Elizabeth, married Prince Philip of Greece and Denmark. It was an occasion that rekindled Britain's feelings of former glory and offered a tentative glimmer of better things to come. *Time* magazine wrote effusively:

> *It seemed that all of London turned out to see a drama which, if somewhat anachronistic, was nonetheless inspiring. The people crowded along Whitehall to see the procession . . . At the Abbey they cheered the arrival of six kings, seven queens and numerous princes and princesses. Over loudspeakers they heard Princess Elizabeth say her vows. For hours they milled around the Palace hoping to see the newlyweds make an appearance on the balcony. Then, feeling somehow as happy as if it had been their own wedding day, they went home, with the quiet reassurance of goodness, tranquility and survival that the British throne means to Britain's people*

Behind all the pomp of the day, there were the inevitable pre-wedding nerves for the bride and groom. Before setting out for Westminster Abbey with his cousin and best man the Marquess of Milford Haven, Prince Philip fortified himself with a gin and tonic, already a royal family favourite. He perhaps needed the hair of the dog after his two stag parties – the first at the Park Suite of the Dorchester and the second with his naval friends at the Belfry Club. Although it is not a matter of public record what Prince Philip drank at his stag parties, his favourite cocktail was known to be the Silver Bullet – a potent and very dry mix of gin, Kummel, lemon juice and sugar syrup. Silver Bullets have largely disappeared now because Kummel, a spiced liqueur flavoured with caraway and fennel, is so rarely drunk these days. To mark the occasion, the Savoy created a more ladylike cocktail. The Wedding Bells was made with gin, of course, cherry liqueur, orange juice and Dubonnet. The Dubonnet was perhaps a nod to the Queen's personal penchant for the French liqueur.

The next morale-boosting post-war milestone was the 1951 Festival of Britain to mark the centenary of the Great Exhibition, where Schweppes had showed off its spectacular mixer fountain and Soyer had pioneered the cocktail bar. Despite ongoing difficulties with the economy, the festival was another sign that the fog of war was lifting. Its director, Gerald Barry, said that he hoped it would prove a 'tonic to the nation', and so it proved to be. The focal point was the newly built Royal Festival Hall, which was filled with uplifting displays of Britain's contribution to industry, art, culture and technology. The area on the South Bank where it took place had been covered in rubble only a year before, and now it was full of ambitious building projects next to the new Waterloo Bridge, which had been rebuilt after bomb damage.

Even with the 'tonic' of the festival, as we know in hindsight, the Second World War did permanently diminish Britain as a world power, and the feeling that its prominence was fading was already tangible. As American Secretary of State Dean Acheson would later point out, 'Great Britain has lost an empire and not yet found a role' – it was a brief but cutting aside that rankled. The *Daily Express* blustered that it was 'a stab in the back' and the *Daily Telegraph* archly commented that Acheson was 'more immaculate in dress than in judgment'. As the country sought the new sense of purpose of which Acheson spoke, gin would now suffer for its strong association with an old-fashioned kind of Englishness. Despite repackaging and marketing attempts throughout the 1950s and 1960s, gin would be increasingly perceived as a thing of the past along with the rest of 'old England' and its empire.

This nostalgia-tinted image made gin the perfect motif for post-war novels that reflected on both old empire and fresh misery. At this time many writers picked up on the centuries-old connotation of gin being a drink for the melancholic. This was not the gin of the Bright Young Things and their outlandish parties, nor the genteel gin of the Surrey tennis club; this was the gin of the brooding and isolated.

Graham Greene, ever capable of evoking exotic lands with aplomb, set his 1948 novel *The Heart of the Matter* in a West African colony that he later revealed to be Sierra Leone. The protagonist, Major Henry Scobie, a British deputy police commissioner posted in this remote corner during the war, muses to himself: 'There was always bad news that had to be broken, comforting lies to be uttered, pink gins to be consumed to keep misery away.' However, Scobie rarely does keep the misery away, even as the Pink Gins keep flowing. He repeatedly returns to the gin bottle at his lowest moments: 'he grinned miserably at his glass, twisting it round and round to let the angostura cling along the curve'. The male and female characters in the novel drink endless variations of gin-based drinks, often out of sheer boredom. Even on his first day at local expat haunt the Bedford Hotel, Wilson, the new inspector in town, finds very little else to entertain him: 'A black boy brought Wilson's gin and he sipped it very slowly because he had nothing else to do except to return to his hot and squalid room and read a novel – or a poem.'

Gin was used memorably not only to set the gloomy scene in Greene's *The Heart of the Matter* but in George Orwell's most famous work, *Nineteen Eighty-Four*, a year later. With all gin's quintessential Englishness, it was a useful way to immediately show the reader that the capital of Airstrip One had once been London. Gin's early connotations of being a kind of 'opium of the people' in seventeenth- and eighteenth-century London made it a very apt choice still as the drink of down-trodden people in the future. In the opening pages Winston Smith, whose miserable existence in a totalitarian regime we follow, uses it to furtively console himself in the middle of the day: 'He took down from the shelf a bottle of colourless liquid with a plain white label marked VICTORY GIN. It gave a sickly, oily smell, as of Chinese rice-spirit. Winston poured out nearly a teacupful, nerved himself for a shock, and gulped it down like a dose of medicine.' Although gin had, of course, become rather refined by the twentieth century, Orwell harked back to its historic incarnation as a cheap, numbing agent. It permeates the air at the gloomy canteen at the Ministry of Truth, where Smith works, with 'a sourish, composite smell of bad gin and bad coffee and metallic stew and dirty clothes'.

Anthony Burgess also wrote a post-war dystopian novel, *The Wanting Seed*, which, unlike *Nineteen Eighty Four*, has been largely forgotten. It envisaged a future of overpopulation, with London sprawling across all of southern England. In Burgess's future, the only alcohol available is a gin so revolting that it can only be stomached when masked by a chemical called 'fruit juice' – fortunately, that prophecy has not yet come to pass.

In literature gin's new role was far from being a chic accessory for the likes of *Brideshead*-style young aristocrats. It was now a prop for the lonely and washed up, as used to great effect in John Osborne's *The Entertainer*. The play from 1957 centred on the moribund career of Archie Rice, a miserable, drunken music-hall performer. Osborne lamented in the preface that 'a significant part of England' was dying along with entertainers such as Rice. As a motif of an old England fading away, gin was therefore a very suitable vice for Rice. One critic dismissed Osborne as an 'embittered Edwardian', which indeed he was, but the play still struck a chord with his 1950s audience.

Although gin sales did gradually recover in the 1950s, culturally, it was floundering. In the 1930s gin had been wild and exciting and was used to innovate new drinks, but now it would be firmly a drink for older generations, as its ability to gather new devotees flagged. The drink aged with the interwar generations until, by the 1960s, it would become a stuffy 'old person's' drink. Luckily for gin, unlike the 1960s, the 1950s were still rather conservative so it was not too out of step with popular culture yet. The upheaval of the permissive society was still to come.

The change from the tipple of the risqué to the tweedy was neatly shown by Noël Coward. What had fuelled his giddy debutantes in the 1920s was now the party drink of leathery, middle-aged women. He explained in a spoken introduction to *A Bar on the Piccola Marina* from 1954 that the song was inspired by a holiday to Capri in which each evening he used to sit on the piazza and 'watch these hordes of middle-aged ladies arriving by every boat, obviously all set to have themselves a ball.' He made one of these middle-aged ladies the subject of his song. With typical playfulness he invented 'a respectable British matron, who discovered in the nick of time that life was for living'.

> *To that bar on the Piccola Marina*
> *Where love came to Mrs. Wentworth-Brewster*
> *Hot flushes of delight suffused her*
> *Right round the bend she went, picture her astonishment*
> *Day in, day out, she would gad about*
> *Because she felt she was no longer on the shelf*
> *Night out, night in, knocking back the gin*
> *She cried 'Hurrah, Funiculi, funicula, funnic-yourself.'*
> [*Funiculi Funicula* is a traditional Neapolitan song]

No thanks to Mrs Wentworth-Brewster and her middle-aged friends, gin did manage to recapture some of its pre-war glamour courtesy of the racy and stratospherically popular James Bond books – even if it did have to share the stage with its new rival, vodka. As a naval man, Commander Bond's choice of gin reflected the traditional military association of the drink, but Bond gave it a glossy, modern touch. In the first book, *Casino Royale*, he famously sought solace in a Dry Martini. He instructed the barman: 'In a deep champagne goblet . . . Just a moment. Three measures of Gordon's, one of vodka, half a measure of Kina Lillet. Shake it very well until it's ice-cold then add a large thin slice of lemon peel. Got it?'

The fact that Bond unusually mixes gin and vodka for his perfect Martini suggests that Ian Fleming, who had himself been a naval intelligence officer, was not sure whether Commander Bond should drink gin, like an officer, or vodka, as a fashionable man about town. Designing his own Martini that mixed the two was the perfect solution as it was also in keeping with Bond's lone-wolf individualism. As Bond tells his CIA counterpart, Felix Leiter, 'This drink's my own invention. I'm going to patent it when I can think of a good name.' The good name that he comes up with is Vesper, after his double-agent paramour Vesper Lynd.

It is now impossible to recreate the Vesper exactly as the French aperitif that Bond specifies, Kina Lillet, changed its recipe in 1986. Its successor Lillet Blanc is available, but has a much lower quinine content, so the drink lacks the requisite bitterness. One of Fleming's favourite bars was at Dukes Hotel in St James's, which still does excellent Martinis. There, Alessandro Palazzi will rustle you up a modern Vesper with gusto from his highly polished Martini trolley.

Although Bond is famed for his good taste in everything from women to Aston Martins, bartenders are horrified by his immortal 'shaken not stirred' order. The consensus is firmly that it should be the other way around. Shaking the Martini will dilute the ice too quickly, as well as clouding the cocktail and creating little ice shards that float on the surface. Many bars, including that of the Connaught, make a point of politely but firmly warning against it.

Peter Dorelli, head bartender of the American Bar from 1984 to 2003, claims to have only shaken a Martini once in his career:

*I remember Dudley Moore came in and everybody
was basically chanting for him to play the piano.
He refused, but it was getting rowdy. I pleaded
with him, and eventually he looked at me and said
he would do it – but only if I would shake him a
Dry Martini – and to make it in front of him. He
knew I would never shake a Dry Martini and he
didn't trust me. It was the only time I shook a Dry
Martini. First and last. We did shake them for
customers, but I would never do it.*

It is reassuring to know that at least Sir Roger Moore, who
began playing Bond in 1973, himself knows how to mix a
decent one. When making one at home he recommends:
'One teaspoon of Noilly Prat vermouth in a jug, swirl it
around, then toss it away. Pour in a bottle of gin and serve
into martini glasses with a twist of lemon. Put the full glasses
into the freezer and serve ice cold.'

Fortunately, Bond was on safer ground with his gin and tonic
order. His method in *Dr No* sounds about right: 'Bond
ordered a double gin and tonic and one whole green lime.
When the drink came he cut the lime in half, dropped the
two squeezed halves into the long glass, almost filled the glass
with ice cubes and then poured in the tonic.'

Beefeater must have been absolutely thrilled when it was
singled out for Bond's Pink Gin in *The Man with the
Golden Gun*, from 1965. Bond specifies the brand, 'with
plenty of bitters', when he is undercover in Jamaica, as
Mark Hazard, Francisco Scaramanga's personal assistant
from London.

Amid all the sadness of Britain's decline, there were signs of lasting improvement ahead in the 1950s. The average wage doubled over the decade, building up to a prosperous 1960s. Keen to capitalise on new consumer-spending power, distilleries stepped up their rebuilding. The new Gordon's distillery was built lower down on Goswell Road, starting in 1951 but taking another three years to get the first production batch running through the stills, and yet another three years before the distillery was totally finished. After careful restoration work, Old Tom, the hand-riveted copper still that survived the Blitz, was one of the three that operated at the new building.

In an attempt to refresh the brand, Tanqueray launched a shaker-shaped bottle, based on their ready-mixed cocktail bottles from the 1920s but they kept the same green glass that they use today, with the seal on the front. However often distillers such as Tanqueray have modernised their packaging, they have always been aware that gin-drinkers love the heritage of the product so none has ever dropped their historical symbols – whether Tanqueray and their pineapple, Gilbey's and their wyvern, Plymouth and the *Mayflower*, or Bombay Sapphire and Queen Victoria.

Beefeater, with its ostentatiously British packaging, did particularly well abroad in the 1950s. By now, Eric Burrough, James Burrough's grandson, was in charge and he focused on export markets. In particular, he often visited the United States to check that Beefeater was stocked in all the most prestigious places. Burrough cunningly capitalised on the mania for everything British and royal, which was prompted by Queen Elizabeth's coronation in 1953. He made the Beefeater image of the yeoman warder from the Tower of

London on the branding even more prominent and took out large, expensive adverts in upmarket American publications. It clearly paid off as Beefeater was served at the finest American hotels, such as the Algonquin in New York, where Dorothy Parker had enjoyed so many Martinis in the 1930s. According to New York's oldest bartender, Hoy Wong, Marilyn Monroe used to come every Wednesday to the fashionable Chinese restaurant Freeman Chum, where he worked, and would order a very dry Beefeater Martini with lunch.

Eric Burrough was doing an excellent job of maintaining the brand's kudos – if not at home, then at least abroad. By 1963, it had become the most widely exported gin in the world. As well as benefiting from clever marketing, Beefeater's unique selling point was that it was a London gin that was made entirely in London. Gordon's and Tanqueray, among others, were sub-contracted to be distilled in the United States. This difference enabled Beefeater to charge a premium price and gave it authenticity and cachet abroad.

Following the trail of Burrough, from 1964 John Tanqueray, Charles Tanqueray's great-great-grandson, undertook his own promotional trips, mainly to Los Angeles and New York. Tanqueray's resulting celebrity endorsements from Bob Hope, Frank Sinatra and Sammy Davis Jr sent sales soaring.

Gordon's, although they did not have an existing family member to act as an ambassador in the same way, also launched an American advertising campaign that made the most of their heritage. Their slogan used on 1960s American posters read, 'Gordon's and Tonic: English invention for coping with the noonday sun', with a picture of a gin and tonic resting under a helmet, in a glass carved with elephants as a nod to the Empire. They even created the character of a 'retired English colonel', who apparently invented the gin and tonic. They told their American audience that, since then, Gordon's had been an 'indispensible ingredient in a host of summer drinks, from Tom Collinses to Orange Blossoms'. Gin's image was working well abroad, but the same could not be said back here.

22: *London Gets Into a Groove, while Gin Gets Into a Rut*

GIN AND COLA
One quarter Gordon's gin to three quarters Cola,
with plenty of ice

BACK IN LONDON, on Carnaby Street and the King's Road, the permissive paradise known as 'Swinging London' was transforming British popular culture. The epithet itself came from a *Time* magazine article in 1966 which proclaimed London 'the world city' of the decade, after it had 'shed much of its smugness, much of the arrogance that often went with the stamp of privilege, much of its false pride'. Britain had indeed also shed an empire, but it did now find a rather different role. Its political influence was waning, but culturally it had never been so pivotal, spreading its youthful exuberance around the world.

Swinging London and its sub-cultures, or 'scenes' as they were called, were all about being fresh and non-conformist. In this brave new world of sex, drugs and rock and roll, gin was rapidly losing its appeal for what should have been its next generation of drinkers. In the 1960s spirit of egalitarianism and modernity, gin's old-fashioned image alienated young people and it suffered greatly for its association with the Establishment.

In the 1950s gin had fared reasonably well, when the fashion for young people had been to look and act as grown-up as possible. Now, as part of the 1960s cult of youth, that behaviour was turned on its head. As fashion designer Mary Quant, who invented the mini skirt, observed, 'There was a time when every girl under twenty yearned to look like an experienced sophisticated thirty. All this is in reverse now. Suddenly every girl aims to look . . . under the age of consent.' Young people yearned to display their flair, individuality and taste. For dedicated followers of fashion their parents' cocktail cabinets, full of dusty bottles of Gordon's and Beefeater, were not the place to start.

Branding built on young consumers became an increasingly complex social language. Products' 'personalities' were carefully crafted through advertising or association with certain 'swinging' people about town, to make distinctions between similar goods. Mick Jagger mocked this growing brand loyalty in the Rolling Stones song '(I Can't Get No) Satisfaction', when he sang that a man 'can't be a man 'cause he don't smoke/the same cigarettes as me'. He played with the idea that young people were defining themselves by the products that they bought.

The hugely successful James Bond film franchise came to epitomise the new consumerism and fetishising of brands. Bond had a particular penchant for premium champagne, such as Krug, Dom Pérignon and Tattinger. He knew what he wanted down to the last detail – even which brand of soda water to order in his cocktails. In Fleming's short story *From a View to a Kill*, in his Americano cocktail Bond 'always stipulated Perrier, for in his opinion expensive soda water was the cheapest way to improve a poor drink'. In the books by Fleming, Bond was a devoted fan of Gordon's, specifying it for his Martinis and Negronis. By the time that Sean Connery came to play Bond in the film of *Dr No* in 1962 however, Gordon's did not seem exciting enough anymore. Now he went for a 'vodka martini – shaken, not stirred'. Even Bond had moved on.

As a relatively new spirit to Britain, vodka was a cultural blank canvas, which made it all the easier for advertising executives to sell to young people. It had none of gin's historical 'baggage'. Its blandness also became a virtue – it was more accessible to new, young drinkers because it had so little flavour and therefore went with anything. Easy house-party drinks, such as vodka with Coke, orange juice or lemonade, were the order of the day. Spontaneity was the new buzzword for entertaining, and cocktails of the 1920s and 1930s were far too fussy.

Although vodka was just as old as gin, it had taken much longer to become popular in Britain. Its international success only began when an American drinks company bought the Smirnoff distillery in Paris in 1934. Then the Moscow Mule cocktail – made from vodka, lime juice and ginger beer – helped to popularise the spirit and demonstrate what it could be used for and finally it caught on in Britain. In the 1960s and 1970s many more vodka brands were launched, and well-timed, witty advertising led to a surge in sales that continues today.

Smirnoff's 'It leaves you breathless' slogan proved particularly successful and was in use into the 1980s. The racy message implied that you could still have your vodka cocktails at lunchtime and your boss, secretary or girlfriend would not catch it on your breath – unlike gin. Posters featured comedian Groucho Marx showing off bottles of Smirnoff hidden in his coat, with the slogan, 'If they don't serve Smirnoff, bring your own!'. Director Woody Allen encouraged drinkers to have a 'Smirnoff Mule' party, and socialite Zsa Zsa Gabor coaxed, 'If you like rocks, darling, try 'em with Smirnoff.' Other vodka brands caught up with the necessity of high-profile advertising and joined the fray, making a very lucrative play for the youth market. Even the most traditional bars were turning their backs on gin. Peter Dorelli of the Savoy admitted in a recent interview: 'It's fair to say that . . . we killed gin in the 1960s – it's popular again now, but back then all the cocktails were vodka.'

Gin brands did attempt a rearguard action through advertising, though with mixed success. Unlike other brands, Pimm's decided to stick to its plummy, older market. One tongue-in-cheek advert read: 'We had to let the west wing go, but thank heavens we can still afford our Pimm's', with a couple standing in the ruins of their castle. Pimm's even ran a writing competition in *Punch* magazine to win a lordship of the manor title by explaining in thirty words: 'I consider it a monstrous crime against nature that I was not born a lord. This is because. . .'

Gordon's went for the younger market, featuring a coquettish blonde woman holding up a glass of Gordon's, and in her other hand she was holding the lead of a Great Dane, with the slogan, 'Next to dogs, I like Gordon's best!' With jokes as bad as that, it is unsurprising that such adverts fell flat. As a direct attempt to push back against vodka as a drink for young people, Gordon's even tried cinema and print adverts in which it recommended mixing it with 'the refreshing cool of Cola'. It is widely agreed that gin and Coke do not mix well, so it was a rather misguided attempt to break out of gin's entrenched association with tonic, and muscle in on sales of Coke with rum or vodka.

To add to gin's woes, in this decade Britain finally became what chancellor William Gladstone had envisaged a hundred years earlier – a nation that drank wine with its food. In 1961 the law had changed to allow grocers and the new supermarkets to sell alcohol all day, and ever since British domestic drinking has been on the increase. This change coincided with a huge variety of wines becoming available from South America, which joined the established European ones. Along with vodka, wine became the fashionable drink of the younger generations. As author Rupert Butler explained, in Wandsworth, where the young Chelsea overspill had moved, all the shopping for 'cut-price plonk and vodka' was a sign of 'what delirious property dealers call the middle-class invasion'.

In fact, it seemed that young people would rather drink pretty much anything other than gin. Rakish novelist Simon Raven advised his peers to abandon it altogether, writing that they would enjoy food much more if they preceded it 'with a light vermouth' rather than 'some vicious concoction of gin (which may be necessary to jolt the middle-aged into civility but is surely dispensable by youth)'. Knowing Raven's views it was unfortunate that the *New York Times Book Review* in 1965 chose to praise his writing as 'as powerful, peculiar and English as pink gin'.

Caught out of step in the changing market, the 1960s and 1970s proved the undoing of many long-cherished gin brands. Victorian dynasties became the victims of takeover bids, with businesses going out of the family for the first time since their founding. One of the first to go was in 1956 when Seager Evans, the gin so beloved by Dickens, was bought up by a New York company. Under new ownership, the whisky side of the company took precedence with the major acquisition of Laphroaig in 1962. By 1970, the name Seager Evans and Co. had been abandoned. Now that their Deptford distillery is a block of flats, little remains of the company. One piece of living history, however, is the Beefeater master distiller Desmond Payne, who began his career there.

In prosperous times, Gilbey's had set up their vast twenty-acre site of warehouses, bottling plants and the distillery at Camden Lock, but in 1963, they had to move out of London for the first time to a cheaper site in Essex. Ronald Gilbey had given up his job on the London County Council to become chairman in 1958, but the family still lost their grip on the board and the company was absorbed by International Distillers and Vintners, which was in turn subsumed by Diageo.

Also in 1963 the Canadian firm Seagram, which has since been disbanded, acquire Burnett's White Satin gin, founded by Sir Robert Burnett in Vauxhall. From 1878 until the late 1950s White Satin had been made in a distillery on Seagrave Road in Earl's Court. Now the long-neglected old building serves as London's first winery, London Cru, and an American company owns the rights to the Burnett brand.

Three years later J&W Nicholson sold the Three Mills distillery, after they had only used it as a beer warehouse since 1941. In the 1970s, the family, headed by Sir Richard Nicholson, sold the remaining business to the Distillers Company – as was the fate of so many of these independent brands.

Pimm's, so consistently popular for over a century, was now struggling too, and most of its cups were phased out. The original No. 1 cup with gin managed to stay on, along with the vodka cup, No. 6, but Nos. 2 to 5 were discontinued after Pimm's was also bought out by the Distillers Company. The No. 3 brandy cup, flavoured with spices and orange peel, had only been recently launched, with the slogan 'Winter brings its own delights'. The public sadly did not agree that Pimm's was one of them, and it was abandoned after the 1960s sales slump. It was only in 2004 that No. 3 was successfully brought back as Pimm's Winter Cup.

Even Gordon's, with its dominant market share, felt the pinch. It was one of the last remaining producers of Old Tom, but ceased production of its 'London Dry Gin with Real Cane Sugar' in the 1960s, after Beefeater had already discontinued its Old Tom in the 1950s.

A small but significant move in the late 1960s was when John Dore & Co. was forced by the local council to move its factory out of Bromley-by-Bow to Surrey. This meant that, for the first time since 1835, the stills for London gin were no longer made in the city. It was a sadly fitting end to the decade.

23: The G&T Loses Its Fizz

NOONDAY REVIVER

A shot of gin, a bottle of Guinness and a dash of ginger beer

THESE DAYS GIN has strong intergenerational appeal, but for the remainder of the twentieth century its famous fans would be distinctly middle-aged and older. The interwar *jeunesse dorée*, who had drunk gin with flair and imbued it with such vitality, were now ageing and they clung to their old drinking habits. Rather than swinging Londoners like Mick Jagger, David Bailey and co., the poster boys for gin were men like prime minister Harold Macmillan, who was partial to a G&T before lunch every day. Gin was still bohemian in the sense that it was part of the London literary scene, but it was now for writers of a certain age such as Graham Greene and W. Somerset Maugham. It felt like the twilight of the drink, and of the people who drank it.

A pivotal member of that older literary scene was publisher Jock Murray of John Murray, Britain's oldest publishing house, who held court with his authors over Dry Martinis in his drawing room at 50 Albemarle Street in Piccadilly. Whether entertaining Freya Stark, Patrick Leigh Fermor or

John Betjeman, Murray, by then in his sixties, always wore his trademark jazzy braces and bow tie. As the place where Murray's family had both lived and worked since 1812, 50 Albemarle Street was the perfect setting for an elegant gin-laced salon, albeit a slightly poignant one for fans of Byron. It was also the place where his memoirs were burned in the fireplace in 1824 when they were deemed too risqué for publication.

The cultural disconnect between the younger generation and their elders in the 1960s was no more apparent than in their drinking habits. A 33-year-old Auberon Waugh wrote an absolutely scathing review of *The Malcontents* by C. P. Snow, an esteemed novelist who at the time was sixty-eight. Waugh complained that not one of the younger characters was realistic and that the youth culture scenes were 'hopelessly incredible'. Waugh found Snow's description of taking LSD particularly risible, criticising Snow for making it 'a sort of cocktail party occasion' – '"Come on, girl. Take a trip" – "Oh, I don't mind if I do" – Lance picked up a bottle and poured a few drops in her gin!'

Author Kingsley Amis, then in his fifties, remained an enthusiastic advocate of gin, while dismissing rum and vodka out of hand. He believed that vodka was merely a spirit 'for the benefit of those rather second-rate persons who don't like the taste of gin'. Like T. S. Eliot, Amis was particularly fond of the now-defunct Booth's gin, which he liked to drink with cold water. As a cocktail, Amis highly recommended a Noonday Reviver. He attributed the concoction to Auberon Waugh's father, Evelyn, whom he greatly admired. It could easily be mixed together at home, with a shot of gin, a bottle of Guinness and a dash of ginger beer.

However, by the time that Amis was recommending this drink from Evelyn's giddy youth, Evelyn himself had died a sad case. He ended his days in a fug of alcoholic lethargy. He wrote in his diary:

> *My life is roughly speaking over. I sleep badly except occasionally in the morning. I get up late. I try to read my letters. I try to read the paper. I have some gin. I try to read the paper again. I have some more gin. I try to think about my autobiography, then I have some more gin and it's lunchtime. That's my life. It's ghastly.*

On the morning of Easter Sunday in 1966, Waugh collapsed and died in the lavatory at Combe Florey House, his home in Somerset, at the age of sixty-three. At least his son Auberon had the sense to reflect that for despair, 'relying on gin is almost certainly not the best cure', as he recalled his father's presence exuding from the library 'in a sort of miasma of Havana cigar smoke and gin'.

The novelist Henry Green, two years younger than Evelyn Waugh, took his melancholia in old age a stage further. He became a recluse leading up to his death, barricading himself in his house on Wilton Place in Knightsbridge with only gin for company. One interviewer who was dispatched to see him there wrote: 'The only move he made was for the separate bottles of gin and water placed on a circular table beside him. He occasionally produced a comb, to draw back strands of hair falling over his face.' Green was horribly reminiscent of American novelist John Cheever's description of a lonely man as little more than 'a stone, a bone, a stick, a receptacle for Gilbey's gin'. He died not long after, in 1973.

Amis, now in his forties, faced his advancing years with a little more humour. He played with the idea that his favourite tipple had become a drink for the washed-up by making his grotesque, gluttonous character Roger Micheldene a heavy gin-drinker in his novel *One Fat Englishman*, from 1963. Micheldene is a pathetic figure, particularly when trying to seduce women: 'He went down the slope to join her. He slid about a bit in doing so, either because of the gin or because he was holding his stomach in so tightly that his legs worked like stilts.' As the novelist David Lodge has since suggested, Micheldene was likely to have been a self-caricature. This idea is leant weight by the fact that Amis's wife, Hilly, used the very phrase 'one fat Englishman' in reference to him. They were on holiday in Yugoslavia after she had discovered Amis's affair with novelist Elizabeth Jane Howard, and in her fury, while he was asleep on the beach one day, she wrote on his back in lipstick: '1 FAT ENGLISHMAN – I F**K ANYTHING'. Their marriage ended shortly afterwards.

Amis's best friend Philip Larkin, also now in his forties, shared his love of heavy drinking. Larkin and Monica Jones, his secretary and girlfriend, could plough through an alarming amount. Journalist A. N. Wilson described days when the couple were on a roll: 'A bottle of sherry for breakfast. A bottle of gin for lunch. An afternoon nap, and then the serious drinking began.' From 1961 to 1971, Larkin was the jazz critic for the *Daily Telegraph* and, along with gin, music was his favourite way to relax. 'Listening to new jazz records for an hour with a pint of gin and tonic', he enthused, 'is the best remedy for a day's work I know.'

Gin also maintained a stronghold as the spirit of choice for a rather different circle – the Cambridge spies. Sir Anthony

Blunt, surveyor of the Queen's pictures and a Soviet double
agent, for all his appreciation of Russian culture, did not
switch to vodka. During the 1960s, Blunt was serving as
director of the Courtauld Institute of Art on the Strand,
where he lived on the top floor. One student at the time
described seeing Blunt, then in his sixties, performing a
weekly routine: 'Every Saturday morning Blunt would sidle
out . . . soon after opening time, shortly to struggle back
laden with carrier-bags stuffed to bursting with gin.'

It was not until Margaret Thatcher's premiership that the
House of Commons would be informed that Blunt had
indeed been the fourth man in the Soviet spy ring. Of course,
there were those who had known long before 1979. The
venerable journalist Geoffrey Wheatcroft recalled: 'In 1973, I
sat in the French pub in Soho with the late Goronwy Rees, a
gifted and blighted figure, who had . . . to say the least, a
problematic connection with the Cambridge circle. After
three or four large pink gins he told me that Anthony Blunt
had been the Fourth Man.' Born two years after Blunt, Rees,
a Welsh author, academic and fellow of All Souls, was also a
spy, according to a KGB defector in 1999.

It was not only a drink for sad, ageing men, but for sad,
ageing women too. Gin became particularly associated with
trapped suburban housewives. It was the calling card of the
unhappy middle-class women in plays such as Alan
Ayckbourn's *Absurd Person Singular*. In it he examines the
marital tension between three couples, focusing on Ronald
Brewster-Wright, a bank manager, and his wife Marion. Most
of the action takes place in the Brewster-Wrights' kitchen, but
Marion is often to be found closeted in her bedroom where
she squirrels away gin. When Marion and Ronald go to visit

their friends Sidney and Jane, Marion is heard grumbling constantly that she needs her gin topping up: 'I've never had such a small gin in my life. Completely drowned,' and later, 'Heavens! Is there anything in here?' when sizing up her gin and tonic.

Abigail's Party by Mike Leigh, another play set in 1970s aspirational suburbia, also tackles marital malaise and petty materialism, this time in Essex. Housewife Beverly hosts a get-together with her estate agent husband Laurence for their neighbours, which turns rather sour. All of the action takes place in their living room as Beverly attempts to impress her guests, and she pours herself and friend Angela generous gin and tonics throughout. Here the G&T finds itself in a world of leather three-piece suites, cheese and pineapple on sticks, and Demis Roussos. In the end, to cap an evening of extreme social awkwardness, mousy divorcée Sue overdoes the gin and ends up vomiting. Across the pond, this type of frustrated housewife character was played most memorably by Elizabeth Taylor as Martha in Edward Albee's *Who's Afraid of Virginia Woolf?* Her husband George, played by Richard Burton, has to bellow at her, 'I will tote your gin bottles out after midnight so no one can see.'

Back in the real world of suburbia, things were little better. Psychologists had been using the term 'suburban neurosis' since the interwar period and as the suburbs themselves grew after the war, so the phenomenon gained prominence. In the 1962 Reith lecture on the BBC Home Service, psychiatrist George Carstairs explained that it commonly befell middle-aged married women who had a 'sense of uselessness, of no worthwhile contribution to make'. Some of these women found refuge from the isolation of their comfortable but sterile new homes in the gin bottle, giving a second wind to the old image of 'mother's ruin'.

The Irish journalist and feminist Mary Kenny described her own boredom-driven drinking as a housewife: 'Television . . . is excellent during the daytime, but once you begin watching TV during the daylight hours, all accomplishment – is doomed. There's nothing for it then but to sit down and drink gin all afternoon. The recent report in *Woman* magazine that the housewives of Britain were turning to drink en masse must be related to this.' Discussing the tedium of looking after her children, she confessed: 'I let them stay up until all hours because I'd sooner drink gin and blather on the telephone than go to the trouble of making them stay in bed.'

For his long-running column 'Low Life' in the *Spectator* Jeffrey Bernard painted a poignant picture of lonely older women living in the Home Counties: 'When the shopping's been done in Hungerford, after the obligatory weekly treat of a hair-do in Wantage, and the Mini's been safely put away in the garage, it's back to the log fire, out with the gin and away into the past.' Bernard made gin-soaked spinsters a feature of his column about his chaotic personal life and heavy drinking. He recalled his famous friends' drinking habits, such as the Welsh artist Nina Hamnett, nicknamed 'the Queen of Bohemia', 'who somehow always managed to have a gin in her hand', as well as the women whom he met in bars around central London on his all-day binges, usually in Soho's grottiest pubs. Bernard's tarts were coarse, tragic figures that were very much the successors to the *Punch* charwoman and the Georgian fishwife. A characteristic Bernard lament was: 'I have frequently had to remove a gin and tonic from a woman's lips in order to kiss her,' or, 'It doesn't matter how many gins-and-tonic . . . you buy women, they still snap at you.' Although perhaps that said as much about Bernard as it did his female acquaintances.

24: Prawn Cocktails and Black Forest Gateaux

WINDSOR ROMANCE
One quarter gin, one quarter amaretto, one quarter mint chocolate liqueur, one quarter passion fruit juice. Add ice, mix, and top with champagne and a strawberry

Created by Victor Gower at the Savoy's American Bar for the wedding of HRH Prince Charles, and Lady Diana Spencer in July 1981

IN THE 1970s gin was almost stagnant in growth and its image was in the doldrums. Michelin-starred chef Nico Ladenis, who opened his first restaurant, Chez Nico, in 1975, allegedly declared that he could not run a place for people who drank gin and tonic because it had become symptomatic of an 'attitude of mind' that accompanied the 'prawn cocktail, grilled Dover sole, Melba toast and Black Forest gateaux'. For a connoisseur like Ladenis, gin was now completely beyond the pale.

In the subtlety of British snobbery, it was recognised by now as a drink for people who were trying too hard to seem upmarket, rather than those who naturally were. The phrase the 'gin and Jaguar belt' came to represent the provincial nouveau riche whose heartland was the mock-Tudor architecture and manicured lawns of the Home Counties. In popular culture, they were epitomised by Margot and Jerry Leadbetter in the sitcom *The Good Life*, set in Surbiton, on the outskirts of London. Their poorer neighbours, the Goods, remark that the only thing the Leadbetters 'buy in bulk is gin'.

In the popular imagination, gin was now predominately associated with Betjeman's twee version of England – of golf clubs, tennis matches and dinner parties. When artists Gilbert and George wanted to poke fun at the notion of 'Englishness' for their work *Gordon's Makes Us Drunk* in 1972, they chose gin as its centrepiece. In the video installation, Gilbert and George sit in their suits by a window looking out on a London street, drinking gin while listening to 'Land of Hope and Glory' by Elgar and 'Morning' by Grieg. With deadpan expressions they slowly pour out the gin, while repeating, 'Gordon's makes us drunk' and 'Gordon's makes us very, very drunk'. It was their way of showing the disparity between the apparent respectability of the gin and tonic, with the classical music in the background and their elegant outfits, and the fact that in essence they were just getting embarrassingly drunk. Gilbert and George said that they chose Gordon's simply because it was 'the best gin' and they added their names to the label, on either side of the royal crest. They also adopted gin and tonic as their own signature drink, as part of their ironic personae as 'living sculptures'. Shoreditch jewellers Tatty Devine had the inspired idea a few years ago of commissioning them to design gin-bottle cufflinks and necklaces with their own names as the label, which you can still buy.

As Britain had lost so much of its international standing by now the British man abroad had become something of a mocked figure, with no empire to back up his pretentions. The gin-swilling 'our man in. . .[whichever exotic location it happened to be]', became a stock character and a 'gin-and-tonic embassy' was a nickname for foreign postings that were largely pointless. The world had moved on, leaving Britain's verandah-dwelling colonialists behind. As Anthony Burgess said of his trip to Singapore in 1970, there was 'no room for Somerset Maugham any more, except for that magic-of-the-east blurb on the Raffles Hotel notepaper'.

It was at Raffles, named after the British founder of Singapore, Sir Thomas Stamford Raffles, that expats had first enjoyed the Singapore Sling. Burgess described that time in the early 1900s, when it had served Gin Pahits to 'the tuans [a respectful term of address in Malay], often with an oeuf colonial [a bloated stomach, usually from alcohol]'. It had once been the city's chicest hangout for the likes of Rudyard Kipling, Noël Coward and Charlie Chaplin, where they could have cocktails and relax in the billiard room. Times had, of course, long since changed, and along with it, the clientele. As Burgess pointed out, 'American and Australian tourists, as well as soldiers on R & R from Vietnam, don't ask for Pink Gins.'

Travel writer Carol Wright painted a similarly changed picture of post-colonial India, although she did find a corner preserved in the Nilgiri Hills, where the cinchona tree plantations had been established a century earlier. There, the town of Ooty was a scene of 'time-frozen Victorian England'. Even though the Raj was long over, there were some cultural remnants: 'Its forever England-ness has been fossilised by the Indians who keep roses pruned in the former Governor's residence . . . and, dressed in tweed jackets and cords, drink their gins and tonic in the Club.' As late as the 1970s, the Tollygunge Club, a country club founded by the British in Calcutta, was reputedly still serving the best Pink Gins in town by its golf course.

Of all the gin drinks, it is the Pink Gin that had particular resonance as a colonial throwback, and even now they have not made a comeback in the way that other gin drinks have. As the age of the Pink Gin-drinker advanced, it lost its exoticism and remained just a vestige of a bygone era.

Whichever drinks fashions came and went there was one stronghold where gin would always be welcome – the royal family. The Queen Mother had set the precedent for the family's gin enthusiasm when she married into it in 1923. Her unusual signature drink was gin and Dubonnet, a wine-based aperitif flavoured with herbs and quinine. Her favourite page, William Tallon, kept a handwritten note by her, which later sold at auction for £16,000, in which she gave instructions for a picnic: 'I think that I will take two small bottles of Dubonnet and gin with me this morning in case it is needed. It is a beautiful day, could we have lunch under the tree – one could have 14 at the table and four at a small table.'

The Café Royal book from 1937 recommended adding the juice of half an orange to the mixture, but the Queen Mother had her own way of making it. She made hers with 30 per cent gin and 70 per cent Dubonnet, with ice and lemon. When she was out at the Savoy, head bartender Peter Dorelli remembered that she liked her gin and Dubonnet in the morning, but a Dry Martini in the evening. Even in her later years, at lunch parties in Clarence House she enjoyed two generous gin and tonics beforehand, followed by a few glasses of champagne with her food.

The Queen inherited her mother's love both of Dry Martinis and of gin and Dubonnet. The latter had staff at Lord's cricket ground frantically searching for a bottle during the Ashes Test in 2009. There was a minor panic the day before, when her staff requested a bottle in advance. The only one in the Lord's cellar was out of condition, and a local off-licence in St John's Wood said that no one had asked for it in thirty years. Her butler managed to locate a bottle on the day, but when he arrived he was barred from coming in, as spectators are not allowed to bring spirits. A few negotiations later and the Queen was finally able to enjoy her drink.

Keeping it in the family, records of one of Princess Margaret's royal visit to Mauritius reveal that her favourite drinks were gin and tonic and whisky and soda, which she preferred to wine and champagne. In the 1980s when her son, Viscount Linley, opened his ill-fated Deals restaurant chain in London, she was often there to lend her support. One of the most high-living royals of recent times, a former manager at Deals said that he mainly remembered her 'telling jokes and drinking plenty of gin and tonic'.

When Victor Gower, head bartender at the American Bar between 1981 and 1985, was commissioned to make a cocktail to celebrate Prince Charles and Lady Diana Spencer's wedding in 1981, he knew that, as a royal drink, he would have to start with a generous gin base, to which he added champagne, Amaretto and passion fruit juice. Gower said that the resulting Windsor Romance was his most memorable creation. For the royal wedding of the Duke and Duchess of Cambridge in 2011, the Savoy made the Royal Tribute cocktail with a gin and Champagne base, maraschino, Martini Rosso and Chartreuse.

The present bartender, Erik Lorincz, stuck to the winning champagne and gin combination when he invented the Diamond Jubilee cocktail in 2012, this time adding orgeat syrup, Earl Grey tea, lemon juice and grapefruit and orange sherbet.

At Rules, London's oldest restaurant, they have created the wonderful Kate Middleton cocktail, a mix of Sipsmith gin with vodka and crystallised violets. They also have a house aperitif of which the Queen herself would very much approve – her favourite Dubonnet, Tanqueray No. 10 and vintage cremant. The royal family do keep the gin tradition going with gusto themselves. They have a Christmas tradition that should be more widely replicated – every year at Sandringham, their estate in Norfolk, the Queen, Prince Philip and Prince Charles celebrate Christmas Eve with Dry Martinis.

Outside the royal family, however, traditional aperitifs have been flagging since the 1960s. Alongside gin and tonic, Cinzano, Martini, Campari and Dubonnet became unloved and outdated. In recent years, Dubonnet has only sold around 9,000 litres a year. With mixed success, these brands tried to revitalise themselves with advertising campaigns in the 1980s and 1990s.

Dubonnet invested in some questionable television adverts featuring American actress Pia Zadora as the 'Dubonnet Girl'. The result was rather embarrassing, with Zadora peering out from behind gauzy curtains and speaking breathily, while her lover made his way over on his motorbike in a dinner jacket, where some Dubonnet and ice awaited his arrival. Also trying very hard to be glamorous again was Martini, with the television adverts reminding people, 'It's there to be discovered,' as the camera zoomed in on a woman's smiling mouth covered in red lipstick.

Not taking itself quite so seriously was Campari, whose advert featured a man in a white dinner jacket chatting up soap actress Lorraine Chase at a Venetian bar. Chase looked elegant in her cocktail dress, but when she opened her mouth she spoke like a Cockney and ordered her Campari with lemonade, upsetting the gentleman's sensibilities. In one of the adverts, he asked her, 'Were you truly wafted here from paradise?' to which she replied, 'Nah, Luton Airport.' Cinzano also went in for a tongue-in-cheek approach that proved a hit with British audiences. In theirs, Leonard Rossiter repeatedly spilled his drink over Joan Collins in various glamorous locations around the world.

Gin suffered particularly in the 1970s and 1980s, not just because of its image and the overall decline in aperitifs, but also because it faced yet more competition at the bar. This was the era of tiki cocktails, such as the Mai Tai and the Painkiller, which were mainly rum-based. The aesthetics of these tropical drinks could not be further from a sleek, clear Martini or a discreet White Lady, with their glasses full of outlandish garnishes, as immortalised by Del Boy from *Only Fools and Horses,* which started on the BBC in 1981. His drinks memorably captured the fashion for garish drinks like Pina Coladas, loaded with syrup, sweet fruit and showy decorations such as paper umbrellas, day glo plastic stirrers and patterned straws. This style was never as popular in Britain as it was in the United States, where it started, but it did help the gap between rum and gin widen still further.

Sadly, the decline in gin's image and popularity became reflected in the product itself. To cut costs, many distillers reduced the alcohol content, which weakened the flavour. Before the EU stepped into put its minimum legal level at

37.5 per cent gins from abroad were reducing their alcohol levels to around 28 per cent.

This tempted British distillers to lower percentages as well to compete on price. Even a big brand like Gordon's was not immune to reducing its alcohol content by 1992, from 40 per cent to the minimum. It also cut back on several products in quick succession. Firstly the Lemon Gin, which had been introduced in 1931. It was produced for fifty-seven years until being discontinued in 1988, along with the Orange gin, and two years later Gordon's Shaker Cocktails were phased out too.

As the distillers continued to suffer, the 1980s saw a new round of families losing control of their business, and distilleries having to move out of town. The Burrough family managed to hang on to Beefeater until 1987, when it was sold to Whitbread. Eric Burrough, who had done such sterling work promoting the brand in America, had died in 1970 and so the board at the time comprised of James Burrough's living grandchildren, Alan and Norman, with their sister, Marjorie Burrough, represented by her husband, Neville Hayman. The Hayman side of the family opposed the sale, but there were some 150 family members who held shares, and the majority voted to go ahead. Tanqueray finally lost its family connection in the 1980s as well, when the last Tanqueray, John, retired. The link with the company started by John's great-great-grandfather was severed. Both Tanqueray and Gordon's are now made in Cameron Bridge in Fife, after first being moved out to Essex in the 1980s.

The formerly independent gin brands that had been bought up by the Distillers Company were swallowed up into an even larger corporation when the Distillers Company was itself acquired in 1986 by Guinness. This created United Distillers, which would go on to become the behemoth that is Diageo. Today, it is the world's largest spirits producer, and owns Tanqueray, Gordon's, Gilbey's, Booth's and Boord's, among many others. It was the end of London's family gin makers.

25: The Way We Drink Now

THE BRAMBLE
50ml Bombay Sapphire, 20ml fresh lemon juice, 1tsp caster sugar, 15ml berry liqueur – (Crème de Mure / Chambord / Crème de Cassis), 1 blackberry, wedge of fresh lemon, and crushed ice

Bombay Sapphire's Bramble recipe

As EVER WITH gin, change was just around the corner. It had long lost its privileged position as Britain's favourite spirit, but there were hints in the late 1980s as to where recovery could come from. The gin renaissance would start at the luxury end of the market, and in 1987 came the first successful launch in decades. Bombay Sapphire heralded a gradual return to form for the whole industry, offering a new template for the stylish new gins that followed.

As it turned out, it would take two Americans to pull gin out of the doldrums. Michel Roux, an advertising whizz who had worked on Absolut vodka, joined forces with Allan Subin, an importer of luxury spirits who was looking to launch an authentically English gin for their home market. Subin had started his gin-making making career in 1959, after a fruitful shopping trip around England during which he had bought up the rights to an old recipe.

At G&J Greenall's in Cheshire, Subin had acquired Warrington Dry Gin, which was created in 1761 by Thomas Dakin, who had founded the distillery. Subin renamed it Bombay Dry Gin and gave it a white label with a picture of Queen Victoria on a plain, clear bottle. His idea of repackaging an historic recipe proved a great success for his Bombay Spirits Company. By 1970, he was selling 100,000 cases a year. This original Bombay Dry is still made at the Laverstoke Mill distillery, which Bombay Sapphire opened in 2014, but in extremely small quantities.

In the mid-1980s Subin had come back to England, looking to repeat this success. To make Bombay Sapphire, a luxury version of the Bombay Dry, Subin worked with master distiller Ian Hamilton, who added grains of paradise and the cubeb berry as new notes. This new gin was delicately scented, with juniper as a background botanical. Although this lighter, more floral approach to flavour is now wide-spread, Bombay Sapphire set that precedent of moving away from strong juniper nearly thirty years ago.

We also now take for granted elegant gin bottles that wear their historical credentials – real or embellished – on their sleeves, but it was Bombay that led the way in creating an attractive balance between heritage and modernity, as well as advertising its ingredients. Its exotic blue bottle is known all over the world, rivaled only by the flat-fronted green bottle of Gordon's. It was the first self-consciously stylish packaging that would appeal to women more than the stocky plain bottles of other gins. The prominent image on the label of the last empress of India Queen Victoria, which harks back to the Raj, has been so successful that few people believe that Bombay Sapphire began in the 1980s, not the 1880s.

Of the classic gins, the venerable Plymouth was one of the first to be resuscitated. Desmond Payne, who worked there, remembers only too well that the 1980s and early 1990s were very 'lean times' when 'vodka was king'. Shrinking investment since the Second World War had lost Plymouth all but its most faithful customers. Eventually, a group of investors clubbed together to buy the ailing company from a large brewer in 1996, hoping to rescue the prestigious Plymouth from closure.

At the time it was a shadow of its former self – only producing 3,000 cases a year, when the distillery was built to make 200,000. Like Gordon's, which reduced its alcohol level to 37.5 per cent, Plymouth had been watered down too. Even though the lower alcohol level meant that they were paying lower duty, Plymouth was still losing £24,000 a month. The new investors took the gamble of paying higher duty to put the alcohol content up to 41.2 per cent. It was then very deliberately renamed Plymouth Original Strength Gin so that old fans knew that it was time to come back. After the repackaging, a PR campaign and a few high-profile gin awards, sales shot up to 150,000 cases by 2003.

By the late 1990s traditional gin-makers that had been just about ticking along for decades were spurred on to compete with the artisanal gins that were springing up. Renewed confidence in gin prompted mainstream additions by distillers such as Tanqueray, Beefeater and Gordon's, who had been shying away from creating anything new. The success of Plymouth and the artisanal gins were encouraging signs that gin was dusting itself off for a comeback. Major brands have been ploughing money into improving their ordinary gin and inventing more complex, premium ones ever since.

Most newcomers from the past fifteen years are handcrafted in small batches, such as Hendrick's and Sipsmith, but Tanqueray was the first big gin-maker to take the risk. As the twenty-first century dawned, it unveiled its Tanqueray No. 10, made in Tiny Ten, a diminutive pot still from the 1930s, which was originally used for trial runs. Tanqueray No. 10 used the fruit of oranges, grapefruits and limes, rather than just the peel, creating a fresher taste that other gins have since emulated.

No. 10 brought Tanqueray back up to the top of its game, and it was later joined by the Tanqueray Rangpur in 2007, a sweeter gin with bay leaves, ginger and Indian Rangpur lime as its top notes. Before Rangpur, Tanqueray had a less successful experiment with releasing its Malacca gin, based on one of Charles Tanqueray's original recipes from 1839. It had a short life span, as gins go, of only four years. Even if the public were not quite ready for a sweet, spiced gin, it did attain cult popularity with bartenders. Because Old Tom gins are so hard to come by, the Malacca made a useful substitute in cocktails. When there was a limited second run of 100,000 in 2012, eager bartenders bought up the individually numbered bottles immediately.

In 2008 Beefeater threw its hat into the premium ring with Beefeater 24, at a punchy 45 per cent ABV, using Chinese green tea and Japanese sencha tea. The teas are blended together and steeped for twenty-four hours, hence the name. More of a radical departure was its Burrough's Reserve, which is closer to a genever as it is rested in oak barrels that once contained the aperitif Jean de Lillet. As a sign of how times had changed in master distiller Desmond Payne's forty-year career, Beefeater 24 was the first chance that he had to make a new gin, because suddenly the interest and the investment was available to do it. Now he has been able to create six new ones in the past five years.

Hayman's, a distiller very closely related to Beefeater, also makes a cask-rested gin. After Beefeater was sold, James Burrough's great-grandson Christopher Hayman set up his own distillery with son James and daughter Miranda. Being from the side of the family that did not want to sell Beefeater, when Christopher Hayman heard that Beefeater's old plant in Essex, which used to make pure alcohol for other companies, was going to be sold, he felt that he had to buy it. This unwillingness to let go of their gin heritage makes the Haymans the country's oldest gin dynasty to still be making its own brand. By 2007, it was ready to release its Old Tom, based on a family recipe from 1860s.

Keeping up on the innovations front, in 2011 Bombay Sapphire developed its East version by adding Thai lemongrass, Vietnamese black peppercorns, and 2 per cent more alcohol. The peppercorn and alcohol kick was made with the American market in mind, in order to cut through their sweeter tonics. Boodles British Gin also now makes an American version, with 5 per cent higher alcohol for the same reason.

The most experimental big name venture came from Bacardi-Martini, the current owner of Bombay Sapphire and Grey Goose vodka. It commissioned an offshoot boutique gin, Oxley, which is made by Thames Distillers in Clapham. A world apart from its usual operations, Oxley is vacuum-distilled in batches of only 120 bottles, and uses all the classics among its fourteen botanicals with a few offbeat additions, such as cocoa, aniseed and the herb meadow sweet. Unlike the other vacuum distillers, however, they manage to distill at sub-freezing temperatures, which takes about six hours.

Gordon's did also have a furtive foray into the premium market with its 40 per cent Distillers Cut, made with lemon-grass and ginger, but it was discontinued after five years. They then splashed out £4 million for a campaign featuring chef Gordon Ramsay as their poster boy. Although still a market leader, sales began to slump at this point. It seemed that the image of Ramsay in his chef's whites being soaked by gin and tonic was not making people reach for their Gordon's.

Perhaps intended as an affordable Hendrick's, in 2013 Gordon's launched the ill-advised Crisp Cucumber gin, which was extremely sweet and not particularly crisp. However, it was not a bid for the luxury market because it maintained the standard Gordon's alcohol level of 37.5 per cent. These days, Gordon's interest in the premium market has been cautious and limited to the packaging rather than the gin itself. It commissioned limited edition bottles by British designers Alice Temperley and Jasper Conran, to entice those younger, wealthy customers that they were hoping for with the Distillers Cut.

Pimm's revival on the other hand showed how powerful a well-judged advertising campaign could be. Its campaign featuring jovial comedian Alexander Armstrong as the Harry Fitzgibbon-Sims character was hugely popular. His plummy English accent and twee clothes seemed to tap into a residual affection for a cosy, upper-class Englishness. 'Pimm's o'clock' became a catchphrase embraced by the public, which is every advertising executive's dream come true. Pimm's presence at festivals, live shows and sporting events every summer has also proved lucrative over the past few years. At Wimbledon, the Pimm's Bus, which has been a feature since 1971, now sells over 300,000 glasses. Last year alone, Pimm's annual sales nearly trebled – partly driven by the warm weather, and by the launch of their Blackberry and Elderflower version.

Apart from the occasional misfire, it is at the premium end of the market that gin found its new niche while vodka has become the new cheap high, the bulk of which is aimed at the youngest possible drinkers. This divergence in gin and vodka means that the majority of vodka brands are no longer pursuing the same drinkers. The introduction of sweeter, flavoured vodkas has made it more accessible than ever for teenagers, whereas most young people find it takes longer to acquire a taste for gin.

Partnerships with soft-drinks brands such as Red Bull have helped influence the young's drinks orders as well, so that they see vodka with a sweet mixer as their default choice. It is usually advertised as a party spirit and is often the cheapest at the supermarket, so it is drunk both as a primer at home and again later in the night when young people are out at night-clubs or bars. This trend is known as 'pre-loading' and accounts for a great deal of vodka sales from shops.

While gin is continuing to grow, vodka is still Britain's biggest-selling spirit, although its sales have peaked recently. Supermarket own-brand vodkas are increasingly taking market share away from the expensive vodkas that claim greater purity and more interesting methods. As they struggle, this again means less competition for premium gin. There are some very inventive vodkas out there, such as Black Cow from Dorset, which is made from milk, and Williams Chase in

Herefordshire, made out of potatoes, but they are few and far between. Many vodka brands use marketing to set themselves apart, but taste-wise, for the majority there is not much difference between them.

What really helped the wave of boutique and premium gins gather such momentum in the 2000s was the flurry of interest in cocktails that followed. While the gin itself was improving, there were also rumblings that the London bar scene was reviving after a long hiatus. Even in the drought of the 1990s, it was always possible to find artful cocktails at London's smartest hotels, but the scene outside the formal hotel bars had fallen by the wayside. Gin cocktails had been sidelined by vodka in the 1960s, and they were yet to recover. However, that was about to change, as the bartenders who are leading the charge today in the 'second golden age of cocktails' were just starting their careers.

Few people have heard of Dick Bradsell, and yet he laid the foundations for the world-class cocktail scene that London is enjoying now. Bradsell's most enduring invention is the Bramble from the 1980s, a mixture of gin, lemon juice, syrup and crème de mûre – a blackberry liqueur. We have him to thank as well for the Espresso Martini and the Russian Spring Punch.

Although Bradsell worked at more salubrious places, the most eventful stint of his long career was as a young bartender at the Colony Room Club, where he stared out. Now closed, the drinking den on Dean Street in Soho was opened in 1948 by Welsh–Portuguese lesbian Muriel Belcher, who was famous for her abrasive hosting style. It was frequented by a wealth of hard-drinking creative people over the decades including Francis Bacon, who painted Belcher three times, Dylan

Thomas, Tallulah Bankhead, Lucian Freud, Christopher Hitchens and Isabella Blow. The joy of the bar was its unpredictable clientele. Before it closed in 2008, it was the place where Damien Hirst served naked behind the bar, Kate Moss worked as an honorary barmaid, and artists paid their bar tabs in paintings. Princess Margaret once popped in for a Pink Gin out of irresistible curiosity.

Bradsell went on to mentor Tony Conigliaro, pioneer of molecular mixology and owner of 69 Colebrooke Row in Islington, and Nick Strangeway, who is the mastermind behind the Hawksmoor, and Mark's Bar in Soho. Strangeway was studying at the Courtauld Institute of Art in the early 1990s when he took up bartending at Fred's Club in Soho, with Bradsell as his teacher. Strangeway became so engrossed in his cocktail-making sideline that he paid his friends to take lecture notes for him while he concentrated on honing his bar skills instead. After graduating, he balanced working in bars with assisting as a fashion photographer. Jaded by all the parties and travelling after a while, making cocktails in London became his fully-fledged career.

At Strangeway's bars there is a clear emphasis on historical English drinks – something that has been emulated in bars all over London as Londoners delve back into their drinking past. At the Hawksmoor, for example, they make Silver Bullets, Corpse Revivers and the Hawksmoor Fruit Cup, which is gin infused with strawberries, vermouth, Lillet Rouge and Angostura. At Mark's Bar they offer 1920s classics, such as the Pegu Club and Ada Coleman's Hanky Panky. Many other bar menus now explain the backstory of each drink too as it adds so much to the experience.

By the early 2000s, bartenders had been elevated to 'mixolo-gists' and the profession took on a new fastidiousness. London has since become a magnet for the world's best barmen, in particular the Italians, including: Agostino Perrone at the Connaught Bar, Simone Caporale at Artesian, Giuliano Morandin at the Dorchester, Salvatore Calabrese at the Playboy Club, Alessandro Palazzi at Dukes and Giovanni Cassino at Brown's Hotel. Between them, they have won countless world-class competitions over the past few years.

Now that gin is relatively expensive and everyone is better educated about the perils of overdoing it, the British seem to have finally struck the balance between enjoying Madam Geneva and allowing her to become their mistress. Nowadays, for most people, gin is a drink of celebration, rather than a necessity of keeping despair, boredom or the cold at bay. That bitter pill of life described by Dr Johnson has, at least in material terms, become less bitter. Over the centuries, this has allowed gin to blossom into a wonderful drink that embodies the best of London, not its bleakest. It has pulled through vilification, severe financial straits and many an image crisis to become more sophisticated and innovative than ever.

Whether you are drinking the cheapest Aldi gin or a glass of the finest Berry Bros. & Rudd No. 3, you have a connection to all the gin-drinkers that have gone before you. So the next time that you are sipping away, think of Thomas Tutty weaving home from the gin shop in Covent Garden, the Thames boatmen warming up with their Purl, Winston Churchill brooding over his Martini at the Dorchester, and Jeffrey Bernard propping up the bar in the dives of Soho. It is 300 years of London life – distilled.

How to Explore Gin Further

GIN STYLES

Several styles exist under the 'gin' umbrella. Classifications can be a difficult business as there is such diversity in each distillery's methods. At its most basic, gin is a spirit produced by flavouring alcohol of agricultural origin, usually grain, with juniper and other botanicals. However experimental distillers wish to be after that they have two golden rules that they must legally adhere to for it to be gin. The alcohol by volume, or ABV, must be at least 37.5 per cent and the flavour must contain a discernable amount of juniper.

The forerunner to modern gin is **genever** from Holland, which is sweeter, more malty and whisky-like, and generally oak-aged. It is referred by many names, including Hollands, jenever or simply Dutch gin. Often served neat and not suitable for many cocktails, it tastes very different to the world's most popular style – London Dry. Genever is made very differently too – starting with a mash of rye and barley malt, which is fermented to make beer. The beer is then distilled to produce malt wine, which is re-distilled with juniper and other botanicals for the final product. The most famous brand is Bols Genever, but it only makes up a fraction of the overall world market.

In the eighteenth century when Londoners began to imitate this Dutch gin, the style that they originally created was **Old Tom**. Like the Genever, it was still sweet tasting, but it was not made using the traditional Dutch methods. Londoners used liquorice as a sweetener at first and later cane sugar, when it became affordable. Old Tom would remain popular in the nineteenth century, but sales nosedived in the early twentieth century, and Old Tom virtually disappeared. Certain cocktails call specifically for it, such as historically correct versions of the Martinez or Tom Collins, but not many. When the Dorchester Bar wanted to make their Martinez the old-fashioned way as their signature cocktail, Giuliano Morandin had to commission an Old Tom to be made by the city of London distillery as there was so little available. Since 2008 its fortunes have been recovering with a modest comeback among the small-scale distillers, such as Hayman's, Jensen's and the splendidly named Professor Cornelius Ampleforth's.

To modern drinkers **London Dry** is the most recognisable style, thanks to its subtlety, lightness and ease of mixing. Although other gins are allowed to, as a legal definition London Dry cannot have any flavours or colours added after distillation. All of the flavour has to come from distilling the botanicals perfectly, and not from tinkering around afterwards. To maintain its dryness, London Dry is also only allowed to contain a tiny fraction of sugars.

Distilled gin is made in a similar way to London Dry but it is allowed to have natural and artificial flavourings added after distillation, and as much sweetener as the distiller wants. If a bottle just says 'gin' without 'distilled' or 'London' in front of it, then it is likely to have been made by compounding. This is when the essential oils from botanicals are simply mixed into neutral alcohol.

Whereas London Dry, and other gin styles. can be made all over the world, **Plymouth** gin must be made in the city walls of Plymouth on the coast of Devon – otherwise it simply is not Plymouth gin. It looks very likely therefore that the Black Friars Distillery will remain the only place in the world where it is made, unless someone has the temerity to set up a rival distillery on its doorstep. It is the only English style to be granted this Protected Geographical Indication from the EU, which means that it can only be made in one place.

Other gin styles with such protection include Vilnius Gin in Lithuania and Xoriguer from Mahon, Menorca's main city. Xoriguer, the Spanish's equivalent of Plymouth, has been made on the island of Menorca since the eighteenth century British occupation when it was a base for Lord Nelson. Very unusually, and unlike the London Dry that the British brought over, the Menorcans make their gin from a distilled wine base rather than grain. One of the few other gins in the world to be made from grapes is G'Vine from the Cognac region of France.

The Spanish, who love their *gin tonica* as much as the British, have many of their own brands, the most successful of which is Larios, which calls itself a 'dry gin' without the 'London'. Other than Britain and Spain, big gin producing countries include the USA and, somewhat bizarrely, the Philippines. It in fact has the honour of being the country that consumes the most gin in the world, which it largely produces itself. The Philippine gin San Miguel accounts for well over half of all the gin that they drink there.

JUNIPER AND OTHER BOTANICALS

After juniper, for a classic London gin the second strongest
flavour should be coriander. A fixative such as orris root or
angelica is also usually needed to hold all the other botanicals together and balance them, but after that distillers can
dabble away with an almost endless choice of flavours
– anything goes, from grapefruit and gentian, to lavender
and lovage. As Ian Hart from Sacred points out, there are
in the region of 500,000 known plant species so the
combinations are virtually infinite – and that is not to
mention all the foods that can be distilled. As Hart puts it,
'As a general rule, if you can smell it you can distill it.' It is
the range of botanicals used that makes gin work so well in
cocktails because there are so many flavours to pick up in
the accompanying ingredients. The botanicals are what
make each gin's taste unique and what really distinguishes it
from plain old vodka.

Broadly speaking, there are four categories of gin flavour.
There are citrusy gins like Beefeater, floral like Bombay
Sapphire, herbal like Blackwood's or Boodles, and spicy like
Tanqueray Malacca, Two Birds or Cadenhead's Old Raj. We
can safely say that even if they are not the strongest flavours
most gins will contain some coriander, citrus fruit, and
angelica or orris root as well as the all-important juniper.

Because juniper is so integral to gin, in its earliest days this
caused confusion as to what gin actually was. Lexicographer
Dr Samuel Johnson thought that gin perhaps came out of the
berries, defining it as 'the spirit drawn by distillation from
juniper-berries'. In the 1783 *English Etymology; or, a
Derivative Dictionary of the English Language* by George
William Lemon the same mistake cropped up again. Lemon

guessed that the very word might 'perhaps just a contraction of JUNIPER, from the berries of which it is distilled'.

Strictly speaking, the main flavour should be predominately juniper for all gins, but many modern ones do not adhere to that. The emphasis with new gins tends to be traditional methods with unusual ingredients. The gin that started the trend was Hendrick's, in which juniper is very understated. These days it can play second fiddle to all sorts of flavours – from Hendricks's cucumber to Hoxton's grapefruit to Opihr's black pepper.

Thanks to independent gin-makers who are pushing the boundaries of what traditional gin tastes like, there is now a gin to suit every taste – from the berry notes in Caorunn, to the elderflower of Warner Edwards Harrington Dry Gin, and the lavender and basil in Berkeley Square. For purists, however, recent experimentation can deviate a little too far from traditional juniper. Hoxton Gin was heavily criticised when it launched in 2011 for its coconut, tarragon, iris and grapefruit flavour, which did not taste enough like 'proper' gin. The knack of creating a novel flavour but one that satisfies gin lovers is a tricky one, with which all distillers grapple.

With all the marketing and attractive packaging, it can be difficult for shoppers to differentiate between the gimmicky newcomers and the strokes of genius. The ultimate test, of course, is simply whether people return to it. Hendrick's has proved a great success since it launched in 1999 and has really opened the doors for non-traditional gins to flourish. In the Hendrick's mix juniper is not a strong flavour at all, but few people criticise it, simply because the flavours are balanced, it is still recognisably gin, and it works well in cocktails. Hendrick's wildcard ingredients are its essential oils, pressed from Bulgarian rose petals and cucumber pulp, but they are delicate flavours and are used sparingly.

For drinkers looking for the familiar, clean-tasting pine hit of juniper, there are some great new gins that are bucking the trend and putting juniper back in centre stage. Sacred has developed its Juniper Gin and Sipsmith released its VJOP (Very Junipery Over Proof) in 2013, which introduces juniper at three different stages of distillation. After three days of steeping the juniper in raw spirit, extra juniper is added to the pot still for distillation, and then infused as vapour through its Carter head still at the end. Adnams Copper House Distilled Gin, made in Suffolk, also has a satisfying juniper hit.

Whichever star botanical a gin prides itself on, any distiller will tell you that the crux of a good gin is to artfully balance the botanicals. The number used varies vastly, from the six to make Berry Bros. & Rudd's No. 3 to an incredible forty-seven for German gin Monkey 47. Combinations of botanicals make new flavours, so even with a small number of botanicals, distillers have the potential to make hundreds of different gins. However, it is not necessarily the case that the more botanicals, the more interesting the flavour – throwing extra ones into the mix will not improve the gin if they mask the others. For example, when putting together premium gin Beefeater 24, Desmond Payne thought to add Darjeeling, but that created a tannin imbalance alongside the juniper and dominated the other ingredients, so the Darjeeling sadly had to go.

Not even if you buy a master distiller umpteen gin and tonics of an evening will he divulge exactly what goes into his gin. However, these are the standard botanicals that most gins use:

JUNIPER

Juniper grows wild in Britain, particularly in the Lake District, north Wales, and on the heaths and cliffs of Scotland. As a member of the conifer family, the berries are fragrant with a bittersweet taste reminiscent of pine. After two years of growth, the berries ripen in early autumn, turning from green to a very dark blue.

Although juniper has been growing in Britain for millennia, it is currently in decline because of overgrazing by rabbits and livestock, and a deadly fungal disease. Mercifully, this is no threat to anyone's gin and tonic, as no commercial distillers use homegrown berries. They do not grow large and fleshy in Britain, so they are imported from Umbria in Italy or Macedonia, where they become rich and oily in the sunshine. A world-leading brand like Beefeater will sniff through around 200 samples of juniper a year to pick the right varieties from that particular harvest. Beefeater need so much of it that they make several juniper blends from different varieties to ensure consistency, because they cannot get enough of one crop to make all of their gin for the year. They will also keep two years' worth of stock at any time to avoid the risk of a bad harvest.

CORIANDER

The second most important flavouring
for a classic gin is coriander seed. Its
essential oil, linalool, creates a warming
sensation with hints of ginger.
Surprisingly, the main citrus flavour in
gin actually comes from the coriander.
It is usually imported from Eastern
Europe, Russia or Morocco and is
harvested in April and May.

CINNAMON

Sweet and spicy, cinnamon comes from
the inner bark of a tropical tree, grown
commercially in Indonesia, Madagascar,
Vietnam and the West Indies.
Historically, cinnamon was considered a
superior spice to its close relation,
cassia.

CASSIA

Like coriander, cassia adds warmth and a
rich mouthfeel – a term that distillers use
to describe the 'texture' of the gin. Cassia
is part of the same family as cinnamon
and grows around Indochina, particularly
in Vietnam, where the aromatic bark is
stripped from evergreen trees and dried.
In Arthur Hill Hassall's series of studies
for medical magazine the *Lancet* in the

nineteenth century he considered cassia to be an adulterant,
but it has long since been embraced as a rightful ingredient.

ANGELICA ROOT

Angelica, part of the carrot family, grows wild near rivers in Britain. However, for gin it is generally harvested from the woodlands of France, Belgium and Germany. It acts as a fixative, marrying the other botanicals together, with a distinct dry, earthy quality.

ORRIS ROOT

Like the angelica root, the orris root is a fixative. They are both used in scent and in gin. It grows primarily in the south of France, northern Italy and Morocco, where it is harvested in the summer when the soil is at its driest. It is found in the bulbs of iris flowers, and can only be extracted after the plant has grown for three years. Once the root is ground to a powder, it releases a strong woody scent.

CARDAMOM

After saffron and vanilla, cardamom is the third most expensive spice in the world, but only a few pods are needed to create a powerful, smoky note. The plant, which belongs to the ginger family, is native to southern India and Sri Lanka, but is now widely grown around the world.

LIQUORICE ROOT

Like juniper and many other botanicals, liquorice grows well in the Mediterranean. Its root is ground into a powder that softens the overall flavour of the gin and adds a more complex sweetness than sugar. It is particularly important for flavouring Old Tom gins.

ALMOND

Harvested in the summer, usually in Spain, almonds are ground to produce oil that gives gin a smooth, rounded feel and evens out the competing flavours of other botanicals.

CITRUS PEEL

Lemon or orange peel gives the gin zing, throwing the sweeter ingredients into relief. Sacred and Tanqueray No. 10 use the fruit itself, rather than the traditional peel, for more freshness. Grapefruit and lime are also growing in popularity these days.

NUTMEG

With its gentle, sweet aroma, nutmeg is used in Boodles British Gin, Portobello Road and Martin Miller's. It is native to the Indonesian Moluccas islands, but it is now produced in the West Indies and Sri Lanka as well. Nutmeg oil contains pinene, which is also a component of juniper so the two work very well together.

GRAINS OF PARADISE

The enticingly named tiny brown grains give off a long-lasting mouthfeel, with an intense peppery taste. The plants grow wild in Nigeria, Ghana and Liberia and their seeds are used a great deal in West African cooking. Also known as guinea pepper, it was used as a cheaper substitute for black pepper in the Middle Ages.

OTHER BOTANICALS

Distillers are often particularly proud of one idiosyncratic botanical that gives their gin the edge, that makes them stand out from the hundreds of others. Dodd's are very proud of the organic honey that they use from London bees, as are Adnams of the hibiscus flowers in the Copper House Gin, while Blackwood's success lies in its Shetland Island sea pink flowers.

Sacred's most exotic ingredient is its frankincense resin from Oman, hence the name Sacred, from the Latin for the frankincense tree, *Boswellia Sacra*. Using frankincense in gin, in fact, is not as peculiar as it sounds. Up until the 1830s, many Europeans mistakenly believed that it was the resin of the juniper tree because the two are so closely related.

HOW GIN IS MADE

Alongside the quality and particular combination of botanicals, how they are introduced into the gin also determines the flavour. Each distillery will tell you that their particular method is the most effective, so how gin is made varies greatly. To create the best possible canvas for the botanicals, the base spirit will usually be grain – either barley or maize.

These days, technology is so sophisticated that the neutral alcohol has virtually no flavour at all. Originally, however, gin's base was very rough around the edges as it was made from anything that contained enough carbohydrate to produce alcohol when fermented.

In brief terms distillation is when the raw grain spirit is pumped into a still, normally made of copper to draw out impurities, and infused with flavour from botanicals. The still works by heating the raw spirit containing the botanicals to draw out their essential oils. Distilling is simply a case of separating the liquids in the still based on their boiling points and under normal circumstances, pure drinkable alcohol will start to evaporate at around 78°C. The process itself works slowly, so that each flavour can be picked out in the final product. The vapours from the botanicals are different weights, so they condense at different times. Volatile flavours, such as citrus fruit, will be the first, followed by woody notes. Juniper itself is very heavy and will come through near the end.

The first 15 per cent of the spirit to come out of the still is known as the heads, or foreshots. This is too low quality for drinking and contains unpleasant chemical compounds such as methanol and acetone. This is funnelled off to be distilled again, before it can be included in the final product, although some distillers discard it altogether. The last vapours to come out are known as the faints or tails, which, like the heads, include unwanted flavours that would give the gin a burning sensation and unpleasant smell. They will also be redistilled or discarded. This leaves the middle cut, or the heart, which is the good, drinkable spirit. One of the distiller's most important skills is knowing exactly where this middle cut will be, so that as many impurities from the heads and tails as possible do not make it into the bottle. At Sipsmith, for example, the middle cut runs for about eight hours, which gives the distiller an indication of roughly when the cut-off should be.

The vast majority of distilleries will make a concentrate of their recipe, which they then dilute to the right strength, which is called the multi-shot method. This increases the amount of gin that one distillation run can make, thereby saving on all the energy that it takes to heat up the still each time. The more old-fashioned approach is the one-shot method, which means that the exact concentration is made for the bottle. This is now very rare because of the expense. Sipsmith and Tanqueray are two of the only big players to use it.

However the gin is made, its alcohol content needs to remain high to be considered premium. This is not only important for gin's mood-altering effects but also for an intense and lasting flavour. The alcohol amplifies the taste so most quality gins, such as Boodles, Sacred, Bombay Sapphire, Portobello Road and Beefeater, will go above the 37.5 per cent minimum and start at around 40 per cent. Generally for a gin to be considered premium, it must be at least 40 per cent, but many go for 42 per cent and higher, such as Whitley Neill, Beefeater 24, Martin Miller's Westbourne Strength, and Dodd's.

Distillers who already make premium gin as their main product use the term 'super premium' to describe gins that are even more rarified – and this group has been climbing the fastest of all. The super premium group would include gins like Tanqueray No. 10 and Bombay Sapphire East, because ordinary Tanqueray and Bombay Sapphire are already considered premium. The punchiest of all are the 'navy strength' gins, at around 57 per cent, such as Hayman's Royal Dock and Plymouth Navy Strength, with Sipsmith's VJOP just nudging ahead at 57.7 per cent.

The last, but surprisingly important, ingredient is water. As it brings the gin down to a safe alcohol level, water makes up a lot of the gin itself. Martin Miller's gin even goes to the length of importing it from Iceland at great expense. Most stay a little closer to home, with Bombay Sapphire bringing theirs from Lake Vyrnwy in Snowdonia, Plymouth from Dartmouth National Park and Sipsmith from Lydwell Spring, one of the sources of the Thames. As gin needs no ageing, after the water has been added, it is ready for bottling immediately.

DIFFERENT STILLS FOR DIFFERENT DRINKS

The stills vary in age, material and how they introduce the botanical flavours. Distillers are very protective of them as they believe the slightest change, even down to the dents, can affect the gin that they make. Accordingly, the stills are incredibly well-looked after and are revered as the heart of the distillery. When Beefeater's number seven still turned a hundred years old in 1998, the staff had a party for it.

Despite their clear fondness for their stills, Beefeater is one of the few distilleries that does not give them names. The City of London Distillery's stills are named Clarissa and Jennifer, after TV chefs the Two Fat Ladies; Thames Distillers' two steel pot stills are called Tom Thumb and Thumbelina; Hayman's gin is made in Essex by Marjorie; Langley's No. 8 gin is made by Connie in the Midlands; Two Birds gin in

Leicestershire has Gerard; and Bombay Sapphire's new ones are called Victoria, after Queen Victoria, and Henry, after the master distiller Nik Fordham's son.

THE POT STILL

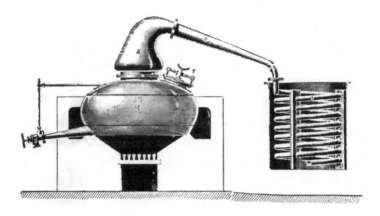

This is an onion-shaped pot in which the raw spirit is heated directly, historically it would have been over an open fire but now it is safely done with a steam jacket. They can take about an hour to heat up and get the spirit evaporating. They have elongated, swan-like necks to extract the more delicate flavours on the way through the still. These alcoholic vapours then condense in a second cylindrical still back to a liquid state by running through pipes surrounded by cold water. This is the most traditional way of making gin, with all the botanicals mixed together in the pot, which is usually made of copper. The advantage of this still is that many of the residual oils from the grain come through into the gin, creating a weightier spirit.

The whole process is in fact carried out twice in a pot still. The first time around, 'low wines' are created – this is a low-quality alcohol, at around 25 per cent ABV. The second time through the still, after the heads and tails of impure spirit have been removed, is when the gin is of a drinkable standard. Pot stills are used to make gins such as Hayman's London Dry and Berry Bros. & Rudd's No. 3, as well as brandy and whisky.

THE COFFEY STILL

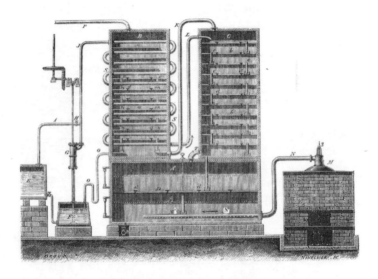

The column or continuous still, invented by Irish customs officer Aeneas Coffey in 1832, is more modern and efficient than its dumpy pot still predecessor. Coffey's tall and thin design allowed for a continuous distillation that created higher strength, purer alcohol in large quantities. Coffey's still uses two columns, one filled all the way up with horizontal perforated plates. These plates allow vapours to pass through, condensing along the way. After the heated raw alcohol and spirit vapours come through the first column, they are condensed in the second. Most gins use this still these days.

THE CARTER HEAD STILL

Created by the Carter brothers, who worked with Aeneas
Coffey, the Carter head is similar to the Coffey, but offers a
different way to introduce botanicals. They are suspended
above the alcohol near the top of the column in a perforated
basket, so that the alcoholic vapour passes through and picks
up the flavour in a light and subtle way. The botanicals have
to be layered very specifically and in the same way every time
for a consistent result. When drinking gin with a mixer, you
may not really notice the smoothness in Bombay Sapphire or
Williams Chase, which both use the Carter head, but it
should come through when drunk neat.

THE HYBRID STILL

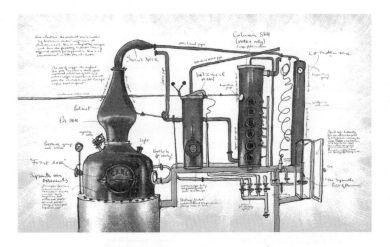

Prudence, Sipsmith's original still, is a unique design of all
three types – a pot, Carter head and Coffey in one. The pipe
that comes out of Prudence's copper pot is curved like a
swan's neck, hence the swan on the Sipsmith label. The gin is
made in the pot section and Sipsmith keep the Coffey part to
make the vodka.

Hendrick's do something more unusual. To make their gin, they mix together two different spirits made from two separate stills. One is a rare 1860 Bennett still from London, of which very few were made, and the other is a Carter head by John Dore & Co, which they bought at auction. Between the two stills, Hendrick's make very small batches of 450 litres. In London Dodd's Gin has the same approach of blending together the spirits of two separate stills – one a traditional copper still, the other a cold vacuum.

VACUUM DISTILLATION

The big benefit of vacuum distillation is that it lowers the temperature of the whole process, which avoids 'overcooking' the botanicals in the heat of normal distillation. Ian Hart at Sacred likens the difference to using freshly squeezed orange rather than marmalade. By reducing the pressure with the vacuum, the boiling points are lowered and the process is more energy efficient. Taking it one step further, Hart takes the time to distil all of his twelve botanicals separately. For this, he has developed his own equipment, which he uses alongside a rotovap – a glass distillation flask that is most often used in molecular gastronomy by the likes of Heston Blumenthal et al. Vacuum distillation is also used by Oxley, which is made at the Thames Distillery, and at the Cambridge Distillery.

GIN O'CLOCK: WHAT TO DRINK WHEN
Decadent morning: Breakfast Martini
Sunny afternoon: Tom Collins
Cold afternoon: Purl
After work: G&T – what else?
Early evening: White Lady
Pre-prandial: Negroni

Post-prandial: sloe gin on the rocks
Party time: Corpse Reviver No. 2
Playing cards: Aviation
Nightcap: genever

GINS TO ADD TO THE COCKTAIL CABINET

CLASSIC STYLE
Hayman's Royal Dock
For a gin and tonic with some proper oomph, stock up on a naval-strength gin such as Hayman's or Plymouth's version. It cuts right through tonic with its 57 per cent ABV.

Gordon's Yellow Label London Dry
Gordon's yellow label higher-strength bottle, at 47.3 per cent, is much more weighty than ordinary Gordon's and can therefore hold its own in sweet cocktails. It is more often found in mainland Europe, but is still possible to track down in Britain. The higher strength is perhaps why Gordon's happens to taste so much better on holiday.

Sipsmith Very Junipery Over Proof
For juniper-lovers, sweet dreams are made of the Sipsmith VJOP. It is probably a little too punchy at 57.7 per cent to drink in a daily G&T, but once in a while it will certainly blow the cobwebs away.

Adnams Copper House First Rate
A charming gin from Southwold in Suffolk, Adnams' First Rate is classically juniper-heavy with a long finish, and at 48 per cent it is the perfect base for a strong Martini or G&T. Its well-balanced botanicals include cardamom and hibiscus flowers to keep it interesting.

Tanqueray No. 10
For an upgrade on ordinary Tanqueray, try this version – a quadruple-distilled, small-batch gin with more alcohol. So named after the dimuniutive still in which it is made, Tiny Ten, the gin has a peppy injection of citrus from fresh orange, white grapefruit and lime. A trusty, fail-safe bottle to keep in the house.

Cream Gin by Worship Street Whistling Shop
Using fresh cream as a gin flavouring dates back to the Victorian era, and you should taste this out of curiosity if nothing else. It is the one that they use in the Black Cat Martini at the Worship Street Whistling Shop, if you want to try it in professional hands. Each bottle contains around 100ml of distilled cream.

No. 3 London Dry
No. 3 is rich in juniper and with only six botanicals it has a satisfyingly traditional flavour. Commissioned by London's oldest continuous wine and spirit merchant, Berry Bros. & Rudd, it comes in an enticing dark green bottle, with a curious key embedded into the front.

NEW WAVE FLAVOURS
Oxley
Made in Clapham, in a vacuum still at -5ºC, Oxley is about as cutting edge as it gets. Its gently sweet ingredients include nutmeg, vanilla and almonds. Like most new gins, much attention has been paid to perfecting the packaging, with its green embossed leather tag and distinctive silver ice-bucket-effect bottom.

Dodd's

From Battersea comes a very warm and smooth gin. With its honey from London bees, it could be too sweet for traditional gin-drinkers, but it is well worth trying. The geometrical label is a tribute to the gin's namesake, entrepreneurial engineer Ralph Dodd. Dodd once warned that a bad spirit 'soon manifests itself in the destruction of its users'. Luckily this is a very good spirit, so there is no problem there.

Beefeater 24

Inspired by tea, this was one of Beefeater distiller Desmond Payne's pet projects and it has turned out to be a lasting success. The twist on ordinary Beefeater is the addition of green tea and sencha tea. In a well-considered nod to its past, its Arts and Crafts-style bottle was inspired by the Royal Doulton ceramics that Beefeater used at the turn of the twentieth century as the factory was its neighbour at the time.

Elephant London Dry

Inspired by the botanicals of Africa, Elephant London Dry is made with pimento berries, devil's claw, lion's tail and baobab, at a generous 45 per cent. Smooth with a hint of sweetness from the thyme and apple, it has a lovely aromatic nose.

Sacred Contemporary Collection

Using Sacred's kit of botanical distillates to blend your own gin (while getting gradually more tipsy and trying to remember what you've used) makes for a great night in. Alternatively, use them separately to add a different flavours to your normal gin and tonic. The pack is made up of six individual bottles of nutmeg, star anise, juniper, cassia, orris root and pink grapefruit.

Blackwoods Vintage Dry

Hendrick's now has some close competition to win the crown of best Scottish gin – Blackwoods, the Botanist and Caorunn are close on its tail. With its marigold, meadow sweet and sea pinks, Blackwoods has a summertime, garden-party feel to it without being sickly, so it makes a pleasant alternative to a drink like Pimm's on a hot day. Blackwoods also make a 60 per cent version – the strongest British gin that you can buy.

Chase's Sloe and Mulberry

Sloe gin is not really a gin at all. It is a sweet liqueur made from sloe berries, but it is so comforting that we will let it off the hook. Usually associated with hipflasks on long walks, sloe gin also makes a great addition to prosecco or champagne. This one is crisp, rich, and not too cloying. A much-forgotten ingredient, the mulberry works extremely well and gives it an intense smell.

NON-GIN FLOURISHES

Vermouth

Much neglected in recent decades, vermouth is back in the cocktail cabinet and winning fans all over again. You will need it for Negronis and Martinis. Sacred makes an excellent new one, but the classics are the Italian Punt e Mes, and the French Noilly Prat.

Kamm & Sons Ginseng Spirit

Alex Kammerling founded Kamm & Sons after working with Martin Miller's to create their Westbourne Strength gin. Rather than simply make another gin, he took the more unusual route of making a bittersweet spirit that does not quite fit into any boxes. Among Kamm & Sons' forty-five botanicals are juniper, ginseng, honey and grapefruit, which work very well in gin cocktails. Here is one way to use it, as suggested by Nathan Merriman when he was at the Savoy:

Summer at the Savoy
30ml Kamm & Sons Ginseng Spirit
30ml Jensen Old Tom gin
20ml camomile syrup
5ml honey syrup
15ml lemon juice
3 basil leaves

Angostura bitters

Only a few drops of Angostura are needed to make a Pink Gin, so the little bottle will be with you a long time. Named after Angostura in Venezuela, the aromatic combination of gentian and spices is in fact made in Trinidad and Tobago. There are other brands of aromatic bitters to experiment with as well, such as Bob's Bitters and Peychaud's.

St Germain Elderflower Liqueur

St Germain comes in a very elegant Belle Epoque-style bottle, and the liqueur itself is marvellous too. It works really well to lift a plain G&T, as well as in more elaborate cocktails. Its sales have grown 75 per cent year-on-year – find out what all the fuss is about.

Dubonnet

For a regal touch to your gin, take a tip from the Queen and add a dash of Dubonnet, an oak-aged French aperitif which is infused with quinine. There is something very comforting about how dated the dark-brown-and-red bottle looks.

Domaine de Canton French Ginger Liqueur
A lovely golden-coloured liqueur made with ginger, cognac, ginseng and honey, Domaine de Canton is not widely available, but it is worth tracking down. Experiment with using it in cocktails, such as a Negroni with Campari and gin, or add half a shot to your normal G&T or Pimm's.

Tipplesworth Pure Cane Sugar Syrup
London-based entrepreneur Frankie Snobel developed this handy syrup to go in her travelling cocktail kits. As a healthier alternative, agave nectar syrup from Mexico is available from specialist shops.

Williams Chase Rhubarb Liqueur
This mildly tart liqueur from Herefordshire is made from Chase's own potato vodka infused with local rhubarb. Sweet but fairly unusual as a flavour, it will add a certain je ne sais quoi to your G&T.

Williams 'Homegrownie':
2 shots Williams Chase gin
1 shot Williams Chase Rhubarb Liqueur
2 shots Aperol

Hix Fix Cherries
If you miss the guilty pleasure of having a cherry with your cocktail, these Morello cherries in Somerset apple eau de vie are the best. It is very tempting to just eat them on their own, but do try to save them for the drinks. The odd shop now sells them, but they are mainly to be found at Mark Hix's restaurants.

Phillips of Bristol cordials

For a Dickensian touch to your gin, try the pink cloves, shrub or lovage cordials from Phillips of Bristol. Like many of these cocktail ingredients, they were originally prescribed as medicines when Phillips started in 1825, hence the austere looking bottles.

Sipsmith Summer Cup

Pimm's is in fact a brand name for a historical type of drink called a 'cup' and it used to be a punchy 40 per cent ABV, or alcohol by volume. These days it is a rather mean 25 per cent, whereas Sipsmith's version is made at 29 per cent – a welcome improvement.

Tonic

Do not forget to experiment with tonics and mixers. Often when people say that they do not like gin, it is actually the tonic they do not like. Try Fever Tree, Fentimans or 6 o'Clock tonic, and Belvoir's pressés.

G&T POINTERS

• Run the fleshy part of whichever garnish you are using around the rim of your glass for a stronger flavour.

• Experiment with using a balloon glass instead of a high-ball to see which you prefer.

• Keep all of your cocktail and G&T ingredients and equipment as cold as possible.

• Try not to drown your gin in tonic. After all, it is the gin that you want to taste – not a mouthful of tonic.

- Gin does not improve with age like some other alcohols. Splash out on a vintage bottle for the novelty, but do not expect the gin to have taken on any special qualities.

It is not just bartenders who have been inspired by the idea of putting a new spin on such a beloved, iconic drink. Gin has become a muse for everyone from chocolatiers to perfumers. From gin bottle advent calendars to Caorunn's gin-scented candles, you can fill most corners of your life with the stuff these days. Whether it is a good thing to smell of gin is debatable, but English scent-maker Penhaligon's has launched Juniper Sling to evoke the heady nights of 1920s London, and soaps, lip balm, and candles scented with Sloane's gin have been a runaway success for small business the Littlecote Soap Co. Gin's influence has also made its way into food, with many luxury chocolatiers such as Hotel Chocolat, Prestat and the London Chocolate Company making delectable gin truffles.

GIN'S LITTLE BLACK BOOK
Modern and not-so-modern gin hotspots – be sure to tick them all off.

THE GRAND OLD DAMES
The American Bar
The Savoy, Strand, WC2 0EU

Try one of the cocktails created here, such as the Hanky Panky, Blushing Monarch or the Windsor Romance. The Clover Club, the Elise and the Croquet Club Cobbler also slip down all too easily. Surrounded by Terry O'Neill portraits, curiosities from its illustrious history and jazz every night of the week, drinking up at the bar makes you feel like a film star. You need to go at least once.

The Connaught Bar
The Connaught Hotel, Carlos Place, W1 3AN

Life is too short to drink mediocre cocktails in forgettable pubs. Save up to go here instead. The Faraway Collins, with No. 3 gin and eucalyptus-infused sugar, is a strong take on a usually bland drink, and the Singapore Swizzle, which features Tanqueray mixed with Benedictine, coconut soda and home-made grenadine, is something you would be hard-pressed to find elsewhere in London. As you would expect from the brilliant, late interior designer David Collins the bar alone is worth going to marvel at. Watch the bartender deftly prepare your Martini at your table, surrounded by Art Deco-style glamour.

Donovan Bar
Brown's Hotel 30–34 Albemarle Street, W1 4BP

Somewhat overlooked, the gin cocktails at the Donovan Bar are punchy but nuanced, as they should be. They do their own version of James Bond's Vesper Martini with Hendrick's gin and Sipsmith's barley vodka, which is delicious. New cocktails arrive on the menu regularly, so it is a great place to keep coming back to, and the soft lighting and luxurious interiors makes it an ideal date venue. Gin-drinking does not come much more refined than this.

Artesian
The Langham Hotel, 1c Portland Place, W1 1JA

You may drink a lot of cocktails, but you will not forget these in a hurry. When it comes to presentation, Artesian pulls out all the stops and it is here that you will find some of the city's most experimental new cocktails, as well as classic glacier-cold Martinis. London enjoys a reputation for being a city of innovative cocktails and this place is one of the main reasons why.

The Dorchester Bar
The Dorchester Hotel, 53 Park Lane, W1 1QA

Early adopters of both Fever Tree tonic and Sipsmith gin, for such a venerable institution, the Dorchester is not at all behind on the latest cocktail trends. Under the watchful eyes of Giuliano Morandin and Simon Rowe, both of whom have been there for over twenty-five years, the cocktails are flawless and popular with a surprisingly young crowd.

The Rivoli Bar
The Ritz, 150 Piccadilly, W1 9BR

Fast winning new fans, the Rivoli has an impressive menu and keeps the presentation imaginative without getting gimmicky. Its dainty mini-masterpieces include the Ramos Fizz (Tanqueray No. 10, lemon and lime juice, vanilla syrup, cream and Solerno Blood Orange Liqueur) and the Angel Face (No. 3 gin, Calvados Père Magloire and apricot brandy, with spiced baked apple). The bar also offers a rare chance to try vintage cocktails using ingredients from the 1960s and 1950s.

The Spaniard's Inn
Spaniards Road, NW3 7JJ

Raise a glass to Dickens in his old haunt, the Spaniard's Inn in Hampstead. As it is close to the Sacred distillery, they tend to stock all of Sacred's latest products and run occasional tasting sessions with its master distiller, Ian Hart. After the long bracing walk from the Heath, you can warm up with a Sipsmith sloe gin toddy.

The Princess Louise
208 High Holborn, WC1 7BW

Sadly there are hardly any authentic nineteenth-century gin palaces, such as Thompson and Fearon's or Weller's in Old Street, to look around these days. However, the Princess Louise in Holborn, built in 1879, has some wonderful gin palace-style features. It was refitted in 1891, so there are details that are more pub than gin palace, but it still offers a glimpse of the original atmosphere. It is extremely popular – mainly with tourists looking for some authentic London Victoriana.

The Princess Victoria
217 Uxbridge Road, W12 9DH

The Princess Victoria is bit of a trek into Shepherd's Bush, but authentic gin palaces are hard to come by these days. Because it was turned into a pub in 1872, not all of the details are strictly gin palace, but this is as close as you will get. Sit in the walled garden in the summer or by the fire in the winter and admire the nineteenth-century features – from the vast windows, to the mahogany bar, to the gaslights outside.

THE NEWCOMERS
The Punch Room
The London Edition Hotel, 10 Berners Street, W1 3NP

A whole bar devoted to punch is, of course, a must-visit. Naturally, the gin ones are the best, and the house concoction is a very drinkable blend of gin, jasmine tea, lemon, orange blossom water and, rather bizarrely, oak moss syrup. As well as the house punch, another eight are available every day, such as An Ode to Mrs Tottenham (Tanqueray, sage and lemon verbena syrup, prosecco and peach puree). A good place for a cosy winter night out, but booking ahead is necessary.

The Booking Office Bar
St Pancras Renaissance London Hotel, Euston Road, NW1 2AR

The Booking Office Bar offers a really delightful historical menu which explains where the recipes come from and how they have been adapted over the decades. Their Gin Punch a la Terrington, with gin, Chartreuse, lemon sherbet and sugar, is a tribute to William Terrington's very early British cocktail book *Cooling Cups and Dainty Drinks*, and there are plenty of other nineteenth-century curiosities in there too. You can order the punches in bowls for twelve people – just as Dickens would have done. The setting of the Victorian ticket hall overlooking King's Cross is perfect.

69 Colebrooke Row
69 Colebrooke Row, N1 8AA

One of the most exciting openings in the city for years, the diminutive bar is always jam-packed with well-dressed yuppies. The high turnover of homemade ingredients, such as vermouth, various syrups and infusions, comes courtesy of cocktail whizzkid Tony Conigliaro who develops bold new flavours in his nearby laboratory, the Drink Factory.

Worship Street Whistling Shop
63 Worship Street, EC2 2DU

Stylish, whimsical and very thoughtfully decorated, the
Whistling Shop conjures up a sense of a long-gone east
London. Its glass-walled 'lab', in which the bartenders make
various ingredients, draws all visitors in for a curious closer
look. The cocktails are generally Victorian-themed, with
offbeat libations such as the Gin and Pep (gin and crème de
menthe aged in oak) and the Black Cat Martini, which uses
their distilled cream gin.

The Star at Night
22 Great Chapel Street, W1 8FR

With an impressive fifty gins (and counting) on offer, this is
an ideal place for a G&T session. They offer various tasting
menus so that you can find your new favourite, and you can
buy the big balloon glasses to take home. Its proximity to the
setting of Gin Lane is a handy reminder not to have a few
too many before heading home.

The Perkin Reveller
The Wharf at the Tower of London, EC3 4AB

Looking out of the floor-to-ceiling windows, you get a great
sense of history being tucked right under London Bridge. You
can picture the Thames Frost Fair out in front of you, and
wish for your own gin and gingerbread for the walk home.
Try the Gin Tea Merchant cocktail, with sloe gin and
Beefeater 24, which comes with a dinky juniper biscuit.

Graphic
4 Golden Square, W1 9HT

If there is a new gin that you have been scouring London for they will certainly have it here, and the staff are totally unpretentious, offering sound advice on where to start with the lengthy menu. As part of its informal atmosphere, it does get noisy and busy. It is a little bit low on atmosphere, but you will not find a bigger selection at any bar in London.

The Northall
Corinthia Hotel, 10 Whitehall Place, SW1 2BD

A grand statement of a bar at a deluxe London hotel like the Corinthia is the ideal place to enjoy a gin cocktail. As with all of these bars, it is the attention to detail that takes it to the next level, with homemade cordials, infusions and bitters, and beautiful presentation, from chunky pewter tankards to elegant flutes. Highlights include the Northall Old Fashioned (Caorunn gin, maraschino liqueur and grapefruit bitters) and the In Grasia, made with Laurent-Perrier champagne and G'Vine, a gin from France made from grapes. Gins from all over Britain are well represented on the menu.

The Whip
50 Davies Street, W1K 5JE

Owned by the Williams Chase distillery in Herefordshire, this brilliant little bar has a very good pedigree, and it shows. If you are casually dressed and not wanting to spend a small fortune, then it is a handy alternative to all the stuffy bars around Mayfair. Ebullient head bartender Jimmy will make you a lovely Frankel Fizz (Williams Chase Extra Dry Gin with Chase Rhubarb Vodka, cucumber and lemon juice) or a Derby Day (Chase Seville Orange Gin, apricot brandy, lemon and mint). The barmen have a real passion for gin and will happily rustle you up a drink off-menu, if there is something that you are really hankering for.

MEET THE MAKERS
The Sipsmith Distillery
83 Cranbrook Road, W4 2LJ

At the new Sipsmith distillery in Chiswick, one of the hyper enthusiastic team will tell you all about what makes their gin so special and show you how Prudence, Patience and Constance work while you sip the fruits of their labours. Ask as many questions as you can think of to people who love gin just as much as you do.

The Beefeater Distillery
20 Montford Place, SE11 5DE

Beefeater, the world's biggest selling premium gin, has been in production at a rather austere-looking factory in Kennington since the 1950s, having moved three times since it was founded in the nineteenth century. Tucked away on a side street of Georgian houses, with a view of The Oval cricket ground, it is a charming pocket of London. The distillery opened to the public for the first time in 2014, with a special edition Beefeater London Garden available from the shop.

The City of London Distillery
22–24 Bride Lane, EC4Y 8DT

Make sure you try lots of obscure gins at this subterranean distillery and bar behind Fleet Street. Founded by Jamie Baxter from the Chase distillery in Herefordshire, the distillery offers tours once a day on weekdays. It also offers a masterclass featuring a tasting of six gins, with a vintage one at the end.

The London Distillery Company
33 Parkgate Road, SW11 4NP

Tours to see where Dodd's gin is made are by appointment only but you will not be disappointed by a trip to Battersea to have a nose around, and marvel at how they keep those copper stills quite so shiny. It is right next to the Doddle Bar, where you can head for a drink afterwards.

TASTINGS AND MASTERCLASSES
Ginstitute
171 Portobello Road, W11 2DY

Learn how Portobello Road gin is made over a Martini or two with jolly host Jake Burger at his homage to a gin palace above the Portobello Star pub. At £100 it is pretty steep, but Burger is generous with the drinks and will give you an entertaining talk on the curiosities of gin. Then, upstairs, in what looks like a school laboratory, he will show you how to blend your own. You can take your juniper masterpiece home with you, as well as a bottle of Portobello Road.

Rules' Masterclass
35 Maiden Lane, WC2 7LB

The masterclasses are held in groups of only four people at Rules, London's oldest restaurant. Because there are so few of you, you can learn to make four classic cocktails each and then a few of your own choice. The beguiling bar itself is worth going to any night of the week as well. Like the Ritz, the emphasis is on a few cocktails, done well. It is ideally placed for thinking back to the rot-gut gin that Covent Garden was awash with when Rules first started in 1798 – and feeling extremely grateful for the cocktail that you are holding instead.

Dukes Bar
Dukes Hotel, 35 St James's Place, SW1 1NY

Book ahead for Alessandro Palazzi's chic Martini master-classes, but drop in any night of the week for an exceptional cocktail. If you are just popping in for a drink, arrive early in the evening to make sure that you bag a seat as it fills up very quickly. The martinis taste so clean and cold, it almost feels like that they must be good for you in some way . . .

Berry Bros. & Rudd
3 St James Street, SW1A 1EG

Although Berry Bros. & Rudd are traditionally wine merchants, due to popular demand they are starting to offer gin tastings. Even more fun are the dining events, such as the Cocktail Dinner in the Long Room, with seasonal food matched to Berry Bros. & Rudd drinks, and a mixologist to talk you through the choices. The Martini Lunches are particularly well-attended, and guests are kept well-oiled throughout.

The Gin Ramble
WSET's London Wine & Spirit School, 39–45 Bermondsey Street, SE1 3XF

For a really comprehensive gin-fuelled day out, sign up for the Wine and Spirit Education Trust's Gin Ramble. It takes an in-depth approach without being at all dry. Your guides take you to at least three of London's distilleries, followed by lunch, a quick cocktail masterclass and a tasting.

Shake Rattle and Stir's Gin Journey
www.shakerattleandstir.co.uk

For a very reasonable £50, ginthusiast Leon Dalloway will take you to some of his favourite gin haunts around the city, on a sort of genteel bar crawl. On the tour, you get five samples of gin and five cocktails, and transport is included.

EXPANDING YOUR REPERTOIRE
The big chains do a really good job of stocking cocktail accouterments and keeping track of the latest gins these days, but for a more enjoyable shopping experience, and to find more unusual ingredients, try these:

Hedonism Wines
3–7 Davies Street, W1 3LD

Do not be thrown off by the name – Hedonism Wines is an absolute trove of offbeat drinks to experiment with. It is one of the few places in London to stock kummel, which you will need to make Prince Philip's favourite, the Silver Bullet. It also stocks rarities such as Canton French Ginger Liqueur, Jade Perique Tobacco Liqueur, the King's Ginger by Berry Bros. & Rudd and Sacred's Rosehip Cup. On the gin front, there are around a hundred at last count, including Gin Mare from Spain and G'Vine from France, alongside vintage bottles from the early twentieth century.

Adnams Cellar and Kitchen
Twelve shops around Britain, including one in Bloomsbury: 30–1 Store Street, WC1E 7QE

Particular highlights at the Adnams shops include their two gins, of course, as well as their Morello Cherry Liqueur and the Winter Spiced Liqueur. There are also all sorts of gadgets that you will find useful for professional-style cocktails. At the one in London, they offer good-value spirit tastings.

Gerry's Wines and Spirits
74 Old Compton Street, SW1 4UW

With its floor-to-ceiling shelves full of spirits that you have never heard of, this would probably be the best place in London to be locked in overnight. Started in 1984, the owner, Michael Kyprianou, made much of his money by buying up confiscated alcohol from Customs. Now Gerry's is rather more discerning and tends to give the next big things their first break. They were the first shop to stock Sacred, and they will no doubt continue to find countless more wonderful, esoteric gins in future.

Amathus Drinks
17–19 Leadenhall Market, EC3V 1LR, and 113–117
Wardour Street, W1F 0UN

As well as lots of lovely gin, Amathus is strong on mixers,
with a great selection of cordials, soft drinks and syrups. If
you are tempted to go for the traditional garnish on your
cocktails, you can buy original maraschino cherries here. Wile
away a few hours on a rainy afternoon pondering the creative
drinks that you could make. They also host free fortnightly
masterclasses that last about an hour.

Harvey Nichols
109–125 Knightsbridge, SW1X 7RJ

It is always a pleasure to browse through Harvey Nichols'
food halls, and the most exciting section is surely the spirits
department. They are usually very quick with buying in the
most fashionable new brands, so if you are on the hunt for a
particular bottle it is a safe bet to start with, and they do
luxurious gift sets too.

OUTSIDE LONDON
There are many distilleries scattered around the country that
welcome curious visitors. The Adnams distillery in Suffolk is
particularly picturesque, as you can see the Southwold
Lighthouse and the North Sea while standing by the gleaming
copper stills. Over in the West Country, Plymouth's attractive
Black Friars Distillery, the oldest working distillery in
England, is also by the sea. The newest and most spectacular
is Bombay Sapphire's Laverstoke Mill on the River Test in
Hampshire.

The Black Friars Distillery
60 Southside Street, The Barbican, Plymouth, PL1 2LQ

If you are in the West Country, do not miss a chance to look around Plymouth's Black Friars Distillery, which was founded in 1793 by the Coates family. The distillery was named after the former medieval monastery before it became a place for more earthly pleasures. It is also claimed to be the place where the Pilgrim Fathers took shelter the night before setting sail for the New World on the *Mayflower,* hence its picture on the label. For not much extra, you can have a tutored tasting as well as the tour. To make a whole afternoon of it, head to the Refectory Cocktail Lounge in the 500-year-old building at the back.

The Adnams Distillery
Copper House Distillery, East Green, Southwold, Suffolk, IP18 6JW

This dinky distillery, where they make all Adnams liqueurs and spirits, looks out over the rooftops of Southwold and over to the lighthouse – there can be few places more charming to sample English gin. At the end of the tour, there is a tasting in the distillery shop, and it is almost impossible not to leave with more than you can carry. As a more expensive option for your visit, you can also blend your own gin with help from the staff.

Laverstoke Mill
Laverstoke, Hampshire, RG28 7NR

Bombay Sapphire has invested in its own beautiful distillery, rather than having it made for them by Greenall's in

Cheshire. From 1723, Laverstoke Mill was used to print bank-notes for use across Britain and the Empire, but it had been lying empty for ten years before Bombay Sapphire transformed it into a state-of-the-art distillery, which has beautiful views from just about every window. Alongside its two-storey-high stills and eighteenth-century buildings, the centrepiece is undoubtedly the glasshouses – one of which is tropical and the other Mediterranean – which are built into the river bed. Designed by Heatherwick Studios, who made the Olympic Cauldron for the opening ceremony of London 2012, they show off to stunning effect the botanicals that Bombay Sapphire use.

Penderyn Distillery
Pontpren, Rhondda Cynon Taff, CF44 0SX

By popular demand, this distillery up in the Brecon Beacons now opens its doors to visitors every day. As well as their gin-making, they share the secrets of their whisky and vodka – with samples included, of course. Booking ahead advised.

The Feathers
16–20 Market Street, Woodstock, Oxfordshire OX20 1SX

Not a distillery, but still well worth a visit, the Feathers Hotel in Oxfordshire is attracting visitors from far and wide, and justifiably so. Ask as many questions as you can think of to people who love gin just as much as you do. It took the hotel three years to build up its world-beating gin collection. Now they have managed to expand to 174 bottles, so clearly they are not going to give up their Guinness world record from 2012 without a fight.

SELECTED BIBLIOGRAPHY

Amis, Kingsley, *Everyday Drinking*

Barnett, Richard, *The Dedalus Book of Gin*

Barr, Andrew, *Drink – An Informal Social History*

Bradstreet, Dudley, *The Life and Uncommon Adventures of Captain Bradstreet*

Clark, Peter, *The English Alehouse: A Social History*

Coates, Geraldine, *The Mixellany Guide to Gin*

Cook, Richard, *Oxford Night Caps: A Collection of Receipts for Making Various Beverages used in the University*

Cooper, Ambrose, *The Complete Distiller*

Dillon, Patrick, *Gin: The Much Lamented Death of Madam Geneva*

Doxat, John, *The Gin Book*, Quiller

Flanders, Judith, *The Victorian City: Everyday Life in Dickens' London*

Gately, Iain, *Drink: A Cultural History of Alcohol*

Grose, Francis, *A Classical Dictionary of the Vulgar Tongue*

Hewett, Edward and Axton W. F., *Convivial Dickens: The Drinks of Dickens and his Time*

Knoll, Aaron J. and Smith, David T., *The Craft of Gin*

Rocco, Fiammetta, *Quinine: Malaria and the Quest for a Cure That Changed the World*

Rogers, Nicholas, *Mayhem: Post-War Crime and Violence in Britain 1748–53*

Solmonson, Lesley Jacobs, *Gin: A Global History*

Tarling, William J. (ed.), *The Café Royal Cocktail Book*

Taylor, Anya, *Bacchus in Romantic England: Writers and Drink, 1780–1830*

Terrington, William, *Cooling Cups and Dainty Drinks*

Uglow, Jenny, *Hogarth: A Life and a World*

Warner, Jessica, *Craze: Gin and Debauchery in an Age of Reason*

White, Jerry, *London in the Nineteenth Century*

PICTURE CREDITS

Gin Lane. Etching and engraving by William Hogarth, 1751. Heritage Image Partnership Ltd./Alamy. p 75

Beer Street. Etching and engraving by William Hogarth, 1751. Heritage Image Partnership Ltd./Alamy. p 78

Sipsmith's hybrid still 'Prudence'. Illustration © Ailbhe Phelan, 2012. p 291

The Coffey or columnar still. Engraving, 19th century. The Granger Collection/Topfoto. p 290

Pot still. Illustration from *Alcohol: Its Production, Properties, Chemistry and Industrial Applications* by Charles Simmonds, 1919. p 289

Fuddling cup. Illustration from *Drinking Vessels of Bygone Days* by G.J. Monson-Fitzjohn, 1927. p 41

A Mapp of the Parish of St. Giles's in the Fields. Engraving, 1755. British Library Board 2014 (Maps Crace Port.15.1.[2.])

Images p208, 209, 243 courtesy Diageo

BOTANICALS

Juniper – © Florilegius/Alamy
Coriander – © Liszt Collection/Alamy
Cinnamon – © Florilegius/Alamy
Cassia – © Florilegius/Alamy